ĀTTUKĀL AMMA

ĀTTUKĀL AMMA

The Goddess of Millions

LEKSHMY RAJEEV

First published in hardback in India in 2016 by Harper Element
An imprint of HarperCollins *Publishers* India

Copyright © Lekshmy Rajeev 2016

P-ISBN: 978-93-5177-706-9
E-ISBN: 978-93-5177-707-6

2 4 6 8 10 9 7 5 3 1

Lekshmy Rajeev asserts the moral right to be identified as the author of this work.

The views and opinions expressed in this book are the author's own and the facts are as reported by her, and the publishers are not in any way liable for the same.

All rights reserved. No part of this publication may be reproduced, stored in a retrieval system, or transmitted, in any form or by any means, electronic, mechanical, photocopying, recording or otherwise, without the prior permission of the publishers.

HarperCollins *Publishers*
A-75, Sector 57, Noida, Uttar Pradesh 201301, India
1 London Bridge Street, London, SE1 9GF, United Kingdom
Hazelton Lanes, 55 Avenue Road, Suite 2900, Toronto, Ontario M5R 3L2
and 1995 Markham Road, Scarborough, Ontario M1B 5M8, Canada
25 Ryde Road, Pymble, Sydney, NSW 2073, Australia
195 Broadway, New York, NY 10007, USA

Typeset in PT Sans, 10/15 by Arijit Ganguly and Supriya Mahajan

Printed and bound at
Lustra Print Process Pvt. Ltd.

The book is offered to my
Āttukāl Amma

The main pongala for Āttukāl Amma cooked by the Thottam singers

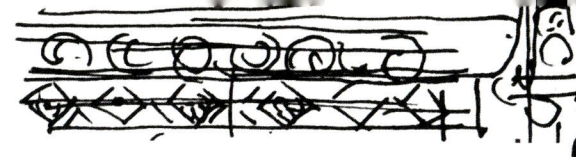

Contents

Preface | **xi**

1. The Temple through Legends | **1**

2. The Dispassionate Gaze of History | **6**

3. Āttukāl Amma | **22**

4. The Origin and Development of the Bhadrakali Cult in Kerala | **38**

5. The Āttukāl Temple | **52**

6. The Commencement of the Ten-day Festival | **64**

7. Āttukāl Amma and Kannaki of *Chilappathikaram*: Different Entities? | **72**

8. Thottam Pāttukār | **88**

9. The Ten-day Festival and the Thottam Pāttu | **100**

10. Āttukāl Pongala | **138**

11. Sahasrakalasham: The Rite of Penance and Ritual Cleansing after the Pongala | **158**

12. Special Offerings to Āttukāl Amma | **174**

13. Daily Rituals of Worship at Āttukāl | **184**

14. The Growth of the Āttukāl Temple and Its Administration | **204**

Notes | **210**

Acknowledgements | **221**

The golden thidampu of Āttukāl Amma

Āttukāl Amma's ceremonial visit to Manacaud Shastha Temple on the night after the Pongala

Preface

I began the search for Āttukāl Amma, spurred on by a challenge during an uchha sheeveli[1] at the Āttukāl Temple. I was standing near the western entrance of the temple, lost in deep thought as the sheeveli procession went past me. A group of women and men, crying out 'Amma!', trailed Her.

I saw the sheeveli idol[2] of the Goddess held close to the chest of a gentle priest lost in adoration, who was taking Her around the temple along the inner circumambulatory path. At that moment, I yearned to be like Her – held close and cherished. As the procession led by this priest came to the outer circumambulatory path, he placed the idol on his head and held on to it with both hands. I had to go farther away from Her and watch – with a fervent longing. From that moment on, She, Āttukāl Amma, the reigning queen in the minds of millions of women like me, began to overwhelm my psyche. The doubt as to whether She is seeing me and whether She knows the sorrows and anxieties of thousands like me, began to gnaw at me.

Before that, I was an occasional visitor to the temple. The feeling that I had something more to do with the temple and the Goddess than merely praying there became deep-rooted in me on that day. I don't know why, but from that day, serious doubts began to raise their heads. Why is She loved this much? Why does the temple festival draw millions of women? Why is this deity so close to so many, irrespective of caste and creed? I came back home and sent an email to my mentor A. J. Thomas telling him that I want to write a book about the Āttukāl Temple.

Over the last four years, I visited the temple very often, entering through the western entrance, passing through by Her side, where Her heart is, till I forgot where I ended and She alone remained.

I began to feel the particular scent of the kumkumam used in the temple all around me when I started to jot down notes for this book. The sweetness of the payasam I received from the temple as prasadam[3] lingered in my memory. I became a regular visitor to the temple; I gradually made friends with the staff, gently inquiring about the temple, the people associated with it and the rituals conducted there. They accepted me as a special visitor soon and everyone greeted me with an endearing smile. Within the first six months, they began asking me: 'What's happening to the book? When will we be able to see it?'

This endeavour gathered enormous strength from the affection and cheering queries of the temple staff. In the span of these four years, the chief priests changed thrice and the temple administration too changed twice. I am indebted to all of them for urging me on, in unknown ways, to complete this book.

I began to observe how every woman is exceptionally happy within the temple precincts – from the richest to the poorest, from the downtrodden to those of the upper crust. I didn't feel it was a temple; it was the sweetest of homes. That's how I feel about the Āttukāl Temple even now. I am sure every woman who comes to the temple shares this feeling. For one thing, there are no restrictions to speak of –

no 'don'ts' about anything. No place for fear, in any way. And bliss in abundance. I also started feeling that Her abode is a place where I can never be sad about anything. This is how the Great Mother began to reveal Herself to me.

I have striven to write down every intense feeling about the Goddess that arose in my heart all through these years, since that first encounter. I wanted to write about the happiness I experienced in this particular temple. I also felt that I had never experienced this kind of happiness anywhere else.

I became a frequent visitor to the temple during uchha sheeveli, listening to the asuravādyam[4] played by the temple drummers and the blowing of the conch amidst the ringing of bells. I would then experience Her moving towards me and pulling out a trident embedded in my chest, and actually see its blood-smeared tips; that would then become the trident in Her hand. This has happened to me hundreds of times in the course of writing this book. I would go to the temple expecting this to happen and it always happened.

I would throw myself before Her, in total surrender, seeking this ecstatic experience. In return, She became my companion. A love that will never walk away from me. Every other tie I had till then – of relationships, of money, of power, of security and safety, everything a woman of my age and stage could think of – was severed with one slash of the sword She wields. Every onslaught of grief, fear and threatening circumstances was warded off by Her shield. The ecstasy of immersing in Her thoughts also enabled me to reach closer to Her in more ways than I could ever imagine. Everything that began to rise in my sankalpa[5] was granted even before they were formed as thoughts. People might call these miracles, but I have learned not to, because She is the only reality for me now, and forever.

Āttukāl Amma is a perpetually accessible Mother, who inspires an almost possessive love towards Her in Her devotees. For example, when I buy a new sari, I feel like wearing it and showing it to Her first. I feel beautiful in Her presence. During the course of writing this book, my small twin children never fell ill. She is the perfect healer; She is the perfect companion; She fills me with a constant state of excitement, making me forget time. There are millions of Her devotees all over the world who cannot physically visit Her, but enshrine Her in their hearts, and offer the annual Pongala[6] wherever they are. I am the privileged one, however, living in Thiruvananthapuram, which enables me to visit Her whenever I wish.

I also remember that my visits to the temple were often made under difficult conditions. I went to the temple at dawn, at midnight and even at 2 a.m. I braved pouring rain and sweltering heat. At times, I was in the midst of enormous crowds. I had also been to the temple when no one was around. Such strange trips provoked serious questions and conflict not only from my loved ones but also in my mind. People would ask me, sometimes jokingly, other times critically and harshly: 'Why do you do this? Would this obsession with the Goddess ever end?' And I would reply, 'It is for Her.' I am not able to rationally analyse this bond between me and the Goddess. My mind is filled with the gratitude of a lifetime towards the Great Goddess for allowing me to be close to Her and to write about Her.

Around the time I completed the book, I asked K. K. Nair, my eighty-year-old guru, who taught me temple tantra,[7] whether I could see the Goddess for real, at least once. His answer, 'No, child, I don't know,' made me weep. After a moment's pause, he said, 'But the Goddess sees you.' Yes, that is enough for me.

This book is my gurudakshina[8] to him.

Finally, it was Kannan Potti, the chief priest at the Āttukāl Temple till recently, who taught me the real prayer I need till my last breath. *Mām madeeyancha sakalamasmal swaminyai Bhadrakalyai thubhyam samyak samarppayami.* (I, everything I have and do, are offered to You, Goddess Bhadrakali.)

There were no authentic sources to tell me more about the temple, but there She was, helping me perceive through darkness, linking together every moment of time. Her sacred name never left my lips ever since; and this book is my offering to Goddess Bhadrakali at the Āttukāl Bhagavathy Temple.

Eswaran Potti carrying Āttukāl Amma's thidampu during the athazha sheeveli

The eight-petalled lotus, the ashtadala padmam, on which the Goddess is invoked and worshipped during Bhagavathy seva

Parameshwaran Pillai face-to-face with the Goddess. Painting by Madanan; model for the young Goddess: Bhadra Rajeev

1
The Temple through Legends

Long ago, in an idyllic village in south Kerala, a miracle took place that has been fondly recounted by generations of devotees. Kerala was not yet a political entity at that time. There were numerous princely states that formed part of what was collectively called as Vanchinad in the south, ruled over by the Āyi kings, the Chera Kingdom in the central regions and the Ezhimala Kingdom in the north. This story unfolds in Vanchinad in a serene little hamlet on the lush banks of the Karamana and Killi[1] rivers, then known as Vanamali and Dakshina Pampa. The region, endowed with natural abundance, marked the confluence of those rivers. The hamlet of Kāvuvila, now known as Āttukāl,[2] close to present-day Thiruvananthapuram, the capital of Kerala, drew its name from the presence of a kāvu, a sacred grove, integral to village life in Kerala.

The Cherukara Valiyaveedu enjoyed pride of place in Kāvuvila as home to one of the oldest and wealthiest Nair families in the village. One of the branches of the family, Mulluveedu, spoke of prosperity – a sprawling traditional Kerala mansion with an imposing padippura[3] and a tulasithara.[4]

The men of Cherukara Valiyaveedu were known for their valour. Their prowess in the martial art of kalarippayattu was put to good use when the then Crown prince of Venad – the soon to be nation state – Anizham Thirunal Marthanda Varma, was attacked by a band of thugs while travelling through the region. He was defended by the warriors of Cherukara. The royal family was also indebted to Cherukara tharavadu for protecting Umayamma Rani,[5] the first woman ruler of Venad, from Ettuveettil Pillamar[6] – the eight families of Nair feudal lords who rebelled against the royal house. As a token of gratitude, Anizham Thirunal Marthanda Varma bestowed many privileges on the Cherukara family when he became king.[7] (These historical events would happen much later than the incident described in the legend below).

The existence of two sacred groves in the region had a strong bearing on the spiritual orientation of the Cherukara family. The larger of the two groves, dotted with gigantic banyans, peepals and poovarasu (Portia tree) that stood in the embrace of winding jasmine creepers, was called thallakkāvu. The smaller one, equally dense, was known as pillakkāvu.

The head of Mulluveedu, an elderly gentleman named Parameshwaran Pillai, used to bathe in the River Killi before the first rays of the sun spread across the sky and perform pujas throughout the day. At one such twilight hour, with the tiny blades of grass swaying at the fringes of the cold waters of the Killi, Parameshwaran Pillai stood in neck-deep water facing the east, his eyes half-shut in soulful invocation of the Goddess in his heart. The Killi flowed on ever so calmly.

As the old man completed his ablutions, he noticed a strange flutter in the river. He felt the undercurrents gain an unruly vigour. He gazed in anxiety as the ripples grew in strength and began to lash against the banks. He had never seen anything like this before. Trying to wade past the waves of premonition, he reached the bank. He noticed the birds rushing back to their nests, their feast of ripe paddy ears forgotten halfway through.

Parameshwaran Pillai knew the ebb and flow of the Killi like the throbbing of his heart. But then a whirlpool seemed to rise from the depths of the river and he struggled to hold himself up as it encircled his frail body. He stood in silent prayer for several moments, and then, as if in response to someone's beckoning, he opened his eyes.

A little girl stood alone on the other side of the river! A wave of anxiety swept over him. Who was this child? From where had she appeared? Could she have fallen into the river and then been washed ashore? Could somebody have forgotten to take her along after the evening bath? He decided to let the questions wait and plunged into the river. He swam as fast as his old limbs allowed him; the little girl waved excitedly at him. As he swam closer to where she stood, she broke into delighted laughter.

On reaching the other bank, he lifted the girl on to his shoulders and began to swim back. He didn't make any queries. He was gripped by the feeling of having found a lost treasure and also by an urgency to ensure her safety. The river was calm then. Parameshwaran Pillai found it easier to swim back.

Reining in his curiosity, he took the girl's tiny hand and walked her to his home. The girl looked barely twelve; she smiled as she watched the old man hurrying down the path, her small hand secure in his grip. The padippura was open and they entered the compound.

Parameshwaran Pillai gazed in wonderment at the girl whose face shone like a jewel. 'Who are you, my dear child?' He asked. There was no reply. He peered into her beautiful eyes and saw a rare glow in them. Their extraordinary brightness disturbed him. He turned his gaze away. He couldn't look into her eyes for long. Was she hungry? Gently, he touched her head, seated her on the veranda, and went inside.

When he returned with milk, beaten rice and plantain, the girl was nowhere in sight. The old man panicked and spent a long time looking for her. She had vanished into thin air. What kind of a test was the Almighty submitting him to?

Parameshwaran Pillai recounted the tale to family and friends. No one would believe him. 'The old man was hallucinating,' they said. He could not sleep that night. After the night-long torment, he fell into a slumber sometime in the early hours.

In that wakeful sleep, Parameshwaran Pillai had a strange dream. The little girl, radiant like a bejewelled deity, was calling him towards her. Then, in a flash, he saw her transform into the dazzling form of Bhagavathy. Bewildered, the old man cried out like a child. Unable to comprehend the spectacle unfolding before his eyes, he bowed in total surrender to the Goddess.

'Son!'

The unearthly voice filled his body and mind with untold ecstasy; tears of contentment welled up in his eyes.

'Why didn't you recognize me when I beckoned to you from the other side of the river? My son, you have been selfless in your devotion, and submitted yourself completely to me. I grant you the privilege of sanctifying a chosen spot in this land where I will dwell as the presiding deity. You may come to the kāvu at dawn. I bless you and this land.'

THE TEMPLE THROUGH LEGENDS

She disappeared.

Parameshwaran Pillai woke up from his dream with an overwhelming sense of bliss. He rose from his mat of woven grass to see the courtyard carpeted with the white flowers of the Nityakalyani jasmine. Parameshwaran Pillai finished his bath and headed to the kāvu with his eyes closed. On reaching the inner sanctuary of the sacred grove, he opened his eyes.

On the leaf-strewn ground of the kāvu were etched three silver lines. Spellbound, he broke into a fervent exaltation of the Devi. Within a fraction of a second, the silvery etchings vanished. He rubbed his eyes in disbelief. But no, the lines had disappeared for sure. Hastily, he picked up a few pebbles and marked the place where he had seen the etchings. His loud prayers to the Devi brought people running to the kāvu. He narrated to them what he had just witnessed.

Thus goes one of the most popular legends revolving around the origin of a temple, where millions throng now. This story took roots in the popular imagination through repetition over a long time.

It is believed that the first shrine was built on the spot where Parameshwaran Pillai saw the silvery etchings; it would later become the temple dedicated to the Goddess he brought home from the river bank. From the beginning, She was fondly addressed as Āttukāl Amma, meaning the Mother at Āttukāl.

My explorations into the mysterious past of Āttukāl Amma uncovered many intriguing facts that point to a more realistic picture.

Āttukāl Temple before reconstruction

2
The Dispassionate Gaze of History

The legend associated with the beginnings of the temple at Āttukāl implies that it was Parameshwaran Pillai who installed the Goddess in the southern portion, called thekkathu, of his ancestral home, Mulluveedu. This is unsubstantiated folklore, and stories of similar nature abound surrounding the founding of many temples including one of the world's richest, the Sree Padmanabhaswamy Temple, which is close to Āttukāl. But no one considers them false, as myths always have an inner core of truth. Believers normally consider such stories true and the scepticism of the historian is not applicable to them. Later, the myth of Kannaki, the epitome of chastity and the protagonist of the Tamil epic *Chilappathikaram*, was incorporated into this tale about Āttukāl Amma's first appearance on the scene.

Except for a few legends and anecdotes that have been handed down over generations, there are no historical records about the origin of the temple or its ownership by a particular family. Whatever the legends and myths may imply, the experience of the devotee is that the constant presence and power of the Goddess overwhelm this place. Everything we witness today at the temple is the result of the contributions of devotees down the ages who worshipped Her deeply, and also that of the millions who worship Her today.

The earlier story about Parameshwaran Pillai installing the deity was expanded to claim that the girl Parameshwaran Pillai brought home was Kannaki on her way to Kodungallur (in Thrissur district of Kerala, where the famous Bhadrakali temple is located) after annihilating the Pandyan king and burning down the city of Madurai! We will unravel that myth in detail, in a later chapter.

There are no written records to confirm that the Āttukāl Temple in its earliest form was the southern portion of the now vanished Mulluveedu, or that it was Parameshwaran Pillai who made a shrine for the Goddess. The important Nair families, who live near the temple precincts, are represented in the temple administration and in the group of people known as the Pāttukār or the sponsors of the Thottam Pāttu,[1] and of the ten-day festival by extension. However, representatives from Mulluveedu are not found in either of them.

The plot of land where the temple's east-facing administrative office functions now used to be the original location of the long-vanished Mulluveedu and Kuruppachan Vilakam families. The office-bearers of the temple trust belonging to the older generation like K.P. Ramachandran Nair, R. Gopinathan Nair, M. Bhaskaran Nair and Mynadu Krishnan Nair had seen Mulluveedu before it was demolished. They state that the temple was not an extension of Mulluveedu. The position of the temple, on the east too, makes it evident that the legend describing the Āttukāl Temple to be a thekkathu or the southern portion of Mulluveedu has no basis in historical fact.

Every Hindu in Kerala has a family temple. Usually it is a temple near the ancestral house but not necessarily owned by the family. The deity of the temple is their kuladevatha, or family deity. No one in the Āttukāl Bhagavathy Temple Trust (ABTT) or among the twelve families that sponsor the Thottam Pāttu claim that the Āttukāl Bhagavathy Temple is their family temple or that the deity is their family deity. Most of the older families around the temple have various other temples as their family temples.

M. Bhaskaran Nair, the secretary of the ABTT when I was writing the book, told me that the trust office was built after demolishing Mulluveedu in the year 1976. The land was purchased by the office-bearers, in the name of the devout seventy-two-year-old Lakshmi Mandiram Narayana Pillai, on behalf of the Goddess, in the year 1973, from the sons of Subhadra Amma Thankachi (daughter of Parvathy Pillai Thankachi) Keshava Pillai, Velayudhan Thampi (Kochuveedu, Sreevaraham) and Kumaran Thampi.[2] The padippura of the demolished Mulluveedu, is preserved in a building near the temple, which currently functions as the local Nair Service Society (NSS) branch office. It is believed that Mulluveedu was sold by its last head of the family to a merchant of Chalai named Keshava Pillai. The year and the person who sold it are unknown; but I was able to gather the documents related to this purchase by the ABTT. Had the temple precincts ever been the property of Mulluveedu, such land transactions would not have taken place without any mention of the family's rights over the temple and its land.

In all government records, Āttukāl village is referred to as Āttukāl pitāka. Sarah Caldwell[3] observes that throughout the medieval period and into the nineteenth century, small traditional kingdoms (or chiefdoms) were located in the foothills and inland areas where paddy production was most intensive. A feudal social organization bonded agricultural workers to landowners, who were mostly of the Nair caste. Each royal house had affinal ties with Brahmin families, whose male members also served as priests in their temples. The fierce Goddess Bhagavathy became the predominant deity of the martial temple owners, to such an extent that each king had his own local installation of the Goddess, who was considered to be a tutelary matrilineal ancestor and protector of his family's personal and political interests.

The historian N. Ajithkumar says that right from the reign of Kulasekhara Perumal, the earliest Chera king, there were citizens' groups which were almost democratic in nature, such as nāttukkoottam, tharakkoottam, desakkoottam and perumkoottam. Similarly, historical records show that the pitāka was the regional organizational system that prevailed in Travancore. During the harvest season, the chief of the pitāka, which included all the layers of society, used to organize the singing of the Thottam Pāttu and other rituals during the harvest festival, in a temporary shrine known as mudippura, erected near the paddy fields. Naturally, the administration of the shrine was the responsibility of this pitāka chief, who was usually a Nair. Nair chieftains in those days were quite independent of the royal seat of power; they used to enact rules and lay down norms connected with the administration which were basically favourable to themselves.[4]

From available historical records, from the physical position of the temple and the ritualistic traditions that are followed there, we can assume that the Āttukāl Temple was a mudippura, or a hypaethral shrine, later converted into a temple. There are several such mudippuras on the banks of the River Killi, which transformed into temples with Brahminical modes of worship later. For example, there are many such shrines in Thiruvananthapuram district like Konchiravila Mudippura, Pazhanchira Mudippura, Mukkolakkal Mudippura, Udiyannoor Mudippura, Jagathy Mudippura and

Karumbukonam Mudippura. Now, people usually do not mention the word 'mudippura' while referring to these places of worship, but some temples have retained the title, for example, Jagathy Mudippura. Through the many conversions and alterations over the centuries, the fact of the Āttukāl Temple being a mudippura is generally forgotten.

Normally, mudippura (literally 'the house where the "mudi" is kept') is the name of the temporary shed where the folded cloth ('mudikkuka' in old Malayalam means 'to fold'), which was worshipped as the Goddess Herself in the fields during the harvest season, was kept. Later, in place of the cloth, crowns made in the same shape, carved from the wood of a live varikka plavu (a variety of jackfruit tree) acquired the name 'mudi'. We usually find a bronze anklet and sword along with this mudi, in almost all Bhadrakali shrines. They are treated as the Goddess's ornaments or as the symbols of the Goddess. Kodungallur Bhadrakali was invoked into these north-facing mudippuras. Facing the north signifies that She was directly gazing at Her father, Lord Shiva in Mount Kailasam, and Thottam Pāttu, which narrates the legend of the Goddess, was sung there.[5]

This ritual of singing the Thottam Pāttu is performed at the Āttukāl Temple and the nearby mudippuras-turned-temples even today. At the time of the festival, a golden brocade cloth, folded in the form of a fan following the old mudippura tradition, is placed behind the idol of the Goddess. The right to starch and iron this cloth rests with a family from the Mannān community.[6] No one knows how and when this practice emerged. It might indicate the persistence of the ancient practice. This folded cloth is seen even in the oldest available photograph of the idol of Āttukāl Amma. There are two swords and a pair of very old anklets inside the sreekovil[7] even today, reminiscent of old times when the Goddess was represented by these things. All this points to the truth that the Āttukāl Temple was once a mudippura or that Āttukāl Amma is a prehistoric village goddess whose origins can't be traced, and so is swayambhoo (self-born) and owned by no particular caste, creed or family.

On the other hand, internal evidence indicates that the ancient abode of the Goddess and its affairs were managed by people belonging to the lower strata of society. There is evidence on record to prove that animal sacrifices were conducted at the Āttukāl Temple even at the turn of the twentieth century. Mahakavi K.C. Keshava Pillai, eminent Malayalam poet and dramatist who died in 1913, in his correspondence with Brahmananda Swami Shivayogi, lauds him for his work *Mokshapradeepam*, owing to the influence of which the evil practice of animal sacrifice was stopped at the Āttukāl Temple. Shivayogi's disciples worked hard to ensure that there were no more blood sacrifices at the Āttukāl Temple.[8]

Further, it may be noted that although the pujas here are presently carried out by Brahmins, the Thottam Pāttu with which the Pongala festival begins, is still sung by low-caste people. The singers were from two sub-castes: Mannān or Vannān (washerman) and Paravan (coconut-tree climbers) and two distinctive and eponymous styles of singing developed: 'Mannāvazhi' and 'Paravazhi'. Gradually, other communities also began to sing the Thottam Pāttu. For instance, Madhu Asan, the main Thottam Pāttu singer today, is from the Ezhava community.

It is noteworthy that a member of the Ezhava community enjoys today the virtually centuries-old hereditary right to sing the hymns in praise of the Goddess, to start off Her festival and to invoke and transport Her from Kodungallur. This is a privilege that places the Thottam singers at a pre-eminent position vis-à-vis the temple and the conduct of the festival. However, it has to be remembered that, 'the Ezhavas or the "excluded caste" were not allowed to enter even the outermost-enclosures of the Hindu temples. They and other lower caste people were denied admission to the temple precincts and were not even allowed to walk along the roads in the vicinity of the temples. They had to worship and make their offerings from distances ranging from fifty to one hundred yards from the outer walls of the temple. Almost all temples had trees or flag-stones to indicate the limit up to which the members of the lower castes were permitted to enter."[9]

Kumaran Asan, the great Malayalam poet and a member of the Sree Mulam Popular Assembly of the princely state of Travancore, raised this issue in the twelfth session of the assembly. He drew the attention of the government to this evil practice, referring particularly to roads in the vicinity of the temples at Vaikkom, Thirunakkara, Sucheendram and a few other places and demanded the removal of the signboards placed near some of these temples, prohibiting the entry of the lower-caste people beyond that point.[10]

Subsequently, the liberal sovereign of Travancore, Sri Chithira Thirunal Bala Rama Varma, promulgated a Temple Entry Proclamation in 1936, granting entry for all Hindus into the temples in his domain.[11] Only then did the social ostracism end, enabling the lower-caste people to enter the temples. But in the case of Madhu Asan, his ancestors had the hereditary right to sing in the temple precincts since ancient times. The same was the case with the other Thottam Pāttu singers whom the Goddess is believed to have given the right to do so – the Vannārs and the Paravans. Those who had the hereditary right to build the canopy with fresh leaves of the coconut palm, known as pacha pandal, belonged to the Thandān community, a backward caste. Likewise, Radhakrishnan Asari and his nephew Appukkuttan Asari, who flag off the ancient ritual of Kuthiyottam from inside the temple, belong to a sub-caste of carpenters, included in the Other Backward Classes (OBCs).

As was the tradition in Bhadrakali worship in the sacred groves in Kerala, fowl and cattle were offered in sacrifice known as kuruthi before this practice was banned by the government. It is believed that animal sacrifice was stopped at the Āttukāl Temple after the early 1890s as mentioned before, but some say it continued until the 1950s or even later.[12] All these point definitively to one conclusion: The temple, beginning probably as a mudippura, belonged, in earlier ages, to all, irrespective of caste or community.

Though many Nair families live around the Āttukāl Temple now, only a few of them – Meleperumpally, Keezheperumpally, Chekkala Vilakam, Vadakke Vilakam, Muthuvila, Velanvila and Muthuvalliveedu – are originally from this area. But they are not directly related to each other. The present-day Nair dominance over the temple administration and conduct of the festival is clearly a recent phenomenon, as testified by a venerable old lady I interviewed. She told me that the Nairs arrogated the right to conduct Pāttu for themselves about fifty years ago. Kurunkudi House was the residence of the Tamil Chettiyars and before selling this property to the Nairs, a Chettiar named Ayyakkutty Pillai used to conduct the Pāttu. Later, when the ABTT was formed, the rules were framed in such a way that the trust membership was limited to the Nairs who had permanent residence in the Āttukāl pitāka, and their children would inherit the right!

We can only surmise that the Goddess's shrine, preserved and protected by various patrons and the villagers, survived the test of time. Almost all of the Āttukāl Temple's records were lost, except the fifty-four-page revenue department document regarding land acquisition. It clearly states that the land where the temple is situated and the land around it was poramboke, land belonging to the government, and was later given to the temple. In the written request to allot the land for the Goddess, the signatures of many people in that area, like the longest-serving melshanti (chief priest) Vishnutheerthan Potti, as well as those of people from the lowest strata of society, appear.[13]

However, the continuance of the practice of very ancient rituals associated with a mudippura like the singing of Thottam Pāttu, Kuthiyottam and guruti (a Brahminical appropriation and refinement of the crude ritual of kuruthi which involved human/animal sacrifice that existed in the Bhadrakali shrines from time immemorial) in the temple, is the only evidence left regarding the temple's antiquity. There are a few elderly scholars like B.C. Balakrishnan and K.K. Nair in Thiruvananthapuram, who refer to the Āttukāl Temple as 'Āttukāl Mudippura' even now. Such references are invaluable, at a time when everything about the temple's origin is shrouded in mystery.

In a few years, those who have seen the relics of the old Mulluveedu House also would be dead, leaving the evolution of the Āttukāl Temple into a great temple in the realm of modern day myth-making. The elderly residents of Āttukāl assert that though the sreekovil of the Āttukāl Temple was renovated in 1964–65, the seat of the Goddess had never been repositioned and this area was never an extension of Mulluveedu.

In the history of the Āttukāl Temple, strands of many lives, great and small, are interwoven, the details of which we may never uncover. Also since Āttukāl was a remote area, it did not attract the attention of kings. So the history of the place and its antiquity, and the history of both the prominent and common people who lived there, faded away from popular memory. Still, a few people remember some of those ancestors. If my inquiries were delayed by a few more years, everything would have disappeared into oblivion.

I have felt many times that it was the Goddess Herself who demanded this journey back in time. The information I gathered from the old people was like recovering a lost treasure. I took incidents such as the links in the story, which had initially eluded me despite intensive search, getting revealed through a fortuitous conversation with someone who had no connection to the topic, as signs of the Goddess training Her attention on this book. In my own childlike ways, I asked Her whether what I had been writing was right or wrong. I drew lots before Her picture, made Kannan Potti do a pushpa prashnam[14] at the temple – when doubts arose.

Who were the first caretakers of the Āttukāl Temple? Who made the arrangements for offering food and puja without any break for a goddess dwelling in a small mudippura and provided the funds for it? In this context, the illustrious name of Shankaranatha Jyotsyar (1790–1858 CE), the astrologer of Maharaja Swathi Thirunal (1813–1846 CE), who played an important role in the growth of the Āttukāl Temple, stands out.

The Advent of Shankaranatha Jyotsyar

Many booklets available in the temple mention the name of Shankaranatha Jyotsyar. He was the husband of Lakshmi Amma, one of the members of the Cherukara Valiyaveedu family. She bore him a son named Shankaran and a daughter, Kamakshi.[15] He was honoured as 'Uthama Purush, Nirmala Budh Joshi Shankaranath, the Spiritual Advisor of His Highness Ranjit Singh, the Lion of Lahore', by Lord William Bentinck, the Governor General of India (1828 to 1835).[16]

Shankaranatha Jyotsyar was the priest at Badrinath Temple earlier and he had written commentaries on various holy texts like *Yogavasishtam* and had translated *Devi Bhagavatham* (incomplete). Books such as *Kashikhandam* and *Gowri-tantram* are also attributed to him. After the death of Maharaja Swathi Thirunal in 1846, Shankaranatha Jyotsyar

Shankaranatha Jyotsyar

continued to serve his successor, the illustrious Maharaja Uthram Thirunal, with distinction. The great scholar breathed his last on the twenty-eighth day of Thulam (13/14 November in the year 1859).[17] A Trust named Sree Kamakshiyamman Trust had been formed by the members of the Jyotsyar's family at their ancestral seat at Karivelloor, in Kannur district of northern Kerala.

It is believed that being an adept in the temple tantra rituals which determine the modes of brahminical worship, Jyotsyar brought in basic changes in the worship and rituals in the Āttukāl Temple, establishing them on brahminical lines. All these would have superseded the existing rituals and custom, which were usual in all mudippuras at that time. From the fact that Jyotsyar named his only daughter as Kamakshi, and that his family deity was Goddess Kamakshi, who was also the deity at his family temple, and that the family trust was named Sree Kamakshiyamman Trust, one can assume that Goddess Kamakshi was his favourite deity as well. Bringing over the bhava of Kamakshi to replace that of the village goddess that Āttukāl Amma was until then would have been close to his heart. At this juncture, one can discern the beginnings of the brahminization of the Goddess of Āttukāl, superimposing on Her the Devi of the Puranas and of *Durgasaptashati*, whom the Brahmins had co-opted long ago. Adopting for Āttukāl Amma the following mantra of Devi from *Durgasaptashati* as used in Devi worship in many Brahminical Devi temples, he would have initiated the changeover. This mantra has become hugely popular with the common devotees of Āttukāl Amma over the years:

Sarvamangala Mangalye Shive sarvārtha sadhike
Sharanye tryambake Devi Narayani namosthuthe

'Prostrations to you, Narayani, who is the auspiciousness of all things auspicious, (who is) the protector of all, who grants the devotee all purushārthas, who is capable of giving refuge to all, and who abides as the three-eyed Goddess.' (Translated by the author.)

This conclusion is corroborated by an incident narrated later in this chapter.

Judge Govinda Pillai

The Legacy of Jugde Govinda Pillai

When this book was on the verge of completion, by a stroke of luck, I was able to find invaluable information about the descendants of Shankaranatha Jyotsyar and the family members of Judge Govinda Pillai who was mentioned in all the booklets about the temple. I was not satisfied with the reply that I got from everyone related to the temple earlier that no member of the Mulluveedu family, the branch of the old Cherukara Valiyaveedu, and of Cherukara Valiyaveedu itself, was alive. I couldn't believe that such a socially prominent family had vanished completely from Āttukāl after being so closely associated with the temple and being involved with the reinstallation of the idol of Āttukāl Amma nearly 150 years ago. A few books in Malayalam describe Judge Govinda Pillai as the person who got the currently worshipped wooden idol of the Goddess made, in the year 1857. But again, there was no proof.

We will meet, in the pages of this book, many individuals whose efforts contributed to the growth of a small mudippura that was situated near a paddy field, into a great, world-famous temple. However, there must have been even more influential people in the past who prepared the ground. I have always felt that the Āttukāl Temple expanded so much, drawing energy from the devotional intensity of such ancestors. Many people have mentioned to me names like Āttukāl Govinda Pillai, Āttukāl Shankara Pillai, Lakshmi Amma and Kalyani Amma, but vaguely – no one knew their relationship with each other. Sadly, the memories of the remaining three or four men from the older generation have faded; Alzheimer's disease has affected them.

Āttukāl Shankara Pillai was a poet, translator and munsiff. In the book *Shankara Kavikal*, written by his son Kunjikrishna Pillai, Āttukāl Shankara Pillai and his father Shankaranatha Jyotsyar are mentioned, but there are no references to any siblings.

Eighty-two-year-old Pankajaskhi Amma of Keezheperumpally (the ancestral family of M. Bhaskaran Nair) who still remembers events with clarity and exhibits the curiosity of a child, turned out to be a mine of information for me in these inquiries. Sitting in the two-hundred-year-old house, the Keezheperumpally, she remembered her mother Rukmini Amma, grandmother Lakshmi Pillai and her great-grandfather Kali Pillai Vaidyan. She recalled that her grandmother Lakshmi Pillai had told her about the temple being damaged by a banyan tree falling on it during a natural calamity. She also said her grandmother had outlived her mother. From her reminiscences, I learned that the earlier idol of the Goddess was damaged by the falling banyan tree. Also, according to her, the temple was renovated and a new idol was made after this incident. Her mother's grandfather Kali Pillai had mentioned that two men from the barber community, then considered an untouchable caste, sculpted the idol from a live jackfruit tree in their compound, wearing wet clothes after bathing in the nearby pond every day. She also added that Cherukara Valiyaveedu, the ancestral home of Judge Govinda Pillai, was situated behind the temple. They were related to the royal family and had Brahmin cooks in their kitchen. The house was known then as Kārakkadu Judgeveedu, recollects Pankajakshi Amma but she doesn't remember what happened to them later.

She also told me that there was a wooden idol even before the time of Judge Govinda Pillai, and the silver decorative piece kept behind the idol was the contribution of someone from the Badrinath Temple, who sent the money to Judge Govinda Pillai's family to get it done. She remembers her grandmother mentioning that it was the idol that got damaged during the storm and Judge Govinda Pillai took the initiative to remake it. We can only assume that the earlier idol or the object of worship Shankaranatha Jyotsyar began with, was later reinstalled and maintained by Judge Govinda Pillai of Cherukara Valiyaveedu, who is also related to Shankaranatha Jyotsyar, and Āttukāl Shankara Pillai.

Mulluveedu, the tharavad of Parameshwaran Pillai of the legend in which the Goddess installs Herself at Āttukāl, was a branch of this same Cherukara Valiyaveedu, but there is no information available about any of its descendants. People of older generations assert that Mulluveedu and Cherukara Valiyaveedu have ceased to exist. However, a palatial house built by Judge Āttukāl Govinda Pillai stands majestically atop a hill at Karamana, near Āttukāl. From the house, the gopuram of the Padmanabhaswamy Temple is visible. One could also get a good view of the Āttukāl Temple, but some apartment buildings now block the temple from view. We visited the judge's great-grandchildren living in that area.

Judge Govinda Pillai, also known as Diwan Bahadur A. Govinda Pillai, was born in the Āttukāl area, in 1849.[18] There are no clear records available about when and why he left Āttukāl and went to the nearby Karamana. Neither he nor his descendants had any presence in the Āttukāl Temple's administrative council; neither was his family among the families that conducted the Thottam Pāttu.

Why and when did Judge Govinda Pillai shift his residence to the hilltop? Why are Āttukāl Shankara Pillai's descendants not in the temple administration now? Bhaskaran Nair and his sister say that they do not know. The locals never inquired about such matters; the members of the judge's family lost their rights over temple administration when the ABTT was formed. No one knows the reason. His descendants expressed disappointment over this, but they never complained. 'We go and see Amma whenever we want, and we do not regret losing the sense of belonging to the temple and its governance,' added the eighty-year-old Anandam S. Nair, the great-great-granddaughter of the judge.

There are rumours that Judge Govinda Pillai was dissatisfied with his marriage; that, since his first wife was not up to his social status and intellectual level, he married again. There is another version which says that he had disagreements with his elder brother and that made him leave Āttukāl. Who was that elder brother? No one knows. In the essays about Judge Govinda Pillai also, there is no clear information on his siblings. In a newspaper clipping whose source couldn't be traced, it is indicated that Kochukrishna Pillai was the elder brother of Judge Govinda Pillai.

When I reached the Tower View Bungalow at Karamana, after making extensive inquiries about Judge Āttukāl Govinda Pillai, I found that Kerala's first TV channel for women, 'Sakhi TV', was functioning from that building. Along with the channel's managing director Sreeraj Menon, executive director Hariprasad, news editors Sajeev C. Warrier and Anupama Kannan, I climbed up to the attic, ignoring the warning that it might cave in, and retrieved the pictures of Judge Govinda

The Chavadi or resting place around the old temple

Pillai and his wife Karthyayani Pillai. We cleaned up the pictures and mounted them on the wall in the main hall. We had a long discussion among ourselves about his social and literary activities. We visited the houses of the judge's grandchildren nearby. These were among the most enriching experiences I had during the course of writing this book.

We also visited the house of the great-grandson of Judge Govinda Pillai. Venugopalan Nair and his wife Sreekumari were elated when I asked them about their forefathers. The only clue Sreekumari could provide was that Kārakkadu Puthenveedu was the family name of the judge's wife Karthyayani Pillai, and she was from Kalady in Āttukāl.

Sreekumari referred to her as Āttukāl Ammoomma. She also told me that her mother-in-law Parukkutty Amma is the daughter of Janaki Amma, who is the daughter of the judge. She was ninety-six when she died and Sreekumari remembers what Janaki Amma told her about the Judge Bungalow. It was constructed when Janaki Amma was five years old and so the house is 130 years old now.

In spite of being a scholar in Sanskrit, Tamil, Malayalam and English, author of several literary works, and a popular judge, time did not grant Judge Govinda Pillai the honour he deserved. As Shooranad Kunjan Pillai, the scholar-patriarch of Malayalam literature, wrote in the *Manorajyam* Special Number

Vishnutheerthan Potti

The sanctum of the old temple during festival time

THE DISPASSIONATE GAZE OF HISTORY

(1989), those who achieved far less than Judge Govinda Pillai became very famous to shine in the annals of history, but Pillai had little luck. Shooranad Kunjan Pillai has also written that the judge's mother Kalyani Amma was from Cherukaraveedu, and his father Sankaran Pandala was from Mavelikkara. The internationally famous playback singer K.S. Chitra is the daughter of Krishnan Nair who is the grandson of Judge Govinda Pillai. It is unclear why members of his family were not included in the temple's administrative council and what caused them to have no significant relations with the main families of Āttukāl, although they were living not too far away.

Eminent historian S. Jayashanker, author of eleven priceless books on the temples of Kerala and retired deputy director of Census Operations, Kerala, has a different take on the Jyotsyar and his descendants. S. Jayashanker is a direct descendant of Shankaranatha Jyotsyar. His mother Karthyayani Amma is the great-great-granddaughter of the Jyotsyar. He told me that Lakshmi Amma and Kalyani Amma of Cherukara Valiyaveedu who were married to Shankaranatha Jyotsyar and Shankaran Pandala of Mavelikkara respectively must have been sisters or first cousins. Their children, Āttukāl Shankara Pillai (1837–91) and Judge Āttukāl Govinda Pillai (1849–1925) who lived during the reign of Maharaja Sree Vishakam Thirunal, were patrons of the Āttukāl Temple. They must have been cousins, as their mothers hailed from the same family, Cherukara Valiyaveedu. The Jyotsyar's only daughter Kamakshi died young. Āttukāl Shankara Pillai married Lakshmi Amma of Thannippanthal House, Paravoor, and had six children. Malabar Shankaran Nair who led the Kudiyān Prasthānam[19] is his grandson. Āttukāl Shankara Pillai's son Kunjikrishna Pillai writes about all these in his book *Shankara Kavikal*, published in the year 1941.

'Why are you not there in the administration or welfare activities of the temple?' I asked S. Jayashanker who is eighty years now. His face lit up with his ardent love for Āttukāl Amma. He said, 'I don't seek publicity. I go there to see my Amma, remember everyone, starting from my great-great-great-grandfather Shankaranatha Jyotsyar, to everyone else in the family who live in different parts of the world. I just go there, join my palms together and pray. I also tell her, "Amma, forgive me if I do something wrong." No one knows me there at the temple.' He smiled, looking at me tenderly.

S. Jayashanker also told me that his grand-uncle Kunjikrishna Pillai (the author of *Shankara Kavikal*) had told him that it was at the small shrine that Shankaranatha Jyotsyar had originally installed and worshipped his thevara vigraham – the idol he carried with him wherever he went. There is no way to check the veracity of this information. We do not know whether it was this same idol of Āttukāl Amma which got established and worshipped over the succeeding decades.

Only two people who currently play a role in the Āttukāl Temple's administration were able to recall some kind of relationship with Judge Govinda Pillai. Radha Bai of Velanvilaveedu informed us that her father Dr A.N. Gopala Pillai was the son of Judge Govinda Pillai's niece. This eighty-two-year-old lady, talking about the offerings made by herself and her late father who was one of the first members of the Temple Trust, revealed that she had inherited the right to conduct the Third Day's Pāttu. She told me how, when she was a child, she used to light the brass lamp in front of the old sreekovil. 'We used to carry oil and cloth to make the wick also,' she added. 'We never watched the programmes during the temple festival because during those times women wouldn't generally go to the festival grounds.

'I remember my father donating an uruli[20] to the temple when he got his first salary as a doctor. I also remember him saying that a part of his salary was used to plaster the chavadi – a long separate portico with tiled roof – in front of the sreekovil. My "jathakam koda"[21] was done at the Āttukāl Temple and it was the first time such a ceremony was conducted there. There is nothing more I need say about the Goddess. I believe She has given me everything.'

She also told me that she had handed over her right to conduct the Third Day's Pāttu to her brothers in 1988.

Eighty-two-year-old Nāru Unithiri from Karivelloor belongs to the family of Shankaranatha Jyotsyar and is actively involved with the temple where the Jyotsyar's Kamakshi idol is kept and the annual Navaratri festival is conducted. He sent me pictures of the small temple at Karivelloor; but what caught my attention was the mantra displayed on a board there. It is the same mantra that is used by millions here at Āttukāl, as the Goddess's mantra, 'Sarvamangala Mangalye ...' We do not know for sure when this mantra began to be used for worshipping a non-Brahminical goddess, but it could be Shankaranatha Jyotsyar who used it here at Āttukāl for the first time, as I assumed earlier. Nāru Unithiri is the one who connected me with S. Jayashanker, who was living very close to my home in Thiruvananthapuram!

Such seemingly eager moments on the part of my interlocutors were frequent during this inquiry, as if people were just waiting to hand over to me valuable insights, connecting me to greater depths and then vanish.

The abhisheka vigraham of the Goddess smeared with kumkumam

Other Important People Connected with the Temple

It is believed that when the revered Chattampi Swamikal (1853–1924) was a child, his mother brought him to this temple to cure him of a skin disease. Chattampi Swamikal is said to have found the temple premises ideal for meditation. The ABTT constructed a shrine for him on the eastern side of the temple in 1992. The piece of land to build the shrine was donated by a group of people in Kuriyathi near Āttukāl in 1965.[22] During the Swamikal's lifetime, the Āttukāl Temple would have passed through the transformation I have been describing.

It is seen in the temple records and photographs that Swami Abhedananda of Thiruvananthapuram (1909–83), a great saint of the twentieth century, who advocated the 'Hare Rama mantra', laid the foundation stone for the renovated Āttukāl Temple. It is he who guided the temple priests to use one of the main mantras of *Durgasaptashati*, 'Sarvamangala

Mangalye...' in the worship of the Goddess in the Āttukāl Temple, with a slight variation [*sharanye tryambake devi (gauri)*]. Suffice it to say that Swami Abhedananda guided the temple priests to continue with this mantra, which could have been introduced at the Āttukāl Temple by the Jyotsyar.

Vishnutheerthan Potti, the Longest-serving Melshanti

Vishnutheerthan was a Brahmin from Tulunadu.[23] His father Sreenivasan was the priest of the Puthenkotta Shiva temple. Though it was the priesthood of Thirunarayanapuram that Vishnutheerthan inherited, the administrators of several temples in Thiruvananthapuram invited him to be the priest in those temples.[24]

Vishnutheerthan's son Devadas, now aged seventy-three, recalls: 'My father became the priest at the Āttukāl Temple at the age of twenty-one in 1915. The temple did have a wooden idol. At that time, the Travancore palace astrologer Punnapuram Krishna Pillai's father, a member of the Āttukāl administrative committee, invited Vishnutheerthan to Āttukāl. He agreed to do a puja at the Āttukāl Temple once a day. He would leave after the puja at Thirunarayanapuram by 11 a.m. and walk along the country road from there, crossing the paddy fields, to reach Āttukāl. He used to return to Thirunarayanapuram in time for the evening puja. He conducted pujas at Āttukāl till 1968.

'It was my father who created an orderly system for the way in which the pujas were to be performed at the Āttukāl Temple. He served Āttukāl Amma until it became impossible for him to do the puja due to old age. He passed away at the age of eighty-eight in 1982.'[25] Devadas showed me the Salagramam – the black fossil from the River Gandaki which Vishnutheerthan used for puja – his walking stick and the cane adorned with silver bands that he brought from Āttukāl. Vishnutheerthan's son still conducts Ganapati homam daily in his house without a break, a practice that was initiated during Vishnutheerthan's lifetime.

K.P. Ramachandran Nair, the current president of the Āttukāl Bhagavathy Temple Trust (2015) and one of its oldest members, fondly remembers his association with the temple thus: 'My father was a member of the Āttukāl Temple's administrative committee. Right from the age of five, I used to spend time at Āttukāl Amma's abode daily, oblivious of the passage of time. Small groups of children including me would wait in the temple compound for the priest Vishnutheerthan Potti's arrival to open the temple. He would come crossing the nearby paddy field holding an olakkuda.[26] He would bathe in the pond close to the temple, open the sreekovil and prostrate before Devi. Then he would remove the previous day's flowers, clean the sacred space and conduct the abhishekam.[27] Afterwards, he would adorn Devi with the fresh garlands he had brought and apply saffron and sandalwood paste on the idol. The puffed rice and banana he brought would also be offered to Devi. Sometimes there would be payasa nivedyam and thrimadhuram.[28] Offerings given by the devotees were also accepted. When he left after closing the temple, he would distribute the prasadam to the children. He followed this routine every day. His main offerings were supplied by the

Vishnutheerthan Potti

ĀTTUKĀL AMMA

traders of Chalai market. His only source of income was the dakshina they gave him.

'The sreekovil I saw during those days was enclosed by wooden jalis and there were metal lamps affixed to it. It had a tiled roof and a small portico. The stones of the walls that enclosed the temple compound were beginning to crack. The skilled handiwork of Vishnutheerthan Potti, was clear on the sandal paste facial decorations on the Goddess's idol.'

A few more elderly residents of Āttukāl whom I interviewed provided me with the different facets of the history of the temple's development. Of them, two elderly ladies deserve to be quoted.

'We used to carry to the temple rice, jaggery and firewood and sometimes the vessel to cook, or the payasam offering for the Goddess during Vishnutheerthan's period,' the ever-cheerful Leela Bai, who is eighty-two years old, recalled. 'I taught the first Brahmin priest's son Devadas in Chalai school. The first occasion I witnessed a massive gathering at the temple was during the 1978 festival season when the ABTT invited K.B. Sundarambal to sing at the Āttukāl Temple, and that remains my most unforgettable memory in connection with the temple. We also used to make garlands for Devi when we were children; and when we hatched chicken at home, we used to offer one from among them to the temple. I believe it's I who first offered a golden thali for Devi on the day of my sister's wedding. Now this has become a very popular offering there.

'Judge Govinda Pillai, who played a major role in renovating the temple after the storm, is my great-grandmother's uncle. The house, Judgeveedu, where a TV channel runs its office now, belonged to him.'

People of the older generation unanimously state that it was Vishnutheerthan who was responsible for the Āttukāl Temple's present glory. It is believed that he was the first Brahmin priest of Āttukāl. There is also another belief that, even before him, the Nambis of Koopakkara Madhom were taking care of the temple's rituals. Koopakkara Madhom was the erstwhile residence of the priests of the Padamanabhaswami Temple.

However, the first known Brahmin priest attached to the Āttukāl Temple is Vishnutheerthan Potti, as mentioned above. M. Bhaskaran Nair and his sister remember (they specify that they have not seen) hearing about someone, maybe a young

THE DISPASSIONATE GAZE OF HISTORY

person, called Ambi Potti (Ambi is not really a name; it is a nickname, rather) in their childhood.

The Goddess's festival, the Āttukāl Pongala, has grown to such proportions that Hindus now consider marriage proposals from the Āttukāl area as a blessing, as I have heard several persons remark, because it will provide a house for them near the Goddess's temple which will enable them to offer the pongala conveniently! People have started using the image of Āttukāl Amma on wedding cards that used to be dominated by the images of Lord Ganapati.

The kodi-archana led by Vasudevan Vasudevan Bhattathirippad

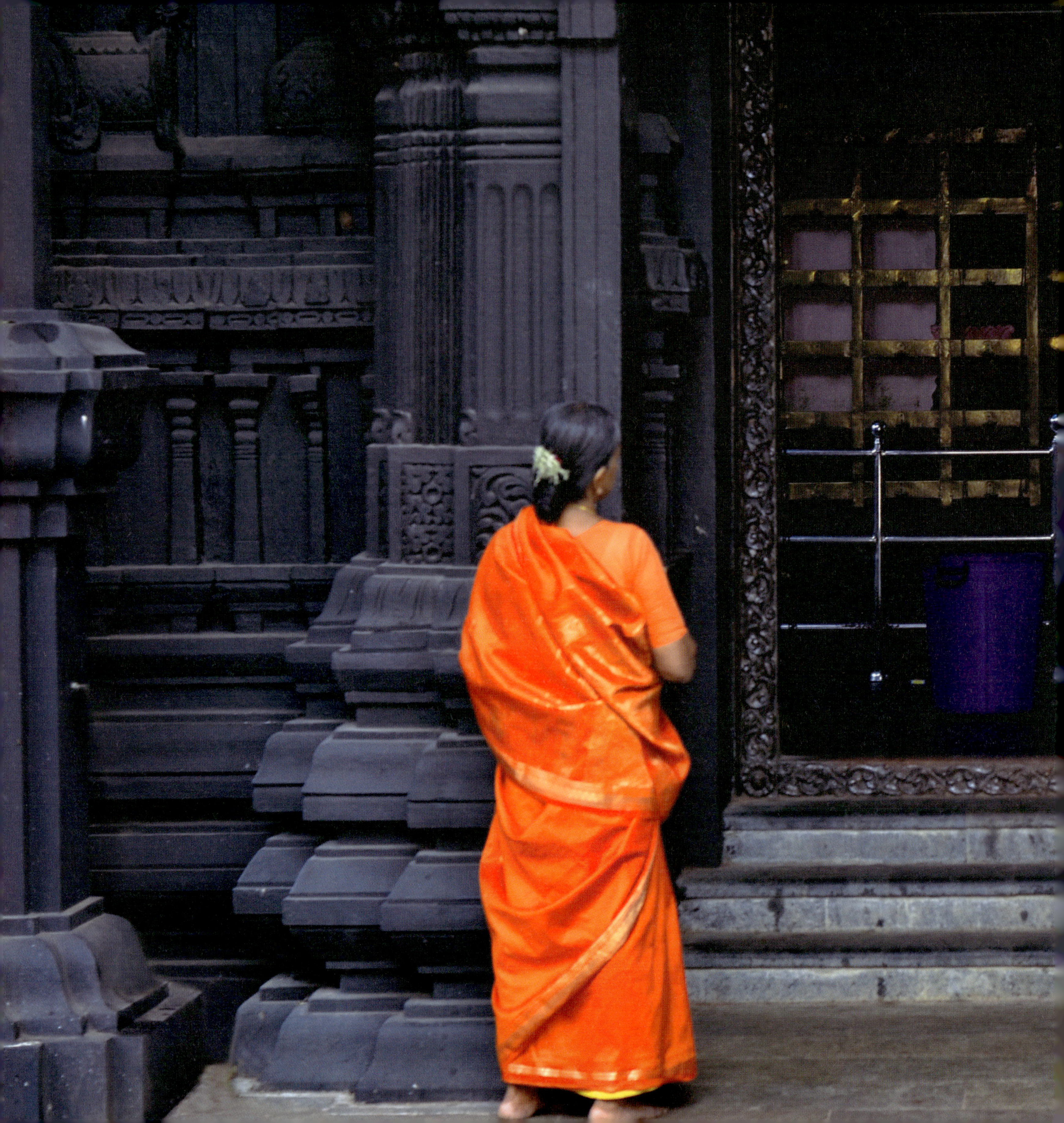

A devotee at the western entrance, in the evening

3
Āttukāl Amma

The main idol of Āttukāl Amma sketched by artist Madanan

Āttukāl Amma is a reality for millions of Her devotees. The manifestation of Her maternal love is reinforced in my consciousness again and again, the latest instance being my ineffable experience of sensing it while watching the Pongala in 2015. I witnessed nearly four million women from all walks of life, without caste and religious barriers, cooking the pongala on simple hearths on roadsides to offer Her. She is the people's Goddess. In my entire life I have never come across a deity this close to the people, mainly women. Is it because the position of women in Kerala is still very insecure and the need for an all-powerful woman, a saviour, is all the more urgent?

I witnessed the barricades-breaking intensity of faith, the outbursts of suppressed pain, agony, and the belief in Her as the saviour of their lives. None, including men, hesitates to break down before Her. I was overwhelmed by the feeling of sheer helplessness, wondering whether I would be able to comprehend what She is to these millions. None can. Anyone visiting Thiruvananthapuram during the week of the Pongala festival would find it hard to believe that it is the capital city of a communist bastion. Despite eight decades of communism, atheism has not really struck deep roots in Kerala's social milieu.[1]

Personally, as a regular visitor to the temple now, the anticipation and the delight that arise in my heart when I arrive at Killippalam (the bridge over the River Killi), and

The picture of the Goddess drawn by artist S. Sitaram in 1968

The ideal devotee, a common sight. Photo: B. Chandrakumar

take the turn to the right to reach the temple, is inexplicable. I am lost in a sort of joy, not devotion, similar to that of a child returning home to its mother after a tiring day at school. The journey from Killippalam to the temple, through the road that runs along the now polluted and considerably shrunk River Killi, is a blissful one. It makes me feel as if Amma Herself is waiting to see me, and not I, as a devotee, am rushing to meet Her.

Eternal bliss pervades this abode of Āttukāl Amma. And the very presence of Her temple has already brought prosperity to the humble village of Āttukāl. There are rows of shops that sell the items needed for many kinds of puja offerings; there are also a few shops that sell tiny silver pieces embossed with the shapes of various body parts and the whole body itself, at the main entrance on the northern side. It is believed that such ālroopams (replicas in silver) are offered to Her for curing various diseases afflicting that particular part of the body. The thundering sound of the offering of kathina-mortars greets us as we enter the temple from the northern gate. There is a continuous stream of women lighting the narangavilakku,[2] on the metal posts with circular tiers to place the lamps. A shop to the right of the entrance sells these lemon lamps filled with oil and wicks. Another interesting sight is the colourful concrete idol of the Goddess on the façade, dressed in the saris devotees offer Her; sometimes we see glass bangles on the idol's hands. The sari is changed seven times a day and the used saris can be bought in auction from the temple authorities.

Āttukāl Amma's moola vigraham (main idol) inside the sreekovil is resplendent with kindness, and, from afar, it appears as a big glow. At the sight of Her, the faces of devotees turn earnest, their palms join, and lips utter Her auspicious names. All they see is Her face shining with a radiant smile and the assurance that She is always there for them. No one would have seen the extraordinary wooden idol of Āttukāl Amma after 1985 when it was encased by the thanka anki, the gold-plated outer covering.

There is no need for devotees to check the details of anything they see there. The thought of Amma is more than sufficient for them, coupled with the glimpse of Her golden face. The devotees have to pass through a fenced passageway to reach the sreekovil. Although every day is crowded, on Fridays, Tuesdays, Sundays and the first of every Malayalam month, the lines of devotees waiting to have a glimpse of Her is really unending. The temple watchmen flank the sreekovil, continuously urging the devotees to move forward. On important days, it is the policemen who perform this duty. The devotees get only a few seconds to look at Āttukāl Amma's visage as they are usually hustled out. Some stop there and gaze at Her and they are gently pushed out!

There are separate queues for women and men, but there is no strict gender segregation. Some people stay back in the nālambalam (the rectangular structure outside the sreekovil); some sit in the space between the sreekovil and the walls surrounding it and recite sacred texts, and some merely stand there, reluctant to go away; some try to get the prasadam from their favourite priest while others remain prostrate until

The abhisheka vigraham of Āttukāl Amma

ĀTTUKĀL AMMA

they are asked to get up and move away. No one is allowed to remain in the nālambalam for very long as it has to be sanctified several times a day.

The idol of Āttukāl Amma is in the form of a maiden sitting on the neck of a Vetalika[3] whose palms She uses as stirrups; Her hair is adorned by myriad serpents; She is dārumayi, having been carved from a live jackfruit tree from the compound of the nearby Keezheperumpally[4] family. She has four arms and holds a trishoolam[5] in the lower right hand, khadgam[6] in the upper right hand, paricha[7] in the upper left hand and chashakam[8] in the lower left hand. Although She is seated, She appears to be supported by the bare-breasted Vetalika who has wide and staring eyes, fangs (damshtras), protruding tongue and long claw-like fingernails. The original idol of the Goddess in Her fierce ugramoorthi[9] aspect, faces north, signifying that She is facing Mount Kailasam, directly gazing at Her father, Lord Shiva. The fact that the earth's axis runs in a north–south direction also seems to be relevant in enhancing the energy involved in the concept of the Goddess's fierceness. The sreekovil is also the seat of the sheeveli vigraham,[10] the abhisheka vigraham,[11] and Her revered swords and anklets (chilambu).

The moola vigraham[12] of Āttukāl Amma is fully visible, unadorned, only during the early morning nirmalyam[13] and when the abhisheka vigraham kept in front of it is moved to the mukhamandapam[14] of the sreekovil to perform abhishekams.[15] Usually the abhisheka vigraham is kept in front of the moola vighraham and the flower garlands used to decorate it veil the sight of the moola vigraham.

It is believed that the wooden idol was made when the rededication was done under the supervision of Judge Govinda Pillai of Cherukara Valiyaveedu. In the wooden idol,

The offering of Narangavilakku (lemon lamp)

ĀTTUKĀL AMMA

She has damshtras but in the thanka anki made in 1985, the damshtras are absent.[16] The upper body of the idol closely resembles a mudi, an enormous crown carved from a live jackfruit tree. In several ancient Bhadrakali shrines, the mudi is worshipped because it is the representation of the Goddess, whereas Āttukāl Amma's idol is a complete one, made of wood.

It may be only after 1897 that the deity was given a visage; before that Āttukāl Amma could have been worshipped in the form of a crown, trident, sword, anklets or kindi, a bronze vessel with a spout, on which njorinjāda, the brocaded white cloth pleated like a hand fan, is installed.[17]

Usually, the idol of a deity is made following the description of His/Her form in His/Her dhyanashloka from ancient texts, which establishes the deity's attributes. The dhyanashloka used here to worship Āttukāl Amma is that of Bhadrakali in Her manifestation after Her annihilation of evil, with the severed head of the demon Darikan in one hand.

Kāleemeghasamaprabhām trinayanām vetālaskantasthitām
Khadgam kheda kapāladārika-shira krutvakarāgreshuja
Bhoota preta pishācha mātrusahitām mundasrajālamkrutām
Vande dushta masoorikādivipadām samharineemeesvareem.

Prasadam for distribution among devotees

The sheeveli vigraham of Āttukāl Amma, carried on the head of a priest

ĀTTUKĀL AMMA

(I bow to the Goddess of the universe who has the radiance of the rain cloud, three eyes, who carries in Her arms a sword, shield, skull and the head of the demon Darika, who is accompanied by all demons, ghosts, spectres, adorned with garland made of skulls, surrounded by the celestial mothers and seated on the neck of the mighty spirit, the Vetala, who dispels all the evil plagues that haunt us. [Translated by Sreejith V.T. Nandakumar.]

But the actual idol of Āttukāl Amma differs in some details from the description in the dhyanashloka. She does not hold the severed head of Darikan here. Learned tantris have informed me that the bhava[18] of the Goddess is usually defined by what was visualized at the time of the deity's first installation. But here, there are no authentic records to show who installed this idol and whether the Kerala temple tantra tradition was followed in the installation of the idol. It is shrouded in mysterious antiquity.

It is possible that there was a very rare and now lost dhyanashloka in Her case. Or it could have been something other than any of these explanations. That is what makes this idol unique. Perhaps the mystique surrounding the deity also explains the astonishing sway of Āttukāl Amma across the world, over millions of women.

However, the temple authorities who were present during the construction of the new sreekovil and the reinstallation of the idol state that it does not have the six-layered foundation, a shadādhāra pratishtha, below the installed idol. This shrine has come a long way since it began to follow a Brahminical form of worship.

In the olden days, the idol of Bhadrakali used to be a chara pratishtha, one which was removed and installed in different spots, whereas now, the idol of Āttukāl Amma is installed as a sthira pratishtha, a permanently installed idol. And yet, it is not a shadādhara pratishtha, like all sthira pratishthas should be.[19] Kanippayyoor Krishnan Namboothirippad, an authority on temple vāsthu, told me that the present

A throng of devotees

ĀTTUKĀL AMMA

sreekovil was constructed under the guidance of his granduncle Kanippayyoor Shankaran Namboothirippad and that, according to vāsthu shastra, the shadādhāra method of installing a deity is not adopted for a deity who had already existed there at a particular spot. It was just a renovation of a shrine of unknown origin.

One could assume that the newly constructed temple has quite unconventionally adopted the brahminical forms which are prescribed only for a shadādhāra pratishtha along with the reinstallation of the idol, although the installation itself is not in the shadādhāra form, merely to imitate the brahminical style, and 'upgrade' itself on par with other great temples. Actually, Āttukāl Amma's is a swayambhoo pratishtha, whose origins are shrouded in mystery, and so, shadādhāra pratishtha and all its ancillary requirements are not necessary here. Only a couple of individuals now alive have witnessed the reinstallation, and they attested that it is not a shadādhāra pratishtha.

But with all these alterations, the antiquity and the unique simplicity of the temple are gradually getting eroded. The use of plastic, fibreglass, asbestos sheets, electric lamps and loudspeakers look incongruous. There are some relics from the past like the carved image of Gajalakshmi on the front portion of the roof of the sreekovil, and a kalluvilakku (multi-tiered stone lamp, offered by Umayamma Pilla of Muthuvalliveedu[20] in 1921), which has since been shifted to the rear of the sreekovil. The temple and the surroundings have also been adversely affected by the increase in the number of devotees.

The temple has no dhvajam or flagstaff. Not even a ritually raised temporary dhvajam is used during the festival

An old photo of the sheeveli procession

The namaskara mandapam before the sanctum.
Tantri Chennās Dineshan Namboothirippad performing puja

here. Every attempt to erect a dhvajam has invariably met with failure. This could mean that the Goddess does not like to have this appurtenance, which is the hallmark of a brahminical temple, for Her own reasons. Usually the flagstaff is the seat of the deity's vehicle and though absent here, pujas are offered to Vetalika, in sankalpa, on an imaginary flagstaff.

In April 1966, the old sreekovil was demolished[21] and the existing wooden idol taken out and installed in a temporary abode called the 'bālālaya',[22] under the supervision of the then tantri of the temple Kuzhikkattu V.V. Bhattathirippad and the melshanti, Vishnutheerthan Potti. The foundation stone laying of the new sreekovil was done by Abhedananda Swamikal, the noted ascetic, who was the disciple of Chattampi Swamikal, and the construction was completed within a year under the guidance of the eminent vāsthu expert Kanippayyoor Shankaran Namboothirippad (1891–1981). The idol of the Goddess was reinstalled inside the new sreekovil with ashtabandham,[23] to the base. Though the installation of the idol here is not according to a shadādhāra pratishtha

ĀTTUKĀL AMMA

The prasadam for Ganapati Homam

Keshavan Namboothiri performing Ganapati Homam

pattern, the position of the idol's installation inside the sreekovil follows the temple tantra traditions.

S. Jayashanker in his book *The Temples of Kerala* says, 'Irrespective of the type of sreekovil, the garbha griha has the shape of a square at the central or rear portion of the sreekovil. For the purpose of demarcating the exact point of the pratishtha, the foremost step is to mark the garbha griha into four padas known as the brahma pada at the centre surrounded one after the other by the deva pada, mānusha pada and pishacha pada. This is done similar to the drawing up of vāsthupurusha mandala. Installation of the idol is confined to the brahma pada or deva pada. The brahma pada and deva pada are subdivided into fifteen and thirteen segments respectively. The pratishthas are done from the eighth segment or the rear, to that of the brahma pada. The positions of important deities however differ. Bhadrakali's idol is usually placed at the centre of the thirteenth segment of the brahma pada with a deviation from the centre.' [24]

It is impossible now to measure the exact position of the installation of the idol inside the sreekovil but the former chief priest of the temple, till August 2015, Kannan Potti, confirms that the above-mentioned order is followed. The thanka anki[25] was removed only once after it was fixed in 1985, when the chānthāttam, naveekarana kalasham and ashtabandham were performed during the period of tantri Chennās Dineshan Namboothirippad (2003–15).

Devotees narrate awe-inspiring anecdotes of miracles, bliss and blessings. During one of our many conversations, Kannan Potti told me that while doing the pujas for Her, he would feel Her presence during the invocation and She would hesitate to go back from the abhisheka vigraham after receiving the puja. He was commenting rather affectionately: 'How could She go back, when there is at least one who calls out "Amma", in the queue?' The assistant chief priest V.V. Kesavan Namboothirippad also told me that he visualises Her as blazing fire.

In 1968, artist S. Sitaram drew a picture of the Goddess. Bhasakaran Nair remembers that the artist made a sketch from the moola vigraham and then based on that figure, created the painting which is reproduced and used currently in various formats by the devotees. His signature 'S. Sitaram, SVPT' (Srivilliputhur) is seen on the old prints of the picture but with the advent of modern technology, people alter the image according to their whims and fancies. This is probably the most extensively reprinted image of any god/goddess in the world. However, this popular, elegantly smiling painting of the Goddess, decked with ornaments is just a recreation of how Sitaram visualized Her. Inside the temple, She has a totally different manifestation – that of the fierce form of Goddess Kali with weapons and protruding damshtras. It has been photographed long ago, with the sandal paste decorations, during the time of Vishnutheerthan Potti.

Words are only a fraction of the feelings the human psyche explodes with and 'Amma' is the perfect word to address Her. I began to call Her 'Amma' along with millions of other women. All are equal before Her, but She is most benevolent to those who worship Her. I have personally felt that our love for Her gives rise to deeper fondness in Her, and She makes Her presence felt, every millisecond, in every living moment. Though we try to rationalize what we experience, they are basically tiny miracles.

Neelakandan Namboothirippad sprinkling sacred water on the congregation

ĀTTUKĀL AMMA

People from all over the country arrive in groups. I have seen foreigners, Christians and Muslim women wearing burqa visiting the temple. When asked, they replied more or less in the same manner. 'We have our own God, but we like this Mother.'

The Upadevatas (The Minor Deities)

The elders at Āttukāl recollect that the small shrine of Ganapati used to be situated to the right of the north-facing Goddess near the sreekovil. Some say that earlier there was a single balikkallu at the agnikon, the south-east corner. The idol of Mādan Thampuran, the Goddess's guard, was on the western side under a palm tree. In January 2000, the ashtamangalya devaprashnam[26] – a major astrological conclave – was conducted by a team of astrologers including Thalayolaparambu Parameswara Menon, Cheppadu K.G. Kaimal, and the temple's official astrologer Konchiravila Vasudevan. In this conclave, a number of defects and problems relating to the temple and

Athāzha sheeveli led by chief priest Kannan Potti

the deity's resulting disposition were perceived. Among the measures suggested for rectifying the defects, resolving the problems, and enhancing the glory of the temple, was the prescription that the upadevatas must be shifted out of the sreekovil and special abodes should be constructed for them. M. Bhaskaran Nair told me that the ashtamangalya devaprashnam revealed that 'Amma wants to be alone'. Also, it was found that as a mahakshethram, or great temple, an idol of Lord Shiva had to be consecrated within the precincts without fail.

Kanippayyoor Krishnan Namboothirippad determined the positions for reinstalling the idols of Ganapati and Mādan Thampuran (the existing idols were used for the reinstallation) and Shiva (a new shivalinga was made) while Pambumeykkattu Vallabhan Namboothirippad fixed the location of the new idols of the serpent gods. Soon, the abodes for these upadevatas were built according to the prescriptions of vāsthu shastra. The Bhadrakali sankalpa here is not 'rurujith vidhanam';[27] the west-facing Shiva is an upadevata as the installation was done much later.[28]

Layers of row lamps were fitted on the bars around these abodes. Domes were constructed and gold-plated. The façade of the temple was covered with copper. On 17 February 2002, the temple tantri Vasudevan Parameswaran Bhattathirippad (the younger brother of Vasudevan Vasudevan Bhattathirippad), along with other priests, consecrated the Shiva idol. Afterwards, on 16 June 2002, the reconsecration of the idols of the upadevatas was done. Within the nālambalam, at the centre of the south-east corner, Maha Ganapati was seated. The Ashtanagas[29] including Naga Amma, Naga Rajavu, Naga Yakshi and Mani Nagam were placed on the right side of the shrine of Ganapati on an elevated platform outside the outer circumambulatory path and Mādan Thampuran was installed on the left.[30]

Cooking everything the Goddess likes is a major activity in the temple. There are two kitchens; one is the sacred kitchen, thidappalli, inside the nālambalam on the south-east and the other one, valiya thidappalli, is on the eastern side of the outer circumambulatory path.

The temple's managing authorities and the ABTT office function on the western side, outside the temple.

Āttukāl Amma occupies a powerful emotional space in the hearts of the people in this region. Her name appears on the hoardings of photo studios, shopping complexes, restaurants, grocery stores, and pharmacies. Hundreds of autorickshaws, lorries and buses plying in the city and around are named after Her. Her picture is everywhere – in homes, in vehicles, institutions, restaurants, hospitals, supermarkets, jewelleries and vegetable markets. Even a casual, first-time visitor cannot miss the omnipresent signs of devotion towards Her. In the din and bustle of the city, the face of Āttukāl Amma smiles benevolently from all around.

Theyyam offering at
Vamana Temple, Thalassery

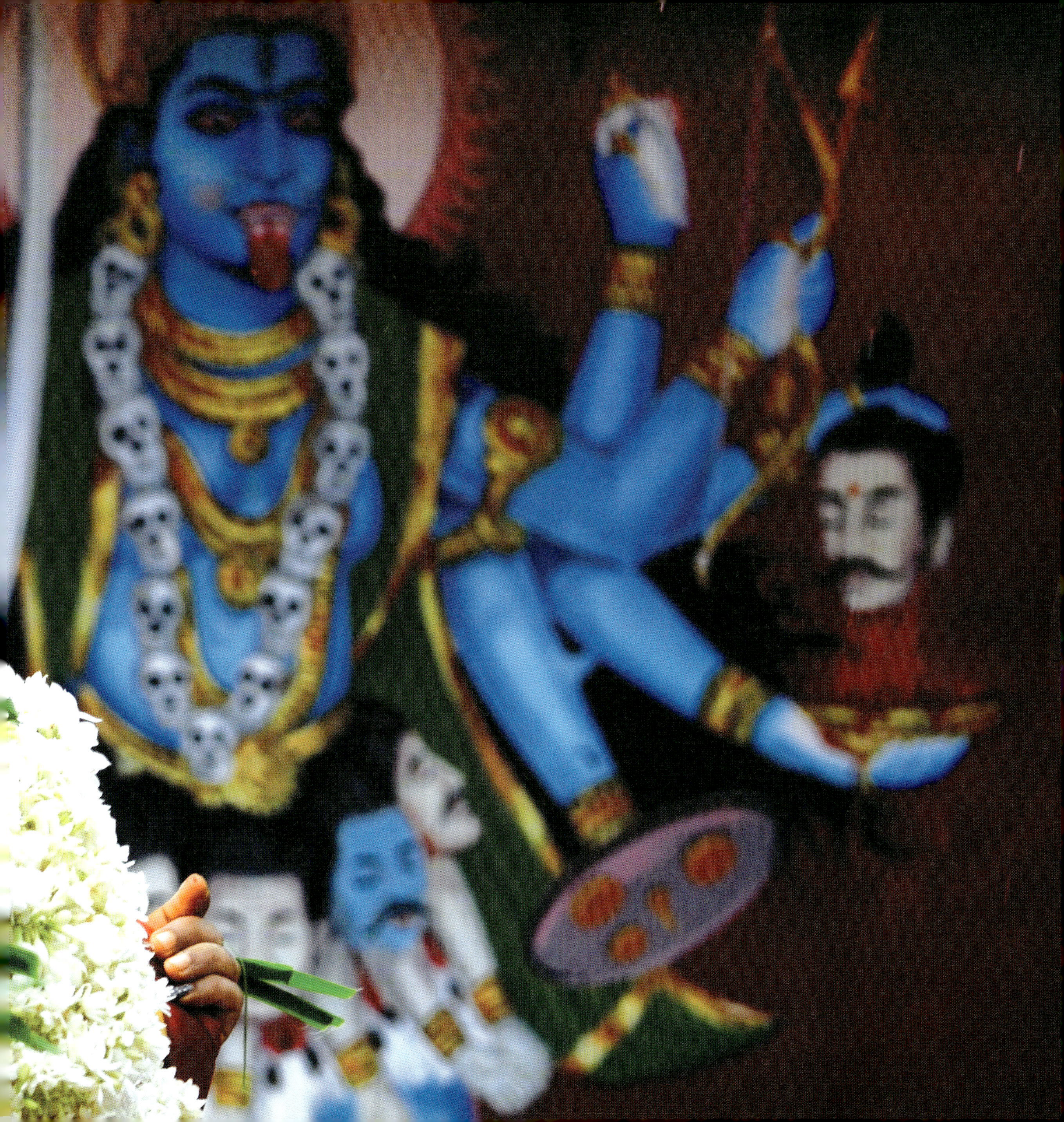

4
The Origin and Development of the Bhadrakali Cult in Kerala

The idol inside the sreekovil of the Āttukāl Temple presents myriad images in the minds of the devotees. During the festival season, journalists, feature writers and television commentators struggle to explain the Goddess, and wrongly describe Her as Kannaki, or Kodungallur Amma. She is, in fact, Bhadrakali, or the 'Auspicious Kali' who annihilates evil.

A number of myths pertaining to the origin of Kerala mention that Parashurama reclaimed this land from the sea, and installed 108 Durga temples and 108 Shiva temples here; however, Goddess Bhadrakali is everywhere in Kerala, with different names. From the Anchuthengu Mudippura on the southern coast near Attingal, and the Sharkkara Bhagavathy Temple at Chirayinkeezhu a few kilometres further east, to the oldest one in Madayikkāvu in the north, in Kannur district, Bhadrakali rules the hearts of Malayalees.

Extensive research has gone into the area of Bhadrakali worship in Kerala and its relation to myths. It has been traditionally accepted that in the many 'kalaris' or kalarippayattu training centres and kāvus all over Kerala, Kali worship was regularly practised from ancient times. She is a living presence in the ballad traditions of the lower castes in Kerala. Almost all of the many and varied ritual theatre forms prevalent in Kerala from the hoary past, are accompanied by songs narrating the same story without much variation – of Goddess Bhadrakali killing a demon named Darikan. The common belief that diseases such as smallpox are cured and all evil spirits and enemies, destroyed by Bhadrakali, is as ancient as the cult itself.

Though the patriarchal Sanskritic tradition tried to marginalize the indigenous cultural values of Goddess worship, Kali is still venerated in every village and worshipped in almost all Hindu homes. Bhadrakali has more significance in Kerala than anywhere else in India.

Brahmanda Purana mentions that Sage Parashurama did the first and primary installation of Bhadrakali in Madayikkāvu, near Kannur in north Kerala. The demon Darikan, whom the Goddess fights and kills, also has his origin in Kerala. Natural formations which devotees believe are remnants of the fort of Darikan, and the cave in which he is supposed to have taken refuge while fleeing from the Goddess, can still be seen near Madayikkāvu.

The origin of Bhadrakali, as millions in Kerala believe, is connected with the narrative of the slaying of Darikan. This asura, armed with the boon of immortality received from Lord Brahma, with the caveat that only a woman can kill him, conquers all the three worlds. No other gods such as Brahma,

Vishnu, Skanda, Indra and Yama could destroy him. Like the asura Raktabija of *Durgasaptashati*, Darikan too had been given a boon that every drop of his blood would emerge as a clone of his. Eventually, Lord Shiva opens His third eye to protect the universe; from within the opened third eye, the form of Bhadrakali emerges, more terrifying and scary than anything the universe had seen.

The origin of Bhadrakali is described thus in *Durgasaptashati:* 'She emerged with an awe-inspiring, earth-splitting roar and a torso as big as the Anjana Mountain, with thousands of hands and faces, glowing and fiery eyes, and weapons in all Her hands. Bhadrakali annihilates Darikan by chopping off his head and, before even a single drop of his blood can strike the ground, She collects his blood in a vessel or skull kept beneath and keeps drinking it.'

Bhadrakali is the family deity of many ancient families throughout Kerala. She is also the tutelary deity of the Nadar community of southern Kerala and Tamil Nadu, and also of the Kodavas of Karnataka.

The history of Kali worship by Keralites is as old, at least, as *Brahmanda Purana*. In the 'Bhadrolpathi' segment of *Markandeya Purana*, the greatness of Bhadrakali is described for the first time. Sarah Caldwell observes: 'The definition of Kali as an Aryan or non-Aryan Goddess (whether tribal,

A scene from Kaliyoottu at Sharkkara Devi Temple, Chirayinkeezhu. Photo: Vineeth Nair

Dravidian, or Asura) is a central concern of narrators for whom She has long been a powerful political symbol. Through the eyes of each devotee, Her identity subtly shifts to conform to the cultural identities that are most meaningful and operative.'[1]

In Kerala, Bhadrakali is not mentioned as a principal deity in canonical texts prior to the sixteenth-century temple tantra text *Seshasamuchhayam* by Chennās Shankaran Namboothirippad. Speaking of the temple tantra texts that explain the philosophical and technical aspects of conducting pujas at temples, *Kriyadeepika*, better known as *Pudayur Bhasha*, composed by Poonthottathu Pudayoor Illam Vasudevan Namboothirippad in Malayalam Era (ME) 518 and *Tantrasamuchhayam* by Chennās Narayanan Namboothirippad in ME 604, do not mention Goddess Bhadrakali. Only in *Seshasamuchhayam* by Chennās Shankaran Namboothirippad, the son and disciple of Chennās Narayanan Namboothirippad, we come across the mention of Her name. It is only in the text *Saparivaram Pujakal*, by Kakkad Narayanan Namboothirippad, compiled much later, in the twentieth century, that the pujas meant specifically for Goddess Bhadrakali are discussed.

Historians contend that the reason for this absence may be that the Bhadrakali form of Goddess Durga had not been worshipped by Namboothiris, the Malayali Brahmin community, till such time that the above-mentioned temple tantra texts were composed, probably because they arrived comparatively late on the scene, and Bhadrakali, the Goddess of the lower castes, could not be assimilated into their predominantly satvik, 'pure,' rituals.

We can, therefore, assume that Bhadrakali is a primordial Goddess, worshipped by non-brahmins from the earliest times and that She was, in the comparatively recent times, appropriated by the hegemonic priestly class and admitted into the Brahminical modes of worship. Myths and folklore are not completely imaginary; there are always elements of historical truth at their centre.

The spread and reach of this unique concept of the Goddess – in which Bhadrakali is the daughter of Lord Shiva, instead of his consort – and its acceptance by generations down the centuries make one wonder if Goddess Bhadrakali did live in this land as a real woman once upon a time. During the course of writing this book, I realized that Kali also was a popular Hindu first name, for women as well as men, some hundred years ago, even in my family.

The idols of Kali installed in the various Kerala temples have different attributes. She is seen bearing in Her hands, sword, shield, human skull, the decapitated head of Darikan, a

Chicken being offered to Bhadrakali Theyyam

silver battleaxe, a small drum, trident, rope, hook, pestle, ring, serpent, conch shell, bow and arrows, spear, and discus.

Her images as portrayed in ancient cave sculptures, bas-reliefs, murals and paintings have four, eight, sixteen and up to sixty-four arms. There are also many different forms of the deity such as Bhadrakali, Karinkali, Muthalappurathu Karinkali, Sumukhikali, Mahakali, Ratrikali, Chamundi, Kandankali (the one originating from the poison Kalakootam in Lord Shiva's throat) Bālabhadrā and others described in various local cult traditions. They got assimilated into one common Goddess, Bhadrakali, and later, into mainstream religion, as Bhagavathy.[2]

Most of the Devi temples in Kerala today are 'Bhagavathy' temples. Bhagavathy is the generic name of the Goddess in Kerala, but each village and each temple add specific first names before 'Bhagavathy' to identify the particular form of the Goddess they worship, for example, 'Āttukāl Bhagavathy'. But, most of these are Bhadrakali installations. Goddess Durga is also known as Bhagavathy.

The First Appearance of Bhadrakali in Sanskrit Sacred Texts

In *Durgasaptashati* attributed to Sage Markandeya, and which is believed to have been written sometime between 400 and 500 CE, the archetypical Kali is first seen. In the eleventh chapter, in the following shloka, the terrifying aspect of Goddess Durga, is presented as Bhadrakali:

Kaliyoottu – the performer impersonates Kali

ĀTTUKĀL AMMA

Jwalakaralamatyugramashesha surasoodanam
thrishoolam pathu no bheether bhadrakali namosthuthe

(May your trident fierce with flames, terrible and causing total annihilation of asuras protect us from all fears! Prostrations to you Bhadrakali!) [Translated by the author.]

The purpose of Her arrival is to kill the demon Raktabija with whom Durga is engaged in battle. The demon's power to create his clones from each drop of his blood that Durga spills on the earth, makes Her create Bhadrakali, who, with Her gargantuan tongue, laps up the blood drops before they hit the earth, and finally kills the demon himself.

An account in *Devi Bhagavatham* goes this way: Bhadrakali was created along with Veerabhadra, when the enraged Lord Shiva struck the ground with His dreadlocks. He does so to take revenge on Daksha Prajapati, when his daughter and Shiva's consort Sati committed self-immolation by jumping into the sacrificial fire at Her father's yagna, unable to bear his humiliation of Lord Shiva.

She has been described variously as Kali – 'the one who blazes like the fire' ('kaluka' in Malayalam means 'to blaze forth'), in one of the many meanings of the word, the one who is dark-complexioned and as Mahakali, the consort of Mahakalan.

Thookkam ritual

The Bhadrakali Legend of Kerala – an Independent Myth

There are several peculiarities in the Bhadrakali myth prevalent in Kerala. While in the rest of India, Kali is considered to be Lord Shiva's consort, in Kerala She is worshipped as His daughter. This can be attributed to the regional variations in myths that keep happening in the retelling of the legends and Puranas. In *Durgasaptashati*, though Devi kills many asuras, Darikan is not one of them. However, in *Devi Bhagavatham*, we come across a mention of Darikan. Furious at the news of Her killing two asuras, Thamrachikshuran and Asilomavidalan, Mahishasura directs his lieutenant Darikan to prepare the chariot for a direct encounter with Devi. This is not supported by the Puranas. There are also opinions that Manodari, the wife of Darikan, is the one who spreads Masuri (smallpox) with the blessing of Shiva and that Kali is its eradicator. In *Devi Bhagavatham*, the name Darikan is never mentioned again, or never used as another name for Raktabija.

There are no references to Shiva's daughter Bhadrakali anywhere in the Puranas, as already pointed out. So, the Bhadrakali legend of Kerala should be seen as an instance of independent myth-making that deviated from the Puranic stories. It was in the *Bhadrolpathi Charitham* that the attempt was made to connect *Markandeya Purana* to the story of Bhadrakali. However, none of the later traditions have any mention of *Markandeya Purana*.

According to N. Ajithkumar, the story of Darikan's slaying is found only in *Keralolpathi*, and it states that Darikan is the reincarnation of Mahishasura. The various names of the Goddess prevalent in Kerala such as Bhadra, Kali, Bhadrakali (in all Her various manifestations), Bhagavathy, Amman, Mariyamman, Mutharamman (and several other 'Ammans' who bespeak the Tamil influence) point to one fact – that it was the Goddess and not the male gods who ruled this land from the earliest times.

It may also be noted that the Keralite Bhadrakali cult was prevalent in various erstwhile kingdoms of what is today the state of Tamil Nadu. There, She is known variously as 'Malayala Bhagavathy' and 'Malayala Bhadrakali.'

Kali ritually falling unconscious during Kaliyoottu

The Sacred Groves and Bhadrakali Worship in Kerala

Kali worship in Kerala may have originated in the form of reverence for Nature as Goddess, in this scenically beautiful

The Mudiyettu at Vellayani Temple

land. Worship of a fierce goddess with attributes similar to those of Kali was prevalent in Kerala even in ancient times. The earliest written texts mention a terrifying tribal goddess called Kottavai, who dwelt in battlefields, deserts, forests and mountains. The traces of old Goddess traditions were preserved in songs and rituals and by the shrines dedicated to the Goddess in the sacred groves called 'kāvus' maintained mainly by the martial and agricultural communities.

Kāvus or sacred groves full of rare trees and plants are an integral part of the Goddess temples in Kerala. Trees and stones are worshipped in these groves which are abodes of Nature spirits. Serpent worship too takes place in the kāvus. The serpent, symbolizing Goddess Kundalini[3] in Tantra, is connected to the Shakta tradition.[4] It is believed that the major Bhadrakali shrines such as Kodungallur, Panayannarkkāvu near Thiruvalla, Madayikkāvu near Kannur, and Vallikāvu near Kottayam, evolved from kāvus or sacred groves. The Kottankulangara Vana Durga Temple in Kollam district is a typical example of the kind of Nature worship that began in kāvus. There, the idol is a black stone that receives sunlight and rain in a roofless sanctum sanctorum, like in most other kāvus. The Arakkal Bhadrakali Temple, also in Kollam district, is known for the faith of the devotees in the unlimited power of Bhadrakali to decimate evil and grant blessings to Her worshippers.

Kali, with Her unpredictable behaviour and primordial appearance represents the organic and dynamic order of Nature; this is in stark contrast to the artificial, static order imposed on society by the Indian caste system.

It has been traditionally accepted that in the many 'kalaris' or kalarippayattu training centres and kāvus all over Kerala, Kali worship was regularly practised from ancient times, even prior to the advent of the Aryans into Kerala. Lokanārkkāvu, near Vadakara in Malabar, which is described as 'the Shaolin Temple of Kerala' by feature writers and TV channel presenters, is the abode of Bhadrakali, whom many heroes of the *Vadakkan Pāttukal* (Northern Ballads), like Thacholi Othenan, worshipped. Lokanārkkāvil Amma is still revered as the tutelary deity of all warriors of the region. The many other Bhadrakali temples and kalarippayattu training centres with Bhadrakali shrines attached to them existing now in Kerala, where non-Brahmin priests perform pujas, bear witness firmly to the ancient Bhadrakali worship in Kerala dating back to pre-Brahmin times.

Ritual Performances and Folk Songs Related to the Bhadrakali–Darikan Myth

Kali is worshipped in Kerala as an embodiment of wrath and fury as well as of protection and preservation. The pervasive emotion connected with Bhadrakali is fear – people are afraid of Her in spite of the protection She assures, says Sarah Caldwell.[5]

The angry Kali, a scene from Kaliyoottu ritual at Sharkkara Devi Temple, Chirayinkeezhu

ĀTTUKĀL AMMA

Kodungallur Bhagavathy, a sketch by artist Madanan

The legend of Darikan is not prevalent anywhere else in India. His story figures in all the songs related to Bhadrakali sung during ritual performances such as 'Darikavadham Thottam', 'Darikan Thottam', 'Kalampāttu', 'Bhadrolpathi', 'Pāna Thottam', and 'Darikavadham Pāttu'. In ritual performances such as Mudiyettu and Paranettu, the encounter between Kali and Darikan forms a major part. This is called Nilaththilporu.[6]

Also, the folk songs in Kerala are steeped in the Kali – Darikan myth. There are folk songs from Travancore, Malabar and Kochi that narrate the story of Kali challenging Darikan bluntly for an encounter (*Vāda Darika porinu vāda/Darika veera porinu vāda...*). In the folk song 'Darikavadham Pāttu' of the Mannān community in northern Malabar this story is fully described. This song also includes the stories of Lord Shiva gifting His daughter Kali to the childless king of southern Kollam, and an anklet of the Goddess leading to the killing of the Pandyan king. (The Thottam Pāttu, which is used to invoke and transport Bhadrakali from the Kodungallur temple to the Āttukāl Temple too has a similar storyline.) It says the Goddess kills Darikan after hearing about his atrocities, on Her way back from the Pandyan Kingdom.

This story, 'Darikavadham', is also portrayed in the 'Pulavrittam' performed immediately before Padayani, an ancient performing ritual art form. Similar ritual art forms like Kalianadakam and Kalikettupāttu of the Paraya community in Thrissur, Kalampāttu by the Pāttukuruppu community, Pallippāna by the Velan community, and all the mantramālas invoking Kali have the same storyline.[7]

In northern Kerala, the ritual dance of Theyyam is an example of the very ancient Bhagavathy (read Bhadrakali) worship surviving over the centuries through folk tradition. 'Muchhilottu Bhagavathy' has the largest following in northern Kerala. Though worship of Shiva, spirits and ancestors also are now part of the Theyyam tradition, its origin is in the Goddess cult.

The ritual theatre form Mudiyettu mainly found in central Kerala, stages the battle between Kali and the demon Darikan. The Mudiyettu actor is believed to be possessed by the Goddess during the performance. Patriarchy diluted this ritual by making it a male-dominated exercise. Women played a crucial role in rituals associated with the Goddess. Female shamans channelled supernatural forces and the Goddess during their trance. They were experts in divination, as oracles. These women, whose ritual activities included dancing, singing and drumming, lived in the hilly forested regions of the Western Ghats. They were the oracles at the Bhagavathy Temple of Kodungallur.

Kodungallur Bhagavathy

Kodungallur Bhagavathy has an important part to play in the Āttukāl Pongala festival. The singers of the Thottam Pāttu invoke Her through their songs and invite Her to Āttukāl, where She takes up residence for the duration of the festival.

The Goddess of Kodungallur is Bhadrakali – in fact She is believed to be the next installation of the Goddess, after the one at Madayikkāvu. The advent of the Goddess of the Kodungallur temple is related to the episode about Darikan narrated above. Even after slaying Darikan at Madayikkāvu and obtaining an abode at Kodungallur, the fire of Kali's fury did not subside and it threatened to engulf the universe. Devotees began singing bawdy songs to fan the sexual desire of the Goddess, and to whittle down Her anger. Although in this story the patriarchal religion relegates the originally tantric Goddess to be Shiva's subordinate, the unusual devotional method of singing sexually charged songs may have had its origins in the tantric practice of considering the Goddess as one's Divine Lover rather than as a Mother Goddess.

In the Kodungallur Bharani festival[8] (so named, because the festival begins on the Bharani asterism in Kumbham, ME, and ends on the Aswathi asterism of the next month Meenam, on which day Devi is supposed to have killed Darikan, making it one of the longest festivals in Kerala, lasting a month), worshippers still sing sexually explicit songs passed down the centuries, and run around the temple dancing, presumably to satisfy the aroused Goddess. On the final day of the festival, which happens on the Aswathi asterism, the ritual called 'kāvu theendal', takes place, watched over by the Raja of Kodungallur, in which the velichappādus (oracles), many of whom are women, run around the temple, singing ribald songs addressed to Bhagavathy. The ritual begins only after getting the signal of permission from the Raja of Kodungallur, who takes up his position under a silk canopy set up on the broad base of a peepal tree in the precincts of the temple. The leader of the lower-caste people is called Palakya Velan, and he is the one who leads the rush of the velichappādus.

'Theendal' literally means 'the entry of the untouchable'. It is believed that from olden days, the raja would permit the people from lower castes to enter the temple precincts and perform this ritual. Conversely, it could have been that, in ancient times, the lower castes used to control the temple; such rituals would have been traditionally performed by them, with the permission of the local chieftain; and they would have succeeded in retaining this hereditary right, in spite of the Brahminization of the temple during later times. Significantly, Brahmin priests keep away from the festivities. The temple is closed for seven days after this ritual, and reopened later after purification.

Though the upper castes still control the temple, the thriving Bharani festival proves that the indigenous non-Brahminical Goddess tradition prevails, albeit through an annual ritual lasting a few hours. During the Bharani Festival, the so-called backward-caste people like the Velas and their chief, Palakya Velan, enjoy an astonishingly predominant status, though granted by the raja.

The Sri Kurumba Bhagavathy Temple, situated half a kilometre south of the present main temple (but included in the temple complex), is considered by many as the moolakshetram (parent temple). The festival procession of the lower-caste people during the Bharani festival begins from this temple. The Kudumbis, a Konkani-speaking farming community, an Other Backward Community spread over central and south-western Kerala (they are of the same stock as the Kurmis of north India), who have Kodungallur Amma as their tutelary deity, frequent this smaller temple.

Kodungallur Amma is supposed to be the third of the Sapta Matrikas, (the seven Divine Mothers) and though there are stone images of the Matrikas, the main object of worship is a large wooden idol of the Goddess with eight arms. At Āttukāl too, the bali stones representing Sapta Matrikas were recently installed to the south of the sreekovil; this is just a replication of what is present in other ancient Bhadrakali temples of Kerala.

Kerala, Goddess's Own Country

Kerala, a state where the Goddess could not be eclipsed by the advent of male deities, still cherishes 'Bhagavathy' or 'Devi' in her various manifestations everywhere within its territory. It is difficult to find a Kerala village without a shrine for Devi. Crowning this Goddess affinity of Malayalee believers, millions of women devotees the world over repose their unalloyed love and trust in Āttukāl Amma, as recorded in the *Guinness Book of World Records* more than once. All this point to one fact: Rituals and temporal aspects apart, Bhagavathy is the all-pervading and protecting Universal Mother.

Kerala Tourism Department's famous slogan declares the state as 'God's Own Country'. However, in ancient days, before the worship of male gods sneaked into Kerala's psyche, the Goddess ruled the consciousness of this land of tall coconut trees, lush green paddy fields and turquoise green backwaters. The patriarchal religion swept over Kerala with the male gods Shiva and Vishnu in the vanguard, concurrent with, or following, the rout of the Jains and Buddhists by Shankaracharya in the eighth century. He revived Hindu faith with its Advaitic teachings based on the wisdom culled from the Upanishads. However, before that, despite the spread of Jainism and Buddhism, Devi worship centred around the several Bhagavathy kāvus, located in villages across Kerala, was the predominant cult. These kāvus and temples still exist and hold their sway over the hearts of Malayalees.

Thottam Pāttu: The singers sitting in the thatched-shed hymn house

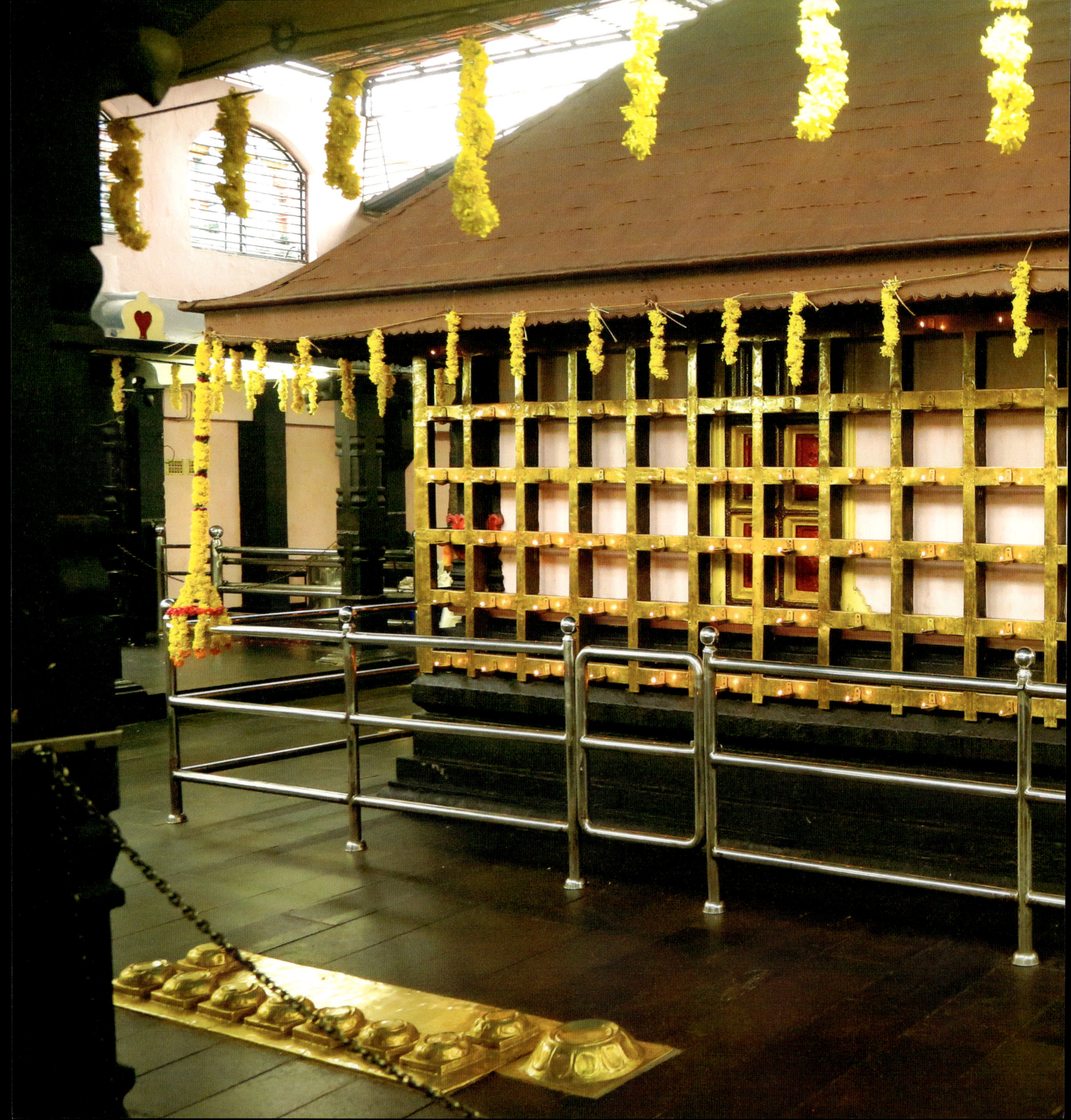

The Sreekovil of Āttukāl Amma, view from the south.

5

The Āttukāl Temple

Kanippayyoor Krishnan Namboothirippad, the temple vāsthu expert who also guided me in my research about the structural aspects of the temple, told me that expansion of the building complex in this manner became necessary because material prosperity, with lots of money and valuables pouring in as offering into the coffers of Āttukāl Amma as Her fame spread far and wide, demanded more sacred space for the devotees flooding there.

Āttukāl Temple,
view from the west.
Sketch by artist Madanan

Along with prosperity, the serene simplicity of the erstwhile mudippura has vanished. The Āttukāl Temple is a mahakshetram, a great temple, now, in terms of fame, structure, riches, the number of people visiting every year, and the Pongala festival that attracts the largest gathering of women in the world. It is a temple that follows Brahminical modes of worship now. But it is not a Brahminical temple or a temple dedicated to Kannaki as is often made out.

We witness the blending of Keralite and Tamil architectural styles in the temple sculptures of Āttukāl today. Keralite temple architecture is mainly wood-based, with pagoda-like roof, and wooden jalis, whereas, in the Tamil style, temples are generally built as massive stone structures, many parts of which are, of late, built in concrete as well. The concrete sculptures painted in gaudy colours mar the earlier serenity and simplicity of the Āttukāl Temple when it was a small mudippura.

A typical brahminical temple follows the architectural norms and rules found in many ancient texts. Even though the deities are different in various temples, the architectural design of temples is more or less similar as in the case of the structure of the human body. Spatially, the Kerala temples follow the general Indian philosophical concepts of the centre, axis, and the human connectedness to cosmic reality, while its implementation in the built form follows the Vedic religious practices.

The Construction of a Brahminical Temple

Before the construction of a temple starts, a square pit is dug at the place where the sreekovil is going to be built. The bottom of this pit is purified by oblations to the Vāsthupurusha. Only thereafter is the installation of the idol done according to the shadādhāra method which is described below:

The ādhārashila, a flat foundation stone with a cavity in the centre, is placed in the middle of this pit. The cavity is then filled with different kinds of grains. Above that, a pot made of copper or stone, filled with gold and gems, is placed. On top of that, a flower carved from granite is placed. Over this flower, a tortoise carved in stone is placed facing the same direction the deity would be facing. On top of this tortoise, a hollow copper tube, the yoganāla, pointing skywards, is kept. Atop this comes the napumsakashila, a stone which is neither male nor female, which represents Earth, one of the five elements. On top of the napumsakashila is the peetham or the base to install the deity's idol.[1] The floor of the sreekovil is built around the napumsakashila.

But at Āttukāl, when the new sreekovil was constructed (1966–67), exactly at the place where the centuries-old thatched structure stood, the shadādhāra pratishtha procedure was not followed. 'The entire place was full of water when we dug up the land to build the new sreekovil. It must have been a paddy field once. So a strong foundation of rocks and concrete had to be built. We completed the work within three months and each rock we purchased from Mayiladi has my touch on it,' M. Bhaskaran Nair said. 'The rajagopuram (main tower) was built over two years from 1973 to 1975, and its foundation goes down as many feet as its height,' he added.

The panchaprakāram scheme is another feature of a Brahminical temple. In temple architecture, prakāram means enclosure or limit, and thus, panchaprakāram, are the five enclosures around the sreekovil. Only great temples have these prakārams. Now, the Āttukāl Temple has five enclosures according to the panchaprakāram scheme. However, some of the structures outside the sreekovil are later additions and do not strictly adhere to the panchaprakāram scheme.

The panchaprakārams are:

(a) Akathe balivattom or the inner enclosure that encompasses the sacred sreekovil, the sopanam, the mukha-mandapam, antarmandalam – the area within a dotted square connecting the twenty-four balikkallus (the stones on which sacrifices are offered to minor deities and spirits), the

ĀTTUKĀL AMMA

The sanctum of Āttukāl Amma

namaskaramandapam and pranālam, the pipe through which the fluids used for the ablutions performed on the idol go out;

(b) The chuttambalam that protects the temple, as it surrounds the temple. It comprises thidappalli (the temple's kitchen) and the place to prepare kalashams (the pots filled with water and other sacred ingredients to anoint the idol everyday), and to make mulayara, the temporary shed, to sow seeds to enhance the chaitanya of the idol, during the sahasrakalasham and other rituals closely connected with the sreekovil;

(c) The vilakkumādam, a wall affixed with rows upon rows of lamps. However, it is absent at the Āttukāl Temple. Very few temples have vilakkumādam;

(d) Purathe balivattom (or the outer enclosure) that comprises valiya balikkallu, balipeethas, kshetrapalan, valiya thidappalli and the sreekovil of upadevatas; and

(e) Maryada, the outer wall.

THE ĀTTUKĀL TEMPLE

Not every temple follows the panchaprakāram closely. Many temples have other combinations like 'a' alone, or 'a' and 'b', or 'a', 'b' and 'd', or 'a', 'b', 'd' and 'e'.[2]

The sreekovil or the prāsādam denotes a 'settling down,' and a seat made for that which has settled down and acquired concrete form, the form of a dwelling, a residence, the seat of God. Here the sreekovil is square in shape, reached by three steps, the sopanam, that lead to the mukhamandpam, the front chamber of the sreekovil. A door from there opens to an inner ambulatory passage, the idanāzhi, an area that extends into a passage around the sreekovil and the front door leading to the sreekovil.

It is usually very hot inside the sreekovil, because it is a very confined space, with only the door for an opening; there are several oil lamps burning and the priest do ārati often within this space. The roof, made of concrete, is covered with

Vishnu Namboothiri decorating the Nagar idols

ĀTTUKĀL AMMA

ĀTTUKĀL BHAGAVATHY TEMPLE
(Not to scale)

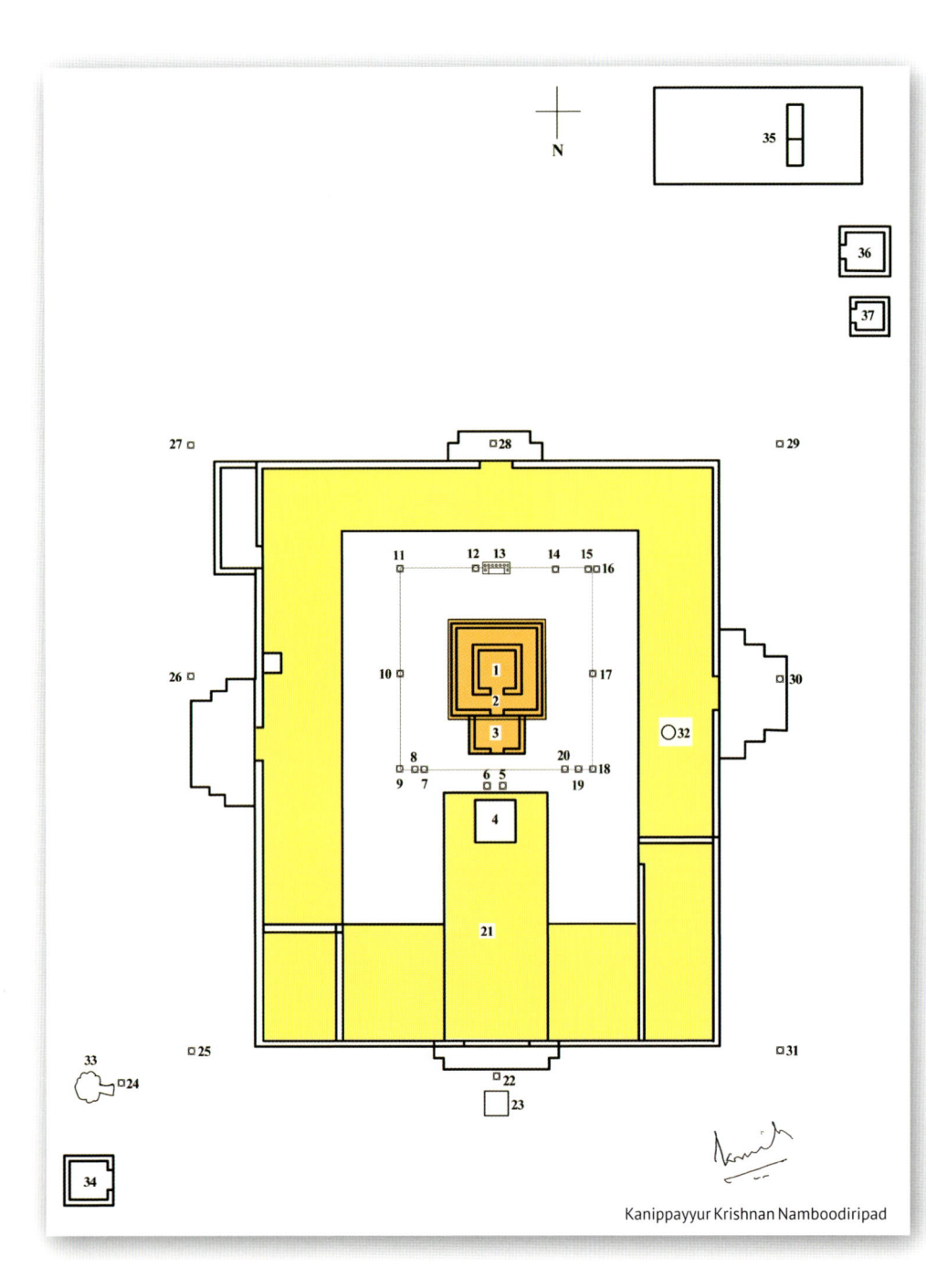

Kanippayyur Krishnan Namboodiripad

1. Devi
2. Idanazhi
3. Mukhamandapam
4. Namaskara Mandapam
5. Soman
6. Vaishravanan
7. Nirmalyadhari
8. Brahman
9. Eeshanan
10. Indran
11. Agni
12. Yaman
13. Sapthamathrukkal. Veerabhadran. Ganapati. (A cluster of 9 stones)
14. Shasta
15. Anandan
16. Niruthi
17. Varunan
18. Vayu
19. Durga
20. Subramanyan
21. Passage - kedavilakku
22. Bheeshanabhairavan
23. Valiyabelikkallu
24. Kshethrapalan
25. Samharabhairavan
26. Asithangabhairavan
27. Rurubhairavan
28. Chandabhairavan
29. Kroheeshabhairavan
30. Unmathabhairavan
31. Kapalibhairavan
32. Palmtree (Old Madan installation)
33. Old arāyal
34. Sivan
35. Nāgar Idols
36. Ganapati
37. Madan

thin copper sheets. The sheltered akathe balivattom (the inner enclosure that encompasses the sreekovil) has a namaskara mandapam located directly in front of the sreekovil.

I was told by Kannan Potti that the west-facing pranālam, through which the water used in abhishekam flows out, has been closed here on the instructions of the temple's tantri. According to temple vāsthu, the flow of water from the sreekovil should be towards the north.

It is important to note that in the books on temple architecture, parallels are drawn between the temple structure and the human body, comparing body parts to sections of the temple. The sreekovil is considered as the head; akathe balivattom, the face; the namaskara mandapam the throat; the nālambalam, the arms; purathe balivattom where the minor deities are installed as the stomach; the outer wall as the knees and ankles; and dhwaja stambham, the flag mast, or the gopuram (the Āttukāl temple has no flag mast, so it might be the gopuram) above the sreekovil as the deity's feet. The proportions that these five structures have to follow have been prescribed in the second chapter of *Tantrasamuchhayam*.

The style of the renovated temple structure reflects myriad sociocultural, economic and religious compulsions of recent times, since the past two to three decades, including the possible interpolation of the Kannaki myth in the narration of Āttukāl Amma's story. In her article, 'Myth and Modernity in a Ritualistic Space',[3] with reference to the Āttukāl Temple, Darshana Sreedhar notes that the architectural arrangement in the temple itself tries to incorporate the earlier Kannaki traditions into the Hindu pantheon. The Kannaki cult is integrated into the Hindu mythic tradition here.

The towers of the Āttukāl Temple and a prayer hall were constructed only a few years ago. The concrete sculptural ornamentations on the rajagopuram reflect the skills of the gifted sculptor Rajaram, a native of Madurai, who lived in Thiruvananthapuram. On the circumambulatory path,

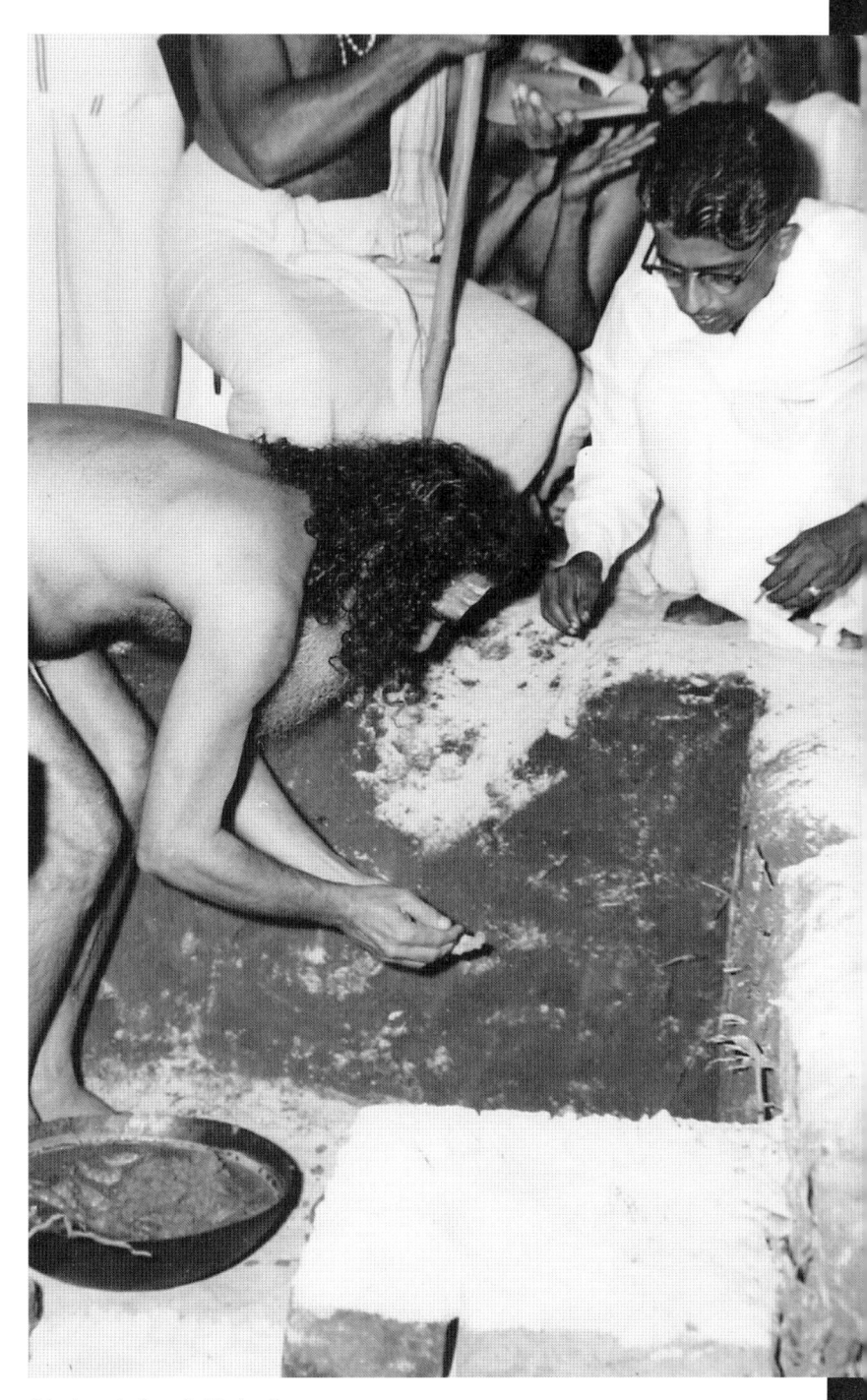

Abhedananda Swamikal laying the foundation stone of the new temple

ĀTTUKĀL AMMA

above the place where thulabhāram is conducted, there are artistic depictions of women in their traditional attire and ornaments, exemplifying the unique, ethnic Malayalee culture. Idols of four bhootas are fixed on the four corners of the chuttambalam. Many important episodes of Sri Ayyappa's story are depicted on the eastern side of the chuttambalam.

On the eastern and western sides of the rajagopuram, several sculptures tell the story of Kannaki with a few variations from the narrative of *Chilappathikaram*, one of them being the killing of the Vaishya who worshipped the Goddess. This is not mentioned in *Chilappathikaram*.

I have been witness to many changes that have occurred in the temple during the past four years. Devotees are not allowed to stand near the sopanam now and the mini stage in the purathe balivattom was shifted to the outer compound. And the work on gold-plating the entire

Kumbhabhishekam for the new temple, performed by V.V. Bhattathirippad

THE ĀTTUKĀL TEMPLE

Abhedananda Swamikal arriving at Āttukāl

sreekovil is in progress. The formerly open compound is covered and the temple protected by asbestos sheets. Tube lights, electric wires, the presence of many plastic baskets, steel scaffolding pipes, etc., mar the beauty and simplicity of the temple precincts. We may not know what will happen to the exterior of the temple in another hundred years but this chapter is written to describe what the Āttukāl Temple now is and what it is not.

Many have asked me about the ever-increasing chaitanya, or energy, and the flow of people to the temple. I have always

ĀTTUKĀL AMMA

felt that it is just the love and affection of the common devotees like me and millions of others, who would do anything for Her, which translates into Her power.

The temple staff carrying thattam nivedyam offered to the Goddess

The temple before the superstructure was put in place. Photo: Gopan Thaliyil

THE ĀTTUKĀL TEMPLE

The commencement of the Thottam singing

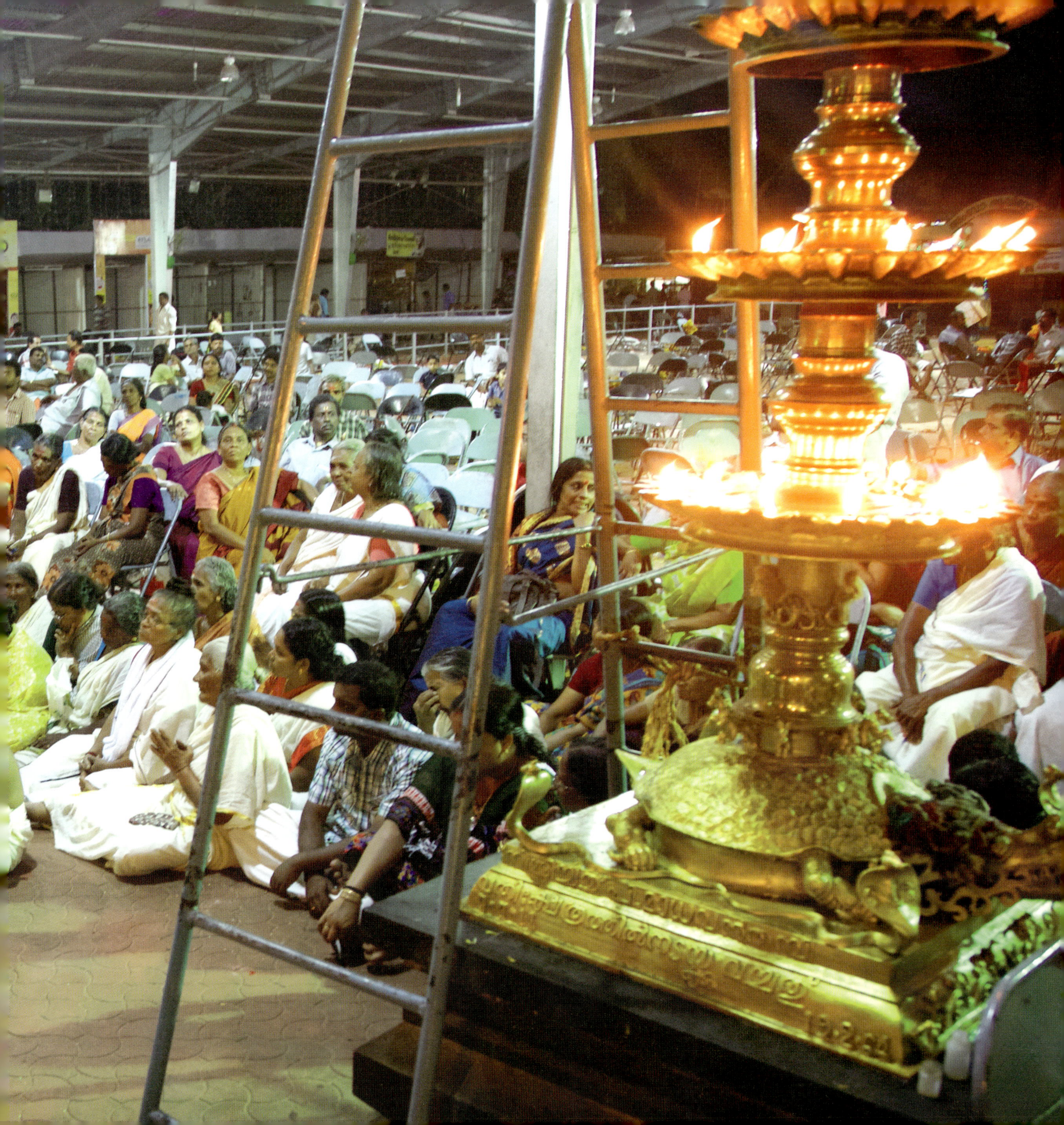

6

The Commencement of the Ten-day Festival

The items used in the purification ritual (Suddhikalasham) before the commencement of the festival

Most Malayalees wait for the Āttukāl Pongala like they wait for Onam[1] or Vishu,[2] the two major festivals of their land. Plans for the celebration are made well in advance. For people living in the vicinity of the temple, no celebration is greater than the Pongala. They renovate their houses, buy new clothes and invite relatives to visit them. The natives of Āttukāl working in faraway lands come back home to participate in this event.

The festival or the utsavam at the Āttukāl Temple commences on Karthika-asterism in the month of Kumbham (Malayalam Calendar) (February–March). The temple follows the lunar calendar; so the date varies every year. The festival lasts ten days and the world-famous Āttukāl Pongala is on the ninth day. The celebrations that accompany the Pongala festival begin with the singing of the Thottam Pāttu by Madhu Asan and his troupe. Thottam Pāttu is a ritualistic hymn narrating the story of Goddess Bhadrakali killing the Pandyan king, who had executed Her husband, wrongly accusing him of stealing the queen's anklets. In the old days, the word 'utsavam' was not used to refer to the festival. People merely said 'The Pāttu has started,' or asked 'When does the Pāttu begin?'

There are three other major Bhadrakali temples on the outskirts of Thiruvananthapuram near the Āttukāl Temple. Of them, the Konchiravila and Mukkolakkal Bhadrakali Temples are important because the deities in those temples are supposed to be Āttukāl Amma's sisters. There are similarities in the way the festivals commence and conclude in these temples, as the same troupe of Thottam singers sings the same ritualistic songs there too. The pongala is an integral part of the festivals there.

The temple astrologer fixes the dates for the festival for the coming year in August–September of the current year – that is, almost six months in advance. A banner announcing the starting date of the festival is put up in the temple precincts on the first of Chingam (August–September), which marks the beginning of the new Malayalam year. The ABTT announces the time to light the pongala hearth also along with this.

Crowds during the festival days

The registration for offering Kuthiyottam[3] starts at this time at the temple's administrative office. The temple buildings are thoroughly cleaned and whitewashed well in advance and the sreekovil literally sparkles during the festival. About a month before the festival, a thin branch of a jackfruit tree is cut and carried to the temple without letting it touch the ground. A peg is shaped out of it and driven into the ground near the Ganapati shrine. This is called kodināttal karmam. Kannan Potti, the chief priest, explained to me that this is a symbolic flagstaff, which safeguards the festival that will commence. This symbolic flagstaff is not to be confused with the dhwajam of the temple.

Vendors of various wares occupy the hitherto empty spaces around the temple; stage performances such as dance, dance dramas and classical music concerts by renowned artistes transform the mood and ambience of the whole locality, almost overnight. There is a special deepārādhana, at midnight during the festival days. Before 2014, the Kuthiyottam boys used to be kept awake by Radhakrishnan Asari, the man in charge of conducting the ritual, to be present during this deepārādhana. However, this practice of keeping the young boys awake till midnight for the deepārādhana was stopped by the temple authorities after the renowned astrologer engaged by the temple, Raman Akkithirippad, conducted a deva prashnam, a conclave of astrologers, and forbade it.[4] The daily rituals at the temple remain the same during the festival days except that the temple remains open till midnight.

The elaborate floral decorations done by the Pāttukār families and the ABTT, the pleated golden brocade, or njorinjāda, kept only during the festival days as a backdrop for the idol, which looks like a halo of Āttukāl Amma, and the phenomenal crowds of devotees that form long, serpentine queues for Devi's darshan are the major changes perceptible

Preparation of the hymn house led by Madhu Asan and Radhakrishnan Asari

THE COMMENCEMENT OF THE TEN-DAY FESTIVAL

during this time. The administrative office and the office-bearers also work nonstop.

For the smooth functioning of the festival and to make the arrangements for accommodation, food and cultural programmes, various committees are formed and a list of volunteers drawn up to assist the respective committees. Government agencies, voluntary organizations and residents' associations join hands to provide assistance to the devotees during this time. A police assistance post and first-aid post are also set up near the temple.

The state government actively assists the Pongala festival. It had sanctioned three crore of rupees to provide better facilities, including infrastructure, for the devotees expected to reach the city for the Āttukāl Pongala festival in 2015.

Purification of the Temple and Premises Prior to the Festival

Two or three days before the Thottam Pāttu and the preparations to ritualy invoke Kodungallur Amma begin in the temporary thatched shed outside the temple by Thottam singers Madhu Asan and troupe, the purification rituals as per the rites of temple tantra start inside the temple. On

The commencement of the Thottam singing – the singers pick up the hand cymbals

67

ĀTTUKĀL AMMA

those special days when the tantri and his group take over the supervision of the temple rituals, the temple seems to acquire greater radiance. Such purificatory rites and rituals that include many homams and abhishekams are meant for the cleansing of the impurities of the temple's structure. The purification ceremony is similar to, but not as elaborate as, the sahasrakalasham, the ritual purification of the temple conducted after the Pongala.

The purification ceremony comprises various homams to propitiate the vāsthu gods and chase away evil spirits, and anointing the idol with twenty-five pots of sanctified water. This is a miniature version of the sahasrakalasham, which is described elaborately in Chapter 11. And after this, shreebhootabali, an intricate version of sheeveli, follows.

There are seven rounds of processions offering havissu (cooked rice, water and flowers) to the bali stones after the puja at noon. The last round of these processions led by the head priest carrying the idol followed by his acolytes, literally dashes ahead and completes the circumambulation of the temple, racing at full speed, all in a single breath, leaving the devotees spellbound. This is called sheeghrasheeveli.[5] This is the offering of havissu to propitiate the evil spirits that chase the idol of the Goddess. The idol is carried inside in a hurry, as if to save it from the evil forces that chase it and the door of the sreekovil is closed. The belief is that, with this, the deity and the temple are ready to receive the pongala.

The special deepārādhana performed after the tying of the Kāppu. The lamp is taken out first to the Thottam singers.

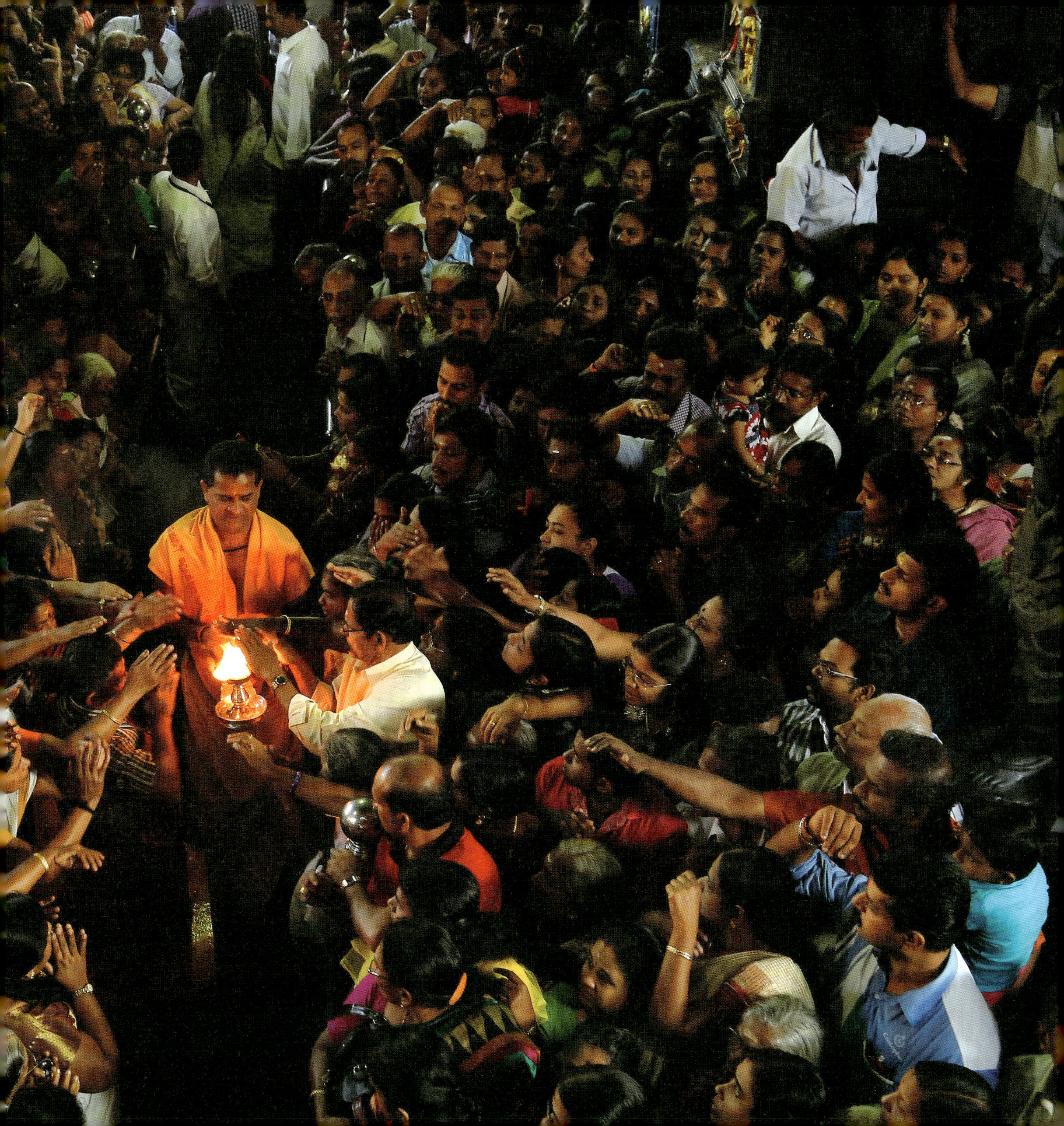

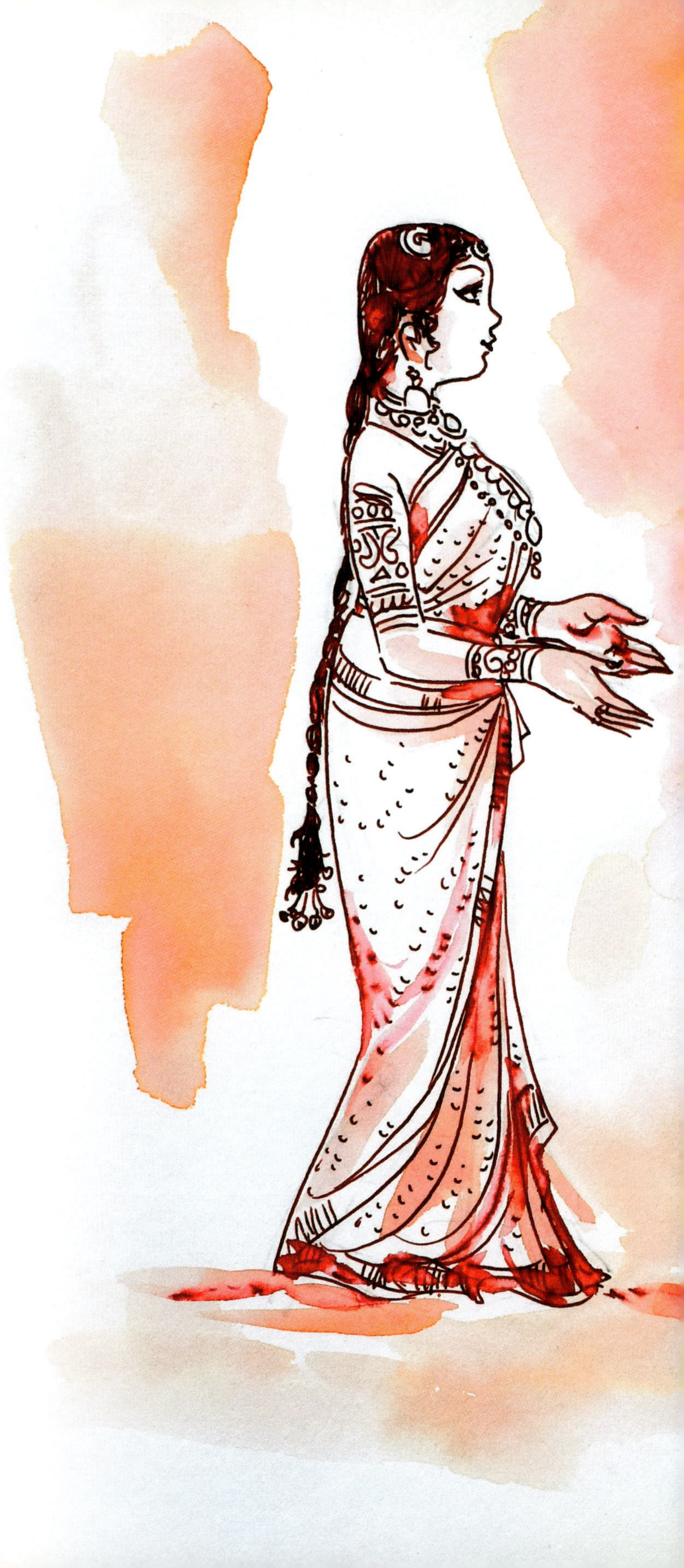

Palakan receiving the anklets
(chilampu) from Kanyavu

7
Āttukāl Amma and Kannaki of *Chilappathikaram*: Different Entities?

All the rituals that are performed inside the temple throughout the year and the crowd that throng the temple everyday look insignificant when the women arrive in their millions to make their own offerings for the Goddess on the day of the Pongala.

During the ten-day festival, the temple and the deity attract wide media coverage. But the media proclaim, without any evidence, that Āttukāl Amma is Kannaki. Song-and-dance productions based on Āttukāl Amma's story depict Her as Kannaki, to popularize the identification of Āttukāl Amma with Kannaki.

Though folklorists and historians in Thiruvananthapuram are convinced that it is not factually correct, the media-created narratives each year in the context of the Pongala gradually find a place in the history of the Āttukāl Temple. The temple's own website repeats this incorrect information. Every attempt to convince the temple authorities to the contrary was met with ruthless opposition – almost to the extent of forcing me to end my research. Obviously, riding piggyback on the well-established and popular myth of Kannaki seemed to be more comfortable to them, than to consider the findings of a historical inquiry by local historians of academic stature like N. Ajithkumar.

The Tamil-style architecture of the temple with the story of *Chilappathikaram* represented through concrete sculptures is equally misleading. Darshana Sreedhar in her essay 'Āttukāl Pongala, Myth and Modernity in a Ritualistic Space',[1] argues that the Kannaki myth vis-à-vis Āttukāl is a recent creation by certain interested groups. In many ways, the temple's website facilitates this wrong myth about the origin by becoming a technologically facilitated 'document' of authenticity and legitimization. This modern framing is not limited only to the temple's website. It also finds its place in the booklets issued by the ABTT and in the temple's architecture.

However, none of this matters to the millions that throng the Āttukāl Temple; for them, She is just Amma, Mother, the Goddess who hearkens to their calls and who alleviates their pain. Those who know who She is, never cared to clarify; those who do not, never inquired. A majority of the devotees don't read anything about Her or know who She is.

But who is this Goddess? Why is She wrongly called Kannaki? Did Kannaki ever visit Āttukāl?

As we have seen in the earlier chapters, the origin myth and the physical structure of this temple have been thoroughly altered. There are, however, a handful of rituals carried over from the past that connects the temple with antiquity. Thottam Pāttu, the ritualistic singing of hymns that heralds the commencement of the ten-day festival, is one of them. The narration is in old Malayalam, which is not influenced by Sanskrit or Tamil; it is the primitive language of Kerala, called Malayāzhma or Malayampazhama.

Thottam Pāttu, the Story of Bhadrakali

The festivals in all major Bhadrakali shrines, known variously as 'kāvu', 'thekkathu', 'ilankam', etc., in southern Kerala, commence with the singing of the Thottam Pāttu. In Malayalam, the word 'thottam' means 'instinct, or something which forms in the mind'. It also means 'spring up' and includes 'improvisation', or a 'hymn or song in praise of a power'. This narrates the legend of Bhadrakali. It is sung by a group of three people led by a singer known as the onnāmpuram, who is also called the Asan; the only accompaniment is a small instrument called kuzhithālam. N. Ajithkumar told me 'Kuzhithālam is one of the most primitive musical instruments found in Kerala and it measures time; actually it denotes the thālam (rhythm) of the thāndavam of Lord Shiva and the lāsyam of his consort; it is apt to be used as an accompaniment in the primitive song, in praise of Goddess Bhadrakali, who is the Goddess of Time itself.'

Of the three-member choir, the two junior singers are seated next to the Asan, in the order of their seniority (randāmpuram, and moonnāmpuram, second and third, respectively) who repeat the lines sung by the Asan. The Mudippura Thottam, the verse offering sung during the festival, has never been written down; singers learn it by rote. Most of the singers of the Thottam songs believe that it is a sin to write these songs down or record them.

Research on Thottam Pāttu is indeed a difficult venture owing to this belief and also due to the regional variations and the overpowering sense of divinity attached to it by the singers. The overriding similarities among them and the absence of any major variation in the theme are pointers to

Goddess Kali with the severed head of Darikan

Kanyavu confronts the Pandyan king with the chilampu

the historical significance of these songs, underscored by the pieces of evidence provided in the book *Malayālathile Pazhaya Pāttukal* (The Old Songs of Malayalam), written in 1917 by Chirayinkeezhu Govinda Pillai. He has divided the main themes of these songs as, (i) the slaying of the asura Darikan, and (ii) the story of the life of a divine virgin, who is Bhadrakali Herself, as the adopted daughter of the king and queen of Thekkum Kollam.

There are five major regional variations in Thottam Pāttu in southern Kerala, and it is usually sung within one day or three days or five days or even forty-one days, depending on the tradition of the temples there. At Āttukāl, the recital of the story is completed within ten days. While C. Govinda Pillai enjoys the unique position as the first to collect and compile these songs in book form, G. Shankara Pillai, who compiled these songs in 1957, says that their division into two parts by Govinda Pillai is wrong and that the Thottam Pāttu is in fact a single song. He also says that *Kerala Sahitya Charithram* by Ulloor S. Parameswara Iyer and *Keralathile Kaleeseva* by Chelanattu Achyutha Menon also repeat the same mistake because they followed C. Govinda Pillai's findings.[2]

I learned that at Āttukāl, the Thottam singers do not sing the first part, i.e., the story of the slaying of Darikan, wherein Kali is described as someone born to kill Darikan. The singers couldn't give me an explanation for this. 'We learned it this way and this is what Amma likes,' Madhu Asan said with a smile.

Thottam Pāttu and the Story of *Chilappathikaram*

Thottam Pāttu, the ritualistic song that heralds the commencement of the festival at Āttukāl, narrates a story which bears close resemblance to the story of *Chilappathikaram*, the epic poem of the Sangam Era of Tamil literature. During the Sangam Era, Kerala had three political centres of power: the principalities of southern Kerala ruled over by the powerful Āyi kings, the Chera kingdom in central Kerala, and the Ezhimala kingdom in the north.[3]

This Jaina epic is believed to have been written at Vanjippattanam (presumed to be at Karooppadanna, near Kodungallur) by Ilango Adikal, a prince of the dynasty that established the first Chera Empire that flourished from third century BCE to the eighth century CE (probably the same time as the composition of *Chilappathikaram*). However, there are different opinions regarding the period of the composition of *Chilappathikaram* and also about Ilango Adikal's identity (R. Parthasarathy, the famous translator of *Chilappathikaram* into English thinks he is almost a mythical figure like Homer or Vyasa). Many scholars have chosen the second century CE as the period of *Chilappathikaram*, but internal evidence such as references to the Alupa kings of the Tulu region, and to the Pala kings of Bengal, push the date much further, from the fifth century to the eighth century, if not later.[4]

Ilango Adikal has brought together the three Tamil kingdoms in the poem: the story begins in Pukar (Poompuhar), the Chola capital, moves through Madurai, the Pandya capital, and ends at Vanjipattanam, the capital of the Cheras. Thus the epic depicts a multidimensional history of the ancient Tamil kingdoms.

After having given up his aspirations of becoming the king by challenging Chenkuttuvan, his elder brother and the powerful reigning king of the Cheras, Prince Ilango Adikal was camping at the temple in Kunavāyilkottam (supposed to be Kunaka or Thrikkanāmathilakam, a couple of kilometers from the present-day Kodungallur Bhagavathy Temple)[5], when a troupe of kuravas, members of a hill tribe, reached there and narrated an amazing event they had witnessed.

They had seen the glorious sight of Lord Indra and his entourage descending from heaven in a winged chariot, approaching a young woman with a torn-out left breast standing under a Venga (Indian Kino) tree. The celestial visitors showed her her husband who was there along with them in the vehicle; they picked her up and ascended heavenwards in the chariot.

The Tamil poet Chāthanar who was present at Ilango's camp, claimed he had already known the story and narrated the tale of a woman who had set Madurai on fire by plucking out her breast and hurling it at the city to take revenge against the Pandyan king Nedunchezhiyan who had her innocent husband executed. Ilango Adikal declared that he would write a lyrical poem on the incident. That poem is *Chilappathikaram*.

In Tamil Nadu, *Chilappathikaram* is claimed as part of an ancient cultural tradition, but the religious practices based on the mythology of Kannaki, the heroine of the poem, survive only in a marginal way. For example, the Chellathamman Temple, near Madurai Meenakshi Temple, was built, according to information which can be found on its website, 'as a tribute to the divine chastity of Kannaki. The temple is built at the place where Kannaki stayed in Madurai. Fire accidents took place often in this area when the temple was built. People believed that the cause of fire may be due to the fury-fire [sic] element in the idol of Kannaki. King Shenbaga Pandyan discussed the issue with his ministers. It is said that Lord Shiva appeared in his dream and advised [him] to install the idol of Mother Parvati in the temple, according to some sources. The king did as advised by [the] Lord and named the [Divine] Mother as Shenbagathu Amman which in later days changed as Chellathamman.' After this event, Chellathamman became prominent and popular. 'First, Puja is dedicated to Chellathamman and then to Kannaki... Kannaki is in the front mandapam with Her anklet in one hand. Women worship Kannaki with tāli and lime fruit garlands.'[6]

This is all that one can find with regard to the worship of Kannaki in Tamil Nadu. Wikipedia says: 'Kannaki Amman is eulogized as the epitome of chastity and is worshipped ... by the Sri Lankan Tamil Hindus.' There is also the mention that she is venerated as Goddess Pattini in Sri Lanka by the Sinhalese Buddhists too.[7] On the other hand, Kannaki is viewed in a negative light by the general populace around Madurai. As I have personally experienced, in the Meenakshi Temple precincts, the mention of the name of Kannaki still evokes strong reproof from even ordinary people rooted in local Pandyan tradition. After all, Kannaki burned their city down once upon a time!

However, Kannaki is very much alive in Tamil popular culture. One of the earliest Tamil epic films, released in 1942, was *Kannagi* directed by R.S. Mani. Another Tamil film *Poompuhar* (1964), follows the theme of the unjust punishment meted out to Kovalan, Kannaki's husband, and Kannaki burning down Madurai city. Several Tamil and Malayalam poets have made Kannaki the subject of their works. 'A statue of Kannagi holding her anklet, depicting a scene from *Chilappathikaram*, was installed on Marina Beach, Chennai. It was removed in December 2001 citing reason that it hindered traffic. The statue was reinstalled in June 2006.'[8]

Eric Miller, an American scholar who traced Kannaki's footsteps from Pukar to Madurai and to the Western Ghats, has a different take on Kannaki. 'In my hometown, New York City, we have a pessimistic saying: "You cannot fight City Hall." But Kannaki proved that you can fight City Hall, and this is the core of the story. That one person with no money, in a place that was not native to her, with no family in sight, could go before the highest civic authority, and speak, and win her case: that is great.' He refutes the charges against Kannaki, that she was harsh towards the residents of the city even when they were supportive of her; that she was fighting an unworthy cause, that of defending a husband who had cheated her. Miller cites a prophecy which says that the Sun God had already marked the city for burning down and Kannaki merely invoked Lord Agni to do it, and it was an act of purification, prior to regeneration. The answer to the second charge is too obvious – any number of good women would pardon their cheating husbands![9]

But the largest variety and number of myths, songs and ritual practices based on the Kannaki story survive not in Tamil Nadu, but in Kerala. The people of Kerala, where the major part of the ancient Chera kingdom flourished, believe that Kannaki was installed at the Sree Bhadrakali Temple at Kodungallur.

Eric Miller in his essay 'Kannaki: Global Symbol of Justice',[10] says: 'Some people here in Kerala might say the *Silappathikaram* was written by a native of the Chera land, which has now become Kerala. But really Kannaki is a Tamil character, she is not a Kerala character, and the story is a Tamil story, not a Kerala story.' This is a wrong point of view, I feel. This character and this story belong both to Tamil Nadu *and* Kerala. On the

Kerala–Tamil Nadu border in the high ranges, at Vannathiparai, near Kumili (inside the Periyar Tiger Reserve, Thekkady), there is a temple on top of the mountain, at a spot called Mangaladevi peak. The Mangaladevi Hill Temple (Mangaladevi Kannaki Kottam) is dedicated to the deified Kannaki.

As a feature in *The Hindu* says: 'Kannaki, according to literary evidence, walked for fourteen days from Madurai to Vengaikanal Nedunkundram, where the temple is now located. From here, she is believed to have reunited with her husband Kovalan. Tribal people, who were witness to the event, reported it to the Chera king, Chenkuttuvan, during his visit to the hilly region. As per legend, the king brought stones from the Himalayas to construct the temple for Kannaki. The king of Ceylon, Kayavagu, attended the consecration of the temple.

'Though it originally belonged to Tamil Nadu, as per the earliest evidence of 1817,[11] it now falls in Kerala territory. It is easily accessible from the Kerala side.'

There is an epigraphic reference to one Mangaladevi Temple in a Perumal Temple at the nearby Gudalur town in Theni district. Kannaki is described as 'Mangala Madanthai' in *Chilappathikaram*. This has led a senior epigraphist to assert that the deity in the Mangaladevi Temple is worshipped as the epic's heroine.[12]

The Mangala Devi Hill Temple is in a dilapidated state now. But from the plinth area and the sub-temples situated on the rectangular outer balivattom, it is obvious that it was a major temple. Whether this is the temple that Cheran Chenkuttuvan built for Kannaki, or, whether that temple is the one at Kodungallur, the capital of the Chera kingdom, is open to further research. Some scholars have assumed that Chenkuttuvan did the installation of the idol of Kannaki at the Kodungallur temple premises.[13] It is interesting to observe here that there is a mention in the *Travancore State Manual* that the Cheras had ruled their kingdom with Kumili as their capital, from the time of Perinchottu Udanan Cheralatan, the grandfather of Chenkuttuvan.[14]

Here it may be useful to narrate briefly the story of *Chilappathikaram* as Eric Miller puts it. In the great harbour city of Poompuhar, on ancient south India's east coast, Kannaki and Kovalan married. Kovalan saw Madhavi, the dancer, perform at court and he went off with her. After an extended period, Kovalan returned home. He and Kannaki walked to Madurai, a distance of about 250 km, to start a new life. There, Kovalan was falsely accused of stealing the local queen's anklet, and the local ruler, the Pandyan king, unjustly put Kovalan to death. Kannaki came to the court and proved that her husband had been innocent of this crime. The king punished himself for the injustice he had done, by simply lying down and dying. Kannaki walked around the city three times, tore off her left breast and threw it against the city wall, and called for the city to burn – but for good people and animals to be unharmed. Agni, the God of Fire, accomplished this. Kannaki wandered westward to the mountains, where some people worshipped her.

In the 'Vanchi kāndam', the third chapter of *Chilappathikaram*, the poet moves from the story of Kannaki to the story of the Chera kingdom where the conqueror of oceans, Chenkuttuvan, is the king. He is resting with his queen Venmāl and his brother Ilango Adikal at the source of the River Periyar (the Mangaladevi Kannaki Kottam mentioned above, and Kumili, the supposed Chera capital according to *Travancore State Manual*, are actually situated in the same region), when the hill tribesmen who witness the miraculous episode at Thirichenkunnu reach there and narrate their story to the king. The queen ordains that Kannaki, the paragon of chastity, should be worshipped as a Goddess. It is also decided that the stone for the idol should be fetched from the Himalayas.

The sages who return from the Himalayas report that the kings of the north, Kanakan and Vijayan, had spoken of the Tamil kings disparagingly. Chenkuttuvan vows to subjugate the kings and make them carry the stone for the temple, as a punishment. When he is about to set out for the Himalayas after a public declaration to this effect, some people reach there carrying oblations from the Padmanabhaswamy Temple of Thiruvananthapuram. After receiving those oblations and wearing them on his person, Chenkuttuvan sets off on his journey. Crossing the River Ganges, he defeats Kanakan and Vijayan of north India and their vassal kings Utaran, Vichitran, Rudran, Bhairavan, Chitran, Simhan, Dhanurdharan, and Shwetan.

Chenkuttuvan chooses the stone from the Himalayas, gets the idol carved, and returns. Kanakan and Vijayan carry the idol. While the party is resting on the banks of the Ganga, Mātalan reaches there and apprises them of the happenings in Madurai after the conflagration.

Vettrivel Chezhiyan, the ruler of Korkka, reaches Madurai, does human sacrifice of a thousand goldsmiths to Kannaki, and takes up the reins of the anarchic kingdom. Kovalan's father, Masuttavan gives away all his wealth and becomes a monk. His wife dies of grief. Kannaki's father becomes a monk too, and her mother commits suicide. Madhavi takes the vows of a nun. She instructs her mother that her daughter, Manimekhalai, should not be initiated into the ways of a courtesan under the devadasi system. Later Manimekhalai also becomes a nun. Her story is narrated in the poem *Manimekhalai* by Chāthanār.

After returning to his kingdom, Chenkuttuvan installs the idol of Kannaki in a temple that he builds at Thiruvanchikkulam near Kodungallur,[15] which later becomes the Sri Kurumba Bhagavathy Temple.[16]

Kannaki and Kodungallur Amma

There is no mention of Kannaki's induction into the Kodungallur temple either in *Chilappathikaram* or in historical records (even though it was supposedly dedicated by Chenkuttuvan with fanfare at the time). It is believed that Kannaki's idol was installed at Sri Kurumba Kāvu in the precincts of the present Kodungallur temple. Later on, her spirit was imported into the deity at the Kodungallur temple, according to another popular belief. Historian V.R. Chandran's following observation somewhat validates this view:

'It is customarily believed that the first dedication took place at Sri Kurumba Kāvu. Later, for certain other reasons – say, due to the Pandyan king's attack, or the Brahmin strategies for domination – it is assumed that it was moved from its primary location to the present temple and placed westward of the existing deity's nada (threshold opening to the sreekovil of the deity) facing northward. They built the nada for the existing deity, which was initially facing northward, as facing the west subsequently.'[17]

P.G. Rajendran, a scholar on the temples of Kerala, has this to say about Kannaki's deification:

'Chenkuttuvan conducted Kannaki's dedication process in the vicinity of the Kurumba Bhagavathy Temple. As *Chilappathikaram* hints, the process took place in the second century. Till date, the Devi's thidambu (replica of the deity) is escorted from this temple.'[18]

The above statements point to assumption that Kannaki's dedication could not have taken place in the Kodungallur temple but it would have taken place in Sri Kurumba Kāvu.

There is another belief that, later on, the deity of Sri Kurumba Kāvu was imported and assimilated into Devi's idol at the Kodungallur Temple. This way, the presence of Kannaki is believed to have reached the Kodungallur temple, providing immense relief to the believers of Kannaki and Kali. Consequently, the belief that the main Kodungallur Bhagavathy Temple is the original Kannaki Temple still persists among many people.

In his book *Keralathinte Samskarika Charitram*,[19] the historian P.K. Gopalakrishnan does a somewhat convincing analysis of how Brahmin domination altered the nature of

ĀTTUKĀL AMMA AND KANNAKI OF *CHILAPPATHIKARAM*: DIFFERENT ENTITIES

the worship of the Goddess, in whom Kannaki was thought to have been merged. According to him, it seems right to believe that at the turn of the seventh century CE, Kannaki, dedicated by Chenkuttuvan, was replaced with Kali due to the spread of the brahminical philosophy and became an object of worship for the Brahmins. Till the end of the seventh century, the Brahmins did not have considerable influence in Kerala. Mezhathol Agnihotri was the leader of the Brahmins who had arrived in Kerala. The foundation for Brahmin influence was laid by seeking the invitations of the kings of Kerala for conducting ritual offerings and carrying forth the message of the Shaiva faith. Since Chenkuttuvan was an ardent follower of the Shaiva faith, he encouraged yagam and other rituals of the Brahmins, as *Chilappathikaram* hints at.

Gopalakrishnan continues his commentary, saying that the seventh century witnessed the gradual advancement of the Brahmins. Brahmin villages mushroomed in between forests and coastal areas. The lands soon became verdant regions. This unprecedented development led the Brahmins to believe that they were the custodians of the earth. When they flourished financially and culturally, and when the Brahminical ideas spread substantially with the help of kings, scholars stepped forward. The belief that salvation could be attained through holy sacrifice and worship grew considerably. Mezhathol's repute as an astute person helped the Brahmins gain in influence.

Gopalakrishnan says that, though it is difficult to take historical cognizance of the story of Parashurama connected to Kerala's origin, leaders of the four regions of Payyanur, Panniyoor, Paravoor and Chengannoor took control over thirty-two Brahmin villages and led them on the path of growth. Four renowned 'thallis' (the kings of northern Kerala called royal palaces and temples, 'thalli') existed in the Brahmin villages spanning from Kottapuram to Chettuva-Kodungallur: they are Methalli, Kizhthalli, Chingapurathalli and Nediyathalli. Apparently, the Kodungallur temple was Nediyathalli. The Brahmin village was not fully able to comprehend and accept the dedication at Kodungallur as well as its rites and rituals. They decided to impose the Namboothiri practices in the worship and rituals of the temple. Mezhathol sought to bring reformation, keeping the existing beliefs and concepts intact. He established a concept of Devi based on the Brahmin faith, combining the figures of the furious Kannaki with that of the fierce Kali to form a deity that was all-powerful and extremely terrifying.

Ever since Cheran Chenkuttuvan dedicated Kannaki as a deity, we have come to learn more about the forms of worship of the early Dravidians, the concept of Devi based on Buddhist theology as well as customs reflecting the intellectual ways of the Buddhist faith.

The Kannaki statue at Marina beach, Chennai

The Brahmins are mentioned in Sangam literature only in a few places. The only king who gave himself completely over to the Brahmin belief system was Palyaney, a Chera king. Brahmins were generally considered a weak community. The immigration of the Brahmins into south India, including Kerala, must have taken place on a small scale in the second century CE. The control of almost all aspects of the temple used to be in the hands of the non-Brahmins. Gradually, from the fourth century onwards, the immigration of the Brahmins gathered pace. And the influence of the Hindu faith increased exponentially. Alongside, the growth of the Jain and the Buddhist faiths came to an end.

By the seventh century, the philosophy of the Brahmins gained almost complete acceptance. They accumulated power and influence, and introduced new changes in the forms of worship and concepts of divinity. To strengthen the concept of Brahminical goddess concept, practices like human and animal sacrifice were abolished along with chicken-slaying; instead, rituals like gurusi (guruthi), raktapushpanjali and splitting of ash ground were introduced.

The Namboothiris eventually took complete control of society at the beginning of the twelfth century. They considered themselves to be the owners of the land. History has it that when competition and avarice among them became rife, Rama Varma Shaktan Thampuran, Maharaja of Kochi (under whose realm the Kodungallur temple was at that time, for a brief period) put an end to the control granted to the Namboothiri-dominated trusts and dismissed the 'Yogātiri' or the Namboothiri chief who had absolute say in the administration of the temples, and took them over and brought them under the direct control of the royal government.

The above analysis by P.K. Gopalakrishnan provides a somewhat clear historical background of how the Jaina culture painted in *Chilappathikaram* was overrun by Namboothiris who absorbed the Kannaki cult into the Goddess cult which they had appropriated from the worship of the pre-brahminical Bhadrakali at Kodungallur.

Did Kannaki Actually Exist?

Eric Miller who walked in the footsteps of Kannaki (and Kovalan), from Poompuhar to Madurai told me in an interview that whether or not the incidents mentioned in *Chilappathikaram*, which he calls Kannaki's biography, occurred in history, 'such incidents occur perpetually in the imaginations of people who know and care about the story. And a story presents people with a model of the past, and a model for the future. That is, people base their characters and actions, their entire worldviews and identities, on the elements of the stories they love.'

M.J. Gentes from the University of Texas in his *Scandalizing the Goddess at Kodungallur* says:[20]

'By 12th century, Buddhism had virtually disappeared and the cult of the Goddess Kali was in the ascendant, (leading to), the re-consecration of Jain and Buddhist sanctuaries as Bhagavati temples...[To make] the nuns leave their residence at Kodungallur, low-caste devotees of Bhagavati were persuaded to throw animals and filth into the sanctuary...It was then rededicated to Bhadrakali and lost its [connection...] with the Jain Goddess Kannaki of the fourth century epic *Shilappadikaram* [The Affair of the Anklet].'

The worship of Kannaki was merged into the Kali cult; and the polluting of the temple during Bharani is a reenactment of the original confrontation between the low-caste women and the nuns, and the taking over of the Jain sanctuary. At Sri Kurumba Kāvu, two narrative traditions portraying the life and attributes of a Goddess exist. One of the Goddesses mentioned is Bhadrakali and Her myth is recited in the Thottam songs. The second set of songs is about the heroine/Goddess Kannaki of the epic *Chilappathikaram*. The songs that

ĀTTUKĀL AMMA AND KANNAKI OF *CHILAPPATHIKARAM*: DIFFERENT ENTITIES

The ruins of the Mangala Devi Temple

praise Kannaki's virtues are used as evidence to identify Sri Kurumba Kāvu as the very shrine described in the ancient Tamil work that was built by the Chera king Chenguttuvan to honor Kannaki. This identification also proves that the original shrine was a Jain sanctuary. Bhagavathy, Kannaki and Kali share some traits and are rolled into one at Sri Kurumba Kāvu; however, separate traditions on each of them survive and are celebrated in songs and ritual practices.'[21]

V.T. Induchudan presents the theory that the true focus of the Bharani festival is Kannaki and that the worship of Kali is suspended during the festival. He concludes that Kannaki's mortal remains lie in the unopened stone tomb that abuts the eastern side of the inner sanctum. 'During the Bharani Festival, a red cloth, one of the Goddess's symbols worn by devotees and given in offering to the Goddess, is hung on the stone wall of the chamber between the tomb and the Kali sanctum. An underground tunnel extends from the chamber under the east portico and surfaces on the eastern side of the shrine grounds. A proscription protects this tunnel, closed and no longer in use: anyone looking into it will go blind, is the story in circulation that is intended to protect this secret.'[22]

Induchudan assumes that at one time, the tunnel was used to bring in neophytes for initiation into the worship of the Goddess. During this initiation, they entered Her courtyard, ritually 'died', and came out 'reborn' after passing through the tunnel. (Similar rebirth tunnels exist in Tiruvilvamala, in south Malabar, and also in the Kailasanathar Temple, the oldest structure in Kancheepuram.) The elderly Atikal (member of a priestly clan) told Induchudan that in the past, the Atikals entered the courtyard through the passage to perform services in the chamber, until it was sealed because of the danger of a cave-in. 'When this practice ceased due to the risk of walking through the passage, services came to be done through the eastern door.'

The famous kāvutheendal takes place on the eastern portico – the starting point as well as the terminating point of the frenzied run – which is normally not used, precisely because worship is directed at Kannaki, the Goddess, whose remains rest inside the east door, Induchudan believes.

It is to be noted here that Kannaki belongs to a literary tradition, both oral and written. But in the deeply rural imagination, such a name would not ring any bells. Dianne Jennet says: 'If you go into the countryside and ask some of them, "Why did Kannaki come here?" they might not even have heard of Kannaki.'[23]

Narrative of the Thottam Pāttu Vs Story of *Chilappathikaram*

It is a mystery as to how the narrative of the Thottam Pāttu sung during the annual festivals in the Bhadrakali shrines of

ĀTTUKĀL AMMA

southern Kerala resembles that of *Chilappathikaram* in the main parts. The popular lore of Āttukāl notwithstanding, in *Chilappathikaram* there is no internal evidence of Kannaki having visited Thiruvananthapuram.

R. Parthasarathy, in the Introduction to his translation of *Chilappathikaram*, opines that Ilango Adikal could be the name of a redactor, a mythical figure like Homer or Vyasa, who wrote down the epic from existing oral versions. N. Ajithkumar believes that the Thottam Pāttu is older than *Chilappathikaram*.[24] Further, Deepu P. Kurup, who is a Thottam Pāttu singer himself, in his doctoral thesis, says that none of us can ascertain when Devi got a song for Herself.

Parthasarathy's observation provides some credence to the argument of N. Ajithkumar, that the narrative in the Pāttus (as sung in the Bhadrakali temples of southern Kerala), is a fictitious rendering of songs sung by Kuravas, the hill tribesmen, at the Kanuvayilkottam Temple. Were the Kuravas singing the Thottam Pāttu? Is this temple the same as the Kannaki Kottam Temple, the Mangaladevi Temple at Vannathiparai, Kumili? No one can be certain.

The structure at Mangala Devi Temple site where a Kannaki idol was installed a few decades ago

ĀTTUKĀL AMMA AND KANNAKI OF *CHILAPPATHIKARAM*: DIFFERENT ENTITIES

According to *Chilappathikaram*, the hill dwellers witness Kannaki's ascension to heaven and narrate the tale to King Chenkuttuvan. His queen, Ilango Venmal, who is also present, requests the king that the heroine of the story be worshipped as a goddess. So, can we assume that the story of Kannaki and Kovalan (that of Kanyavu and Palakan) was sung as a ballad much before Ilango Adikal wrote it in a style that suited the poetic traditions of that time?

Kanyavu Vs Kannaki; Palakan Vs Kovalan

In *Chilappathikaram*, Kannaki is the daughter of a mariner, married to the Vaishya youth, Kovalan, who broke marital fidelity by taking Madhavi, the devadasi dancer, as his mistress. However, in Thottam Pāttu, Kanyavu (the female lead corresponding to Kannaki of *Chilappathikaram*) is Goddess Bhadrakali, the daughter of Lord Shiva.

In Thottam Pāttu, Bhadrakali wants to remain a virgin after marriage but in *Chilappathikaram*, Kovalan and Kannaki lead a blissful conjugal life. In Thottam Pāttu, Devi's tempestuousness comes out most clearly in Her violent rage against Her future husband, and Her adoptive father whom She annihilates by closing Her left eye (for details see the chapter summarizing the Thottam Pāttu). How does one explain this terrible reaction of Devi? She is furious because both are associated with the attempt to get Her married. How can the Goddess Bhadrakali, Lord Shiva's daughter, marry a mortal?

There are no references to Madhavi, the courtesan who seduces Kovalan, in the Thottam Pāttu sung in south Kerala temples. The Pāttu does mention the bad habits Palakan acquired before getting married. But the relationship between Kanyavu and Her husband Palakan has almost no correspondence to the servile and chaste wife of the *Chilappathikaram* who dotes on Her husband, taking him back unconditionally when he returns from the arms of his paramour.

The incident of Kovalan asking for the anklet to be sold in the market has its correspondence in the Pāttu, but in the reverse order. The contrite Kovalan, who has squandered all his wealth and is left with Kannaki's anklets, asks Her to give it to him so that he can go to Madurai, sell it and raise some funds to restart his business. On the other hand, in the Pāttu, Kanyavu asks Palakan to go to the market and sell the anklet along with many other valuables to make money for expanding his business.

Whereas Kannaki of *Chilappathikaram* flies into an all too human rage and confronts the Pandyan king Nedunchezhiyan (it may be noted that in Thottam Pāttu, the king's proper name is never mentioned – it's always just 'Pandyan') about Her husband's unjust execution, and calls upon Lord Agni to burn Madurai as she hurls Her torn-off left breast at the city walls, and it comes to pass, and Kovalan is subsequently resurrected by Lord Indra, Kanyavu of Thottam Pāttu, in a fit of rage hearing the news that Palakan, Her husband, has been wrongfully executed by the Pandyan king of Madurai, rushes to the spot and resurrects Her husband by Herself. (Vannārs, the washermen, who kept Palakan's body intact, is blessed by Devi, who also gives them the right to sing the Thottam Pāttu at night). She then confronts the goldsmith who lied to the king, chops off his tongue and kills him. Then She beheads the king. The queen too falls at her husband's feet and dies. Kanyavu then closes Her left eye, setting the city on fire. A great conflagration follows. Presently, Kanyavu proceeds to Mount Kailasam with the severed head of the king in Her hand and shows it to Her father, Lord Shiva, and hangs it next to the head of Darikan whom She had slain in an earlier episode of the Thottam Pāttu. She pleads with Her father to give Her a permanent abode at Kodungallur, which He grants. Devi goes to Kodungallur with the resurrected Palakan, establishes Herself as Kodungallur Amma (Sri Kurumba, Bhadrakali), and sets up a shrine nearby for Her husband.

It is interesting to note a striking difference in the episode of the king's death: in Thottam Pāttu, Devi kills the king, whereas in *Chilappathikaram*, the king dies of shock upon learning from Kannaki about the injustice he inadvertently meted out to Kovalan. Kannaki is escorted to heaven by Kovalan, but in all the oral versions of the Thottam Pāttu, Devi is the Supreme Power who is able to resurrect Her husband.

In fact, there is not even the mention of the name Kannaki or Kovalan anywhere in Thottam Pāttu. As already stated, the heroine is Kanyavu and the hero, Palakan ('the virgin' and 'Balakan' – literally the youth). In *Chilappathikaram*, Kovalan is the son of Masuttavan, the Vaishya merchant of Pukar. But in Thottam Pāttu, Palakan is the son of King Marayar of Vadakkum Kollam. Kannaki is the daughter of a mariner in the same city; but the virgin in the Thottam Pāttu is the daughter of Lord Shiva and the adopted daughter of King Narayanar of Thekkum Kollam. And there is no mention of Cheran Chenkuttuvan in Thottam Pāttu, or of the building of the temple at Kodungallur. The Pāttu, on the other hand, mentions that Lord Shiva guides His daughter to create Her own abode at Thiruvanchikkulam.

There is an inner contradiction that is running throughout these parallel narratives, if one argues that the story of Kannaki is a mere work of fiction. There exist pieces of evidence (however steeped in legends they may be), like the particular spots in the city of Madurai where Kovalan was beheaded (Kovalan Potal), where Kannaki and Kovalan stayed at Purancheri (the spot where the Chellathamman Temple is situated), the Kannaki Temple at Mangaladevi where Cheran Chenkuttuvan is thought to have installed Kannaki as has been confirmed by highly respected diviners (the rival one at Kodungallur notwithstanding), and a definite route that Kannaki took on her westward journey to the Chera Kingdom after burning down the city of Madurai, walking non-stop for fourteen days, and reaching under the Venga tree, where she resurrected Kovalan (the route which Eric Miller followed).

If the Thottam Pāttu story had preceded the Kannaki story, how then could her story have found a place in the Pāttu? How does it come to pass that in Thottam Pāttu too, the villain of the piece is the Pandyan king? These contradictions add to the fascinating mystery of one of the most outstanding woman characters in the most recent of ancient Indian epics.

The common belief that Kannaki was consecrated into a deity at the Kodungallur temple has been modified by scholars in the field in different ways, as already seen. It is worth mentioning here that Ilango Adikal who had converted to Jainsim and become a monk, seems to have altered the original story to suit his mission. Also, this explains why the tempestuous and fiery Kanyavu (if at all he based his epic on the narrative of the supposedly pre-existing Thottam Pāttu), is depicted as the meek wife Kannaki.

There is, however, a curious connection between the chilambu (anklet) that plays a central role in the story of *Chilappathikaram* and Bhadrakali worship in Kerala: Bhadrakali is invariably represented by a pair of 'chilambus' and 'vāl' (sword) in Her shrines throughout Kerala.

Unravelling the Mystery: A Possible Explanation

The deity of Āttukāl is definitely not Kannaki of *Chilappathikaram*. But Kodungallur Bhagavathy in whom Kannaki's Chaitanya is thought to have been assimilated, is invoked and transported to Āttukāl at the beginning of the ten-day festival, worshipped throughout, and sent back at the end – all these through Thottam Pāttu. Kannaki has got almost inextricably enmeshed in the narrative.

We could look at these anomalies and anachronisms from a totally different angle. There is internal evidence in the Thottam Pāttu sung at Āttukāl to suggest that emendations do take place, in the course of time, as the narrative is sung by the singers down the centuries. The first of its kind which includes a glaring anachronism, in view of the fact that the story would have taken place more than 2,000 years ago, is this: In the fourth day's Pāttu, there is mention of Kanyavu hearing the cannon shots from the ship of Palakan to notify Her of his arrival, reciprocating to which Kanyavu also fires the guns of Her ship. As a matter of fact, it was the Portuguese who brought cannons and other guns to India, after the arrival of Vasco da Gama in 1498. The use of cannons for the first time in India was in the first battle of Panipat in 1526, when Babur, the Mughal, used cannons to defeat the numerically superior army of Ibrahim Lodi. Clearly, the Thottam singers added this piece to the song, somewhere in recent centuries.

Another emendation, once again involving an anachronism, is the occasion in the ninth day's Pāttu, on which Devi grants the contrite Pandyan queen the deity-hood, 'Mukkolaykkal Muttharamma', and the use of a thatched-roof shrine, while She Herself reserves the right to use a tiled-roof sanctum sanctorum! Tiled roofs, as we know, are a comparatively recent addition, only after the arrival of the German Christian Missionaries, in the sixteenth century.

What I want to point out here is the tendency of the Thottam singers to add details from comparatively recent events into the Pāttu, during the course of their singing, over the centuries. They could actually have added the parts in which Kanyavu sends Palakan to sell the wares in the Pandyan kingdom, Palakan selling the anklet, the court goldsmith lying, the king executing Palakan, and Kanyavu's revenge, taking all these strands of narratives from Chialappathikaram itself, as this was a story prevalent in these parts over the last twelve centuries at least. This way, Kannaki and Kanyavu would remain two different entities; likewise, Kovalan and Palakan too would be two different persons. It would just be that over the centuries, the singers of Thottam Pāttu would have added to the narrative some interesting parts of Chilappathikaram, which struck their fancy. These are conjectures – much less a hypothesis – but this could explain the strange resemblances in both the narratives.

Scholars agree that the current form of Kali had evolved from the warrior Goddess, Kottavai, an ancient Dravidian deity. Bhadrakali of Thottam Pāttu is also a warrior Goddess. The Pāttu has elaborate descriptions of battle scenes, full of bravery. The source material of the Pāttu might have originated when a courageous heroine like Kannaki appeared in the midst of a people steeped in the Kottavai legends. By constructing a temple and consecrating an idol of Kannaki, the epitome of chastity, the Chera king Chenkuttuvan enhanced Her already heroic image and perpetuated Her story in popular perception. We can safely conclude that the blending of the worship of the warrior deity Kottavai and Kannaki's story, set the stage for the emergence of a divine heroic song.[25]

According to Deepu P. Kurup, the comparison of Bhadrakali Pāttu and *Chilappathikaram* can be summarized thus: The plots of Bhadrakali Pāttu and *Chilappathikaram* are similar, but both have unique narrative styles. Bhadrakali Pāttu does not rely on *Chilappathikaram* in terms of subplots, characterization and event descriptions. It has original subplots and series of events to strengthen its central theme. It has attained an autonomous existence like the Thampuran Pāttu, Vil Pāttu and Chattu Pāttu.

Bhadrakali Pāttu was created independently as part of the tradition of hero worship prevalent in southern Kerala. It is not an imitation of Ilango Adikal's *Chilappathikaram*. It is an independent work based on the heroic legend of Bhadrakali, running parallel to *Chilappathikaram*. None of the heroic ritualistic songs of southern Travancore can be considered to be copied from any classical poem. While *Chilappathikaram* shows the characteristics of a classical work, Bhadrakali Pāttu is only a ritualistic song. It has a moral outlook which inculcates thoughts of divinity and fear of sin. However, *Chilappathikaram* does not seem to follow a similar moral or ethical line. It is concerned rather with the Jaina values and ethics.[26]

Nevertheless, the Thottam Pāttu which is sung in the forecourt of the sreekovil of Āttukāl Amma now, and will be in the future too, is the ever-tinkling mysterious anklets of the Goddess of Āttukāl.

The Thottam singers of yesteryears

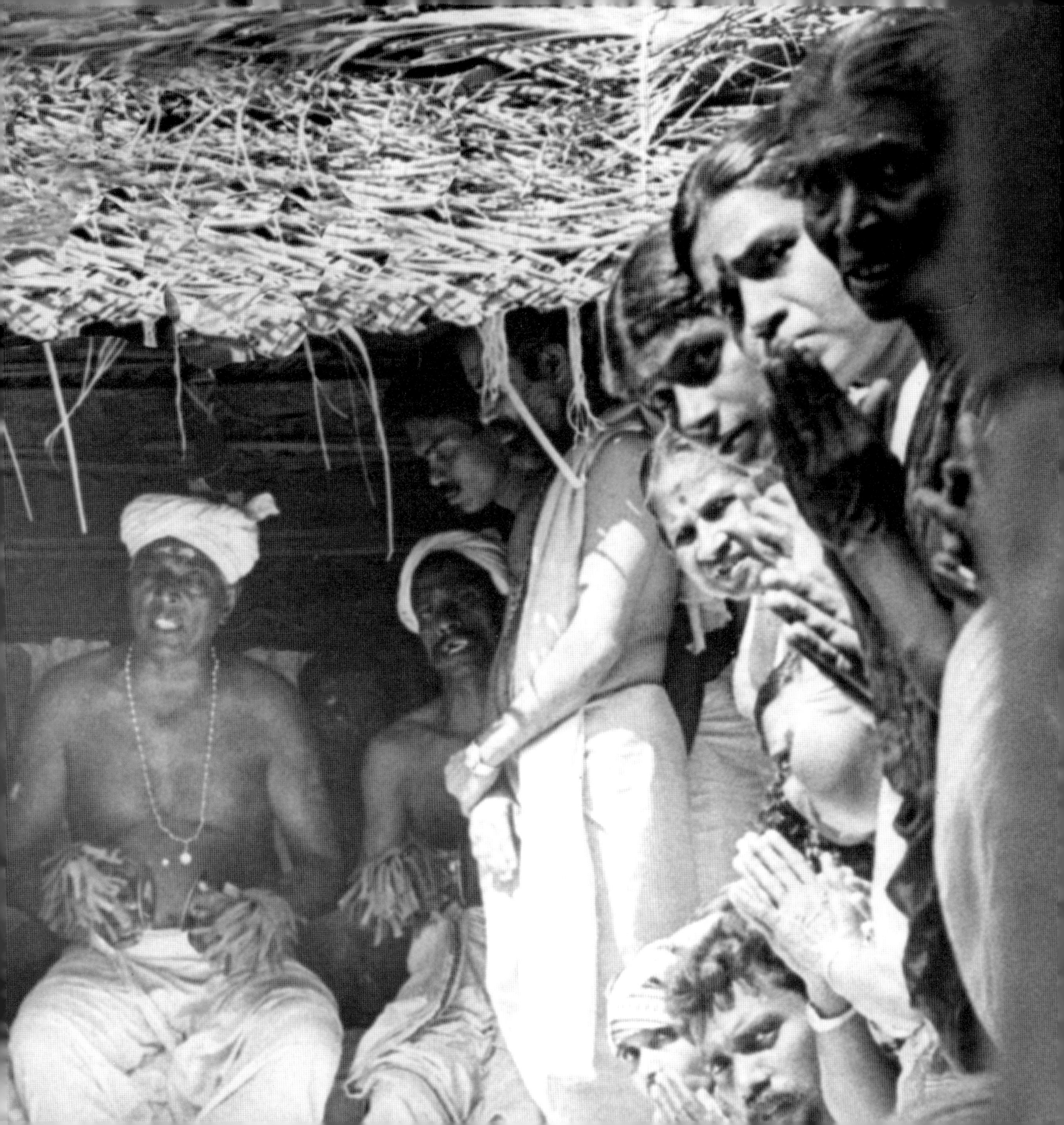

8

Thottam Pāttukār

When the ten-day festival commences at Āttukāl, one can't miss the humble, temporary green-thatched 'hymn house' and the three earnest-looking men sitting inside it, who sing in the mornings and rest in the afternoons. I came across a few very old women and two or three men sitting around the hymn house. They were not familiar to me, but I could tell they knew it was the story of Āttukāl Amma that was being sung. I heard them ululating when important events in the Goddess's story were narrated in the song. All those faces were imbued with the glow of a life lived in the love of the Goddess of Āttukāl.

A toothless, glee-filled grin was their reply to most of my queries. They have only a vague idea about the story; but they believe that the singers are possessed by divinity while they sing the story of Āttukāl Amma. The Pāttukār are much revered during the festival and people prostrate before the hymn house and offer oil, flowers, garlands or money as if the hymn house was a temple. The right to conduct pujas in the temple is now the prerogative of the Brahmins; the right to sing the Pāttu still rests with people belonging to the lower castes.

The Preparation of the Hymn House

The three-member troupe led by Madhu Asan begins the preparations much before Thiruvananthapuram city at large – the temple precincts specifically – begin to be immersed in the spirit of the Āttukāl Pongala. We see Madhu Asan, the main singer, and his assistants Manoharan, Anand and Madhu Asan's son Mahesh, preparing the hymn house after the Rahukalam (inauspicious time of the day) is over on the day before the festival begins. Measuring forty-one steps out from the main door of the temple, the spot for the hymn house is fixed. Now the place is marked on the floor using different coloured tiles so that they don't need to mark it every year. The work is carried out by Madhu Asan and his troupe. Radhakrishnan Asari, who is in charge of conducting the Kuthiyottam ritual, also participates in the construction. Nine coconut-leaf stems are laid out seven steps apart. Green coconut leaves are woven over them. Thus, the green-thatched shed of the singers comes up inside the temple precincts. In the middle of the shed, a platform is fashioned using fresh soil that serves as a seat. Madhu Asan confines himself to this narrow space till the ten days' Pāttu is over. He curls up and goes to sleep after 1 a.m. every morning in that confined space on the platform.

The Pāttukār address Āttukāl Amma with the liberty of a family member. They refer to Her with extreme fondness using words such as kilavi,[1] avaru,[2] moothamma,[3] etc. The entire world has changed, the temple has changed and the status of the Āttukāl Temple and the kind of crowd that gathers there have changed but the Thottam singers continue to retain their age-old methods of worship. In the

Madhu Asan and his troupe singing the Thottam Pāttu

course of the past four years, I persuaded Madhu Asan to sing a few lines for me whenever I met him, but he politely refused each time saying that if he sang the Thottam, the Goddess would arrive on the spot. I was rather frightened imagining Goddess Bhadrakali appearing in my living room or at the temple or on the road!

The elders at Āttukāl remember renowned Thottam singers Govindan Asan of Kunnathuveedu and his associate Ambi Asan of 'Valiyavilakam' (which could be the name of the plot of land where his house was located); they used to tie a red silk cloth around their heads while singing the Thottam. It is believed that they sang this unique hymn every year for sixty-five long years. Madhu Asan is the great-grandson of Kochan Asan and the son of Govindan Asan. Kochan Asan had dedicated himself entirely to the Thottam Pāttu, at the portals of the Goddess at the Konchiravila temple, who is considered to be the elder sister of the Goddess of Āttukāl. One day, Kochan Asan finished the singing for the day at the Konchiravila temple and collapsed dead in front of the Goddess. Madhu Asan's reminiscences about his own

Madhu Asan lost in the praise of the Goddess

lineage do not stretch beyond a hundred years. Madhu was not yet fourteen when he first accompanied his father to sing the Thottam Pāttu at these temples. 'I do not have specific memories,' Madhu says, unable to recall the beginnings of his life of homage at the feet of the music-loving Goddess.

Piety and deep emotion surge on the face of Madhu Asan, when he describes his passion for the ritual. After forty-one days of rigorous observances including sexual abstinence, he stays in the hymn house he has constructed in the temple grounds. For the last twenty years, Madhu Asan has been the one to invoke Kodungallur Amma, and request Her to make Āttukāl Her abode during the Pongala festival. Then, with the aid of only the chenju or kuzhithalam, and his own devotional fervour, he transports Her through the Thottam Pāttu, and installs Her in Āttukāl.

The Thottam Pāttu Commences

Early in the morning, before the starting of the first day's Pāttu, Madhu Asan and his troupe can be seen decorating the hymn house. They spread five plantain leaves before it. The first of these is meant as an oblation to Ganapati. The main items of oblation are paddy, coconut, bunch of coconut flowers, flowers and the chenju. Paddy, polished raw rice, parboiled rice and bunches of areca-palm flowers are placed on the leaves. Before they start the song, they sprinkle water using a flower on Ganesha, the Goddess and Guru (Jupiter). After that, torches made from the dried spathe of coconut-flower pods are placed on the five plantain leaves. A big vettukatthi (a machete-like implement used by coconut tree climbers to cut down coconut bunches) is also placed under one of the banana leaves.

THOTTAM PĀTTUKĀR

Midday repose of Madhu Asan in the hymn house

Three pairs of cymbals and a single one, are offered to Ganapati and the singers take the three pairs when the Pāttu begins. The three singers sit down to start the singing. As the tiny hand-held chenju is sounded in a particular fashion, it resonates in the depth of the mind of the listeners. When the Pāttu begins at a chosen auspicious hour, the crowds start gathering in the temple premises. At this time, the ABTT members, temple administrators and members of the organizing families can be seen hurrying about, attending to every detail of the proceedings.

The Thottam singers have learnt the songs in the oral tradition, as already mentioned. Madhu Asan sits at the left end of the hymn house facing the sanctum, and the acolytes who make up the chorus sit at the right end. The chorus traditionally sings after the Asan. They all wear the starched dhoti given by the temple and the thorthu, a thin cotton towel, is wound over their heads like a turban.

Taking up the chenjus and pressing them to their chests, the Asan and his fellow singers bow before the deity in worshipful prayer. They start singing in the hymn chamber they have constructed, their minds rapt in the narration of the heroic deeds of the Goddess Bhadrakali; they transcend their daily sorrows and tribulations and immerse themselves in the rapture of the Pāttu. The Pāttukār stay at the temple and continue their abstinences over the next ten days. The whole ritual is primordial.

ĀTTUKĀL AMMA

The Pāttu begins thus:

> Hail to the sky that spreads face down
> Hail to the earth that lies supine,
> Hail the Great Ganapati,
> Hail my teacher,
> Hail the learned minstrels, who invoke,
> Hail the good audience who listens to the noble tale.

The invocation of Kodungallur Amma begins. Her imaginary skyward journey from the Kodungallur temple has been described exceedingly well in the song. The fond and devotion-filled humble appeal – that Goddess Bhadrakali should come forth from wherever She is, the hilltop, the depths of the ocean, in the flower, in the river, in the tree, in the forest, in the stream, in Kodungallur, or anywhere else in the universe – moves the listeners deeply.

The Pāttukār sing their hearts out in a tone of total surrender and supplication. The tune and music are in consonance with that mood, as if they do not have any other refuge than the Goddess. They follow the time-hallowed way of singing, touching only on the natural, rudimentary music inherent in the song, and using just the chenju as accompaniment.

The Thottam songs have existed in the oral tradition and were handed down from generation to generation over the centuries and are considered holy and inviolate by the Thottam singers. The unwritten rules, as described by Madhu Asan, are that the Thottam singing should not be recorded or copied down in words, as they believe that it will offend the Goddess. However, of late, excerpts of it are videographed by pushy TV reporters and telecast, indicative of the erosion of values that has crept in through the mindless application of modernity that disregards tradition and beliefs.

In 2014, the temple administrators decided to record, for the first time, the Thottam songs harkening perhaps to the call of 'modernity'. However, the camera developed glitches at the very beginning of the venture and the administrators abandoned their plan to record it. I too gave up the plans of transcribing and interpreting the songs, letting the Pāttu, with no recorded history, reside securely, its sanctity inviolate, in the minds of Madhu Asan and his troupe.

Besides, I had to face the limitation of just being a listener of the Pāttu from afar, as I was not allowed to stand near the singers or follow their time schedule. The singers are in a totally restrained mood during the brief intervals they use to take rest. I couldn't ask them where and how

The pair of Kāppu made of Panchaloha, and the thread made of pineapple fibre

they end a song, as folk songs do not yield to interpretation easily – they differ from version to version. I also realized that there are details that they never tell anyone. And the songs are not audible enough due to the loud devotional music or film songs played from various loudspeakers in and around the temple precincts during the festival.

The preparations of Kodungallur Amma to visit the Āttukāl Temple are described thus in the song: She decorates Herself by wearing three thousand serpents in Her locks, accompanied by Her retinue of all birds and animals and Her fearsome attendants. She moves through the sky to Mount Kailasam. After paying obeisance to Her father, Lord Shiva, She arrives at Āttukāl and the Pāttukār create an imaginary canopy with their songs to welcome Her. That canopy, as described in the song, is decorated with tender coconut leaves, jackfruit leaves, mango leaves, bunches of raw plantains, ripe plantains and tender palmyra nuts. After washing the spot with a mixture of cow dung and water 1,008 times, worshipping it with 1,008 flowers, after spreading 1,008 plantain leaves, arranging 1,008 consecrated oblations to Lord Ganapati, and lighting 1,008 eight-piece lamps, the Goddess, along with Her retinue, will be installed at the north portal of the temple. I would always visualize the gigantic figure of Bhadrakali with a trishulam in hand standing at the temple entrance, pleased with the arrangements to receive Her!

Kāppu kettal (tying of the Kāppu – a small bangle-like ornament made from panchaloha, a compound of the five metals such as gold, silver, copper, lead and zinc) marks the arrival of Kodungallur Amma and the beginning of the ten-day festival. This ritual is also considered a token of the promise of the devotees to conduct the festival in a befitting manner.

Words cannot portray the ambience in the temple at this time. The singers continue their fast-paced singing. They declare at the sreekovil that the Kāppu would be tied at the preordained time. For those who are present on the occasion, it is a moment that will fill their lives with a thousand bright lamps, as long as their memory lives.

Till the pāttukār sing of the presence of Kodungallur Amma, there is all-round silence. The stillness in the throng is suddenly broken by a shout of 'Amma!' in a voice which could be a heart-rending sob or the shriek of a crazed devotee. It is the voice of Ramachandran, an employee of the temple. That sets off an explosion of sound – mortar crackers, pealing bells, percussion ensembles, and the loud chanting of the devotees. It's a breathtaking moment filled with ecstatic divinity and the throbbing of pure, vibrant energy. The power is so physically real that it makes the body shiver. The entire place is suffused with the excitement of Kodungallur Amma's arrival.

'How do you know it?' I asked Madhu Asan, and he just said, 'One can sense the arrival of Amma,' and looked at the distance with eyes filled with tears. I think I almost felt Her arrival too, so I didn't want to seek further proof.

Bliss and graciousness fill the atmosphere. 'Someone has arrived, She's special, She's divine,' is the feeling one gets, something which I personally experienced. The belief is that, gratified by the decorations and the obeisance, the Goddess of Kodungallur resides for the next ten days in the sreekovil and blesses Āttukāl by accepting the special pujas and rituals in Her honour.

The donning of the Kāppu is not a temple tantra ritual, and is performed in Āttukāl and other Bhadrakali temples of southern Kerala. One of the Kāppus is fastened on the tip of the sword of the Goddess kept inside the sreekovil and the other, on the right wrist of the head priest. Once the Kāppu is tied, the head priest cannot leave the temple precincts until the Kāppu is untied from the sword and from his wrist on the tenth day. The thread with which the Kāppu is tied is made from pineapple leaf fibre,

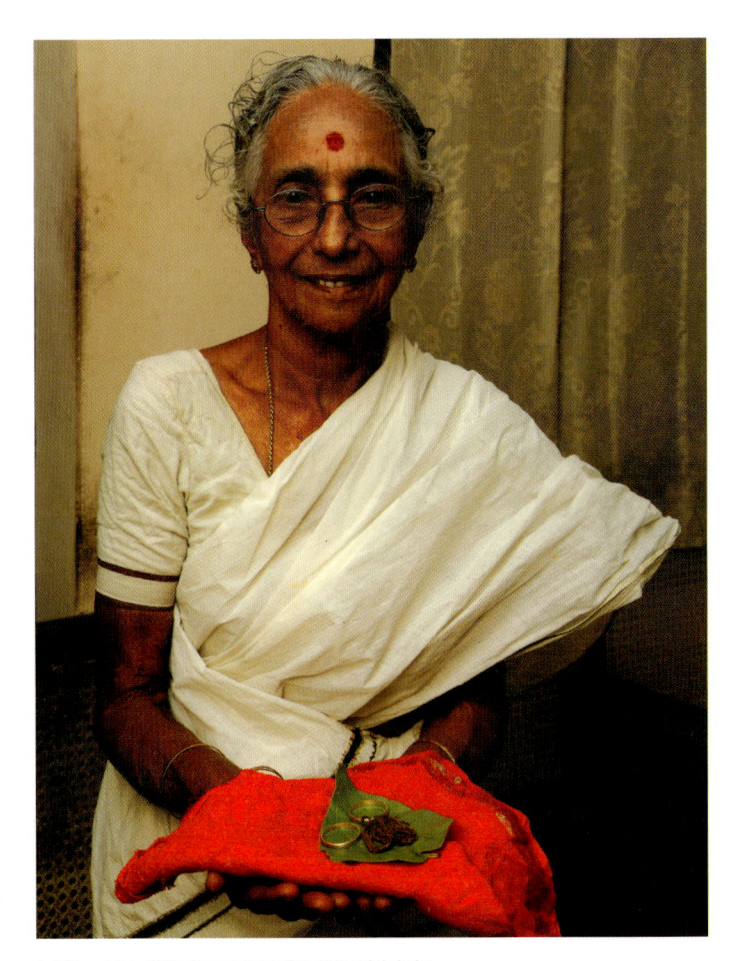

Lalithambika of Nediyavilakom Family, which is in charge of conducting the first day's Thottam Pāttu

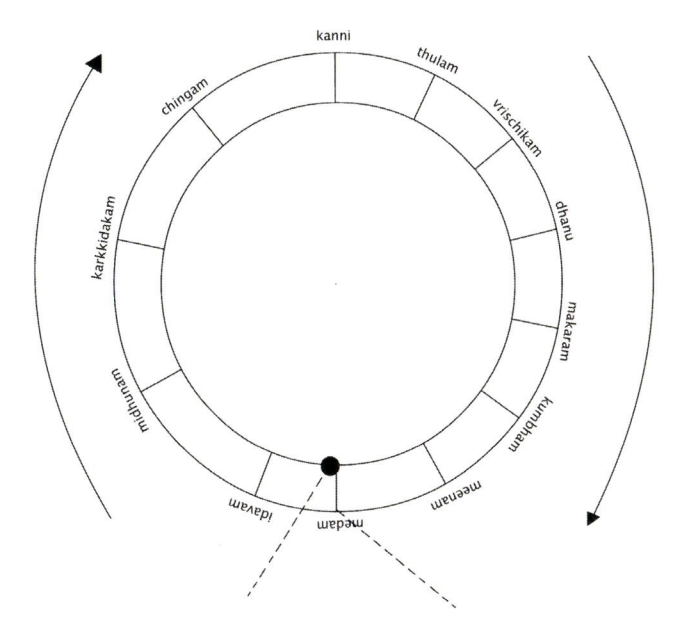

Divination using split coconut

dipped in turmeric paste. For the past four decades, a devotee called Sarasamma has been making this thread.

A pair of Kāppus used to be made by the ABTT annually for the ritual, but gradually it began to be made by the family that conducts the first day's Pāttu. Interestingly, the right to conduct the first day's Pāttu had been rotated, till 1968, among Balan Pillai Madhavan Pillai of Keezheperumpally family, Shivashankara Pillai of Kalluveedu, and Krishna Pillai of Nediyavilakom. For the last thirty-nine years, Krishna Pillai's daughter, Lalithambika and her husband Prabhakaran Nair, have been sponsoring the Kāppu kettal and conducting the first day's Pāttu. The paditharam, or the dakshina given to the Pāttukār, the floral decorations and the expenses for the puja on that day are also borne by them.

After the Kāppu-tying ceremony is over, the special oblations for the Goddess start and the prasadam is distributed among the devotees. It consists of thirumadhuram,[4] aravana,[5] a beverage called pānakam made with lime, honey, melted jaggery, cumin seeds and ground cardamom. This oblation is specially meant for awe-inspiring deities such as Narasimhamoorthi and is considered to have therapeutic effects.

There is a deepārādhana using multiple lamps and the offering of pānakam as nivedyam. The right to seek the first blessing from those lit lamps, as per the tradition of Āttukāl, belongs to the Thottam singers. Then, Madhu Asan breaks a coconut with the single stroke of a Vettukatthi, to divine whether the Goddess is happy with the proceedings so far. If the coconut is cut neatly into two equal halves, it is assumed that the deity is pleased.

Divination by breaking of a coconut is an ancient practice. The Pāttu mentions this kind of divination by cutting a coconut into two equal halves and making predictions for the future, based on how the cut edge on the 'face-half' (the coconut vaguely resembles the human face, with two eyes and a mouth) appears. The circular cut-edge is assigned the

The conclusion of the Thottam Pāttu on the tenth night of festival

twelve houses of the horoscope (see picture). The divination is made by observing which rāsi on the edge is prominent, and which is not. This sort of divination used to be done before the beginning of auspicious activities. The ritual of cut-coconut divination takes place at Āttukāl before the Pāttu starts, to see whether Kodungallur Amma is pleased with the celebration at Āttukāl upon Her arrival. This ritual is repeated after the singing is finished at the end of the ten-day festival, to see whether She approves of all the pujas and oblations and worship done during the festival. After this part of the ritual is over, general predictions are made. For example, if the Edavam rāsi is ascendant, indicated by the cut edge of the half-coconut in this rāsi remaining prominent, there will be incessant flow of wealth for those who are in that rāsi.[6]

The Thottam songs, narrating the story of the Goddess and Palakan, Her husband, continue to be sung for ten days, eliciting corresponding rituals in the temple on each day, reflecting the different stages in the narration. There are no significant variations in the temple rituals except on the seventh day on which the death of Palakan is narrated. Then the temple is closed for a couple of hours as a mark of respect to the dead Palakan. Pujas are delayed for that duration; Goddess's idol atop the gopuram is covered with a cloth, and no new saris are draped on Her as is the practice. On all the ten days, there are crowds, especially of old people, surrounding the singers, listening eagerly to the songs.

After the festival is over and the Kāppus are removed, the right to take them back and store them also is vested with Prabhakaran Nair and his family. Earlier the Kāppu was in the possession of the temple. Along with the Kāppus, this family also has to give more than forty banana plants and bunches of tender coconuts for decorating the temple, and also provide the material for preparing the oblations.

It can only be surmised that Thottam Pāttu was in existence ever since the Goddess was installed at Āttukāl. Gradually, the expenses for the Thottam singing and the festival on each day were met by different families. Somewhere down the years, the right of conducting the Pāttu began to be vested with twelve Nair families of the locality. The first day's Pāttu used to be an offering from Krishnan Kutty Nair of Valiyaveedu family before the 1950s. No one has been able to find out who were conducting the Pāttu before that time but the local people I interviewed told me that people from other communities also used to conduct the Pāttu some fifty years ago.

The Thottam singers do not seek attention or remuneration for this song-offering to the Goddess – they consider the singing as their duty towards the Goddess and, for that reason, they are much revered in the temple.

The singers carry on the same way on all ten days, dealing with different sections of the story, which will be discussed in the next chapter. It is also the privilege of the main singer to cook the pongala for the Goddess when it is telecast live on the Āttukāl Pongala day. We can see the ABTT members, ministers, local political leaders and top police officers surrounding the pongala hearth right in front of the hymn house and cameras capturing every moment till the pongala boils over. The pongala is cooked with raw red rice, coconut scrapings and rasakadali or palayamkodan pazham (local varieties of high-quality plantains). Ghee is added at the end. It doesn't contain jaggery, yet it is mildly sweet. During the course of writing this book, I have had the good fortune of receiving it and tasting it as soon as it was offered to the Goddess.

On the tenth day, when the Pongala and the Goddess's visit to the Manacaud Shasta Temple are over, it is time to untie the Kāppu from the Goddess's sword and from the chief priest's wrist. This ceremonial seeing off of the Goddess of Kodungallur is done through the Thottam Pāttu and it is called Polippāttu.

In olden days, the Pāttukār were primarily from two sub-castes: Mannān (washerman caste) and Paravan (coconut tree climber caste) but now people from various other communities also learn to sing the Thottam songs. In the Malayalam month of Medam, Madhu Asan teaches the songs in a temporary hymn house in a paddy field near his house. He told me that he trains all those who aspire to learn the song, irrespective of caste and creed. The training lasts for forty-one days, from six to eight in the evenings. He believes it is ordained by the Goddess and the right people would certainly arrive during the time of need. Though Thottam singing is generally an inherited right, he didn't insist that even his own son should learn to sing Thottam songs. When this annual musical worship of the Goddess is over, Madhu Asan reverts to his job – that of a daily-wage manual labourer. He is uneducated but singing this hymn of over ten thousand lines makes him a divine presence during the festival.

The next chapter contains the detailed narration of each day's Pāttu.

The conclusion of the Thottam singing called Polippāttu

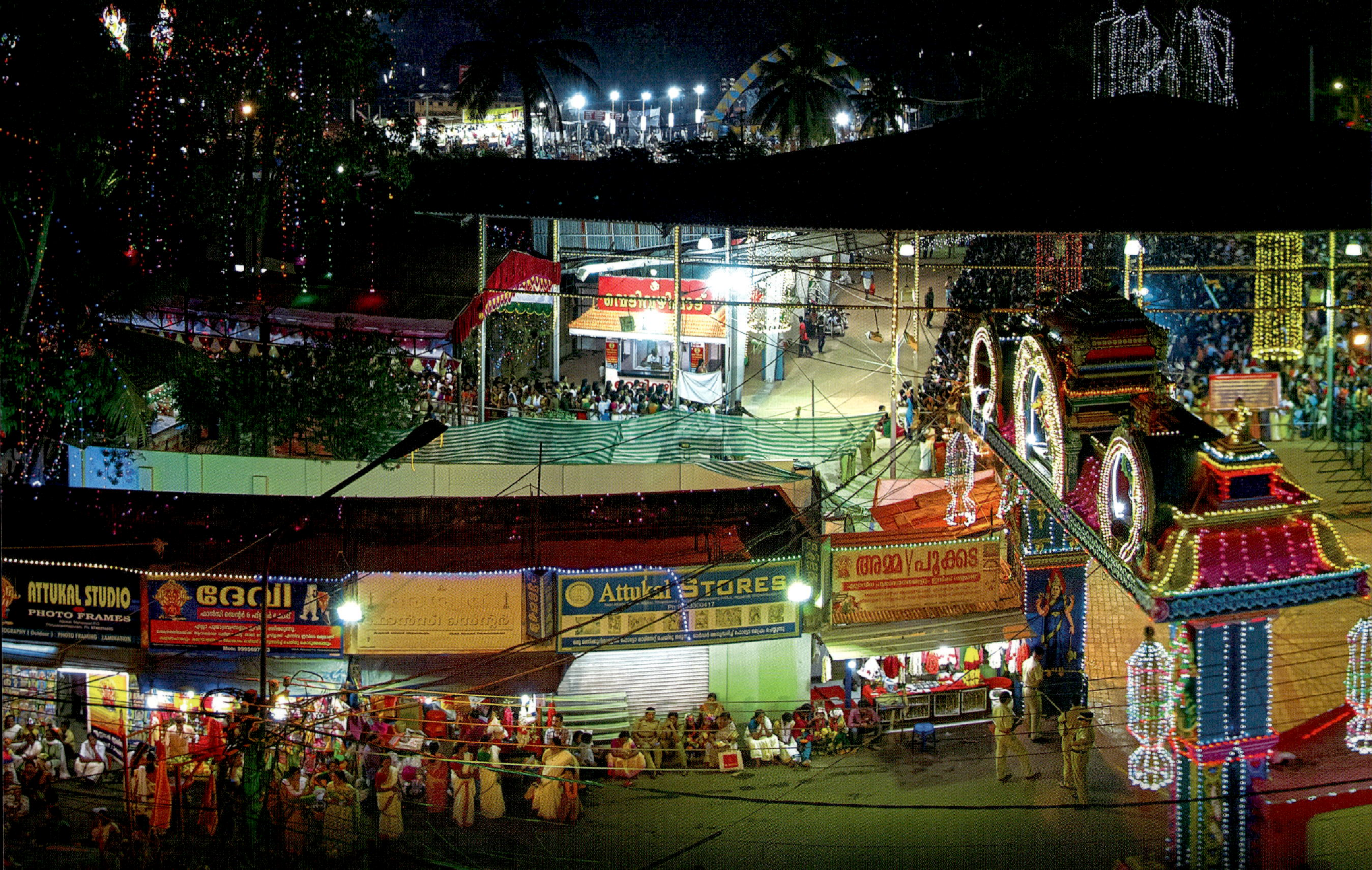
ATTUKAL STUDIO
PHOTO FRAMES
Attukal STORES

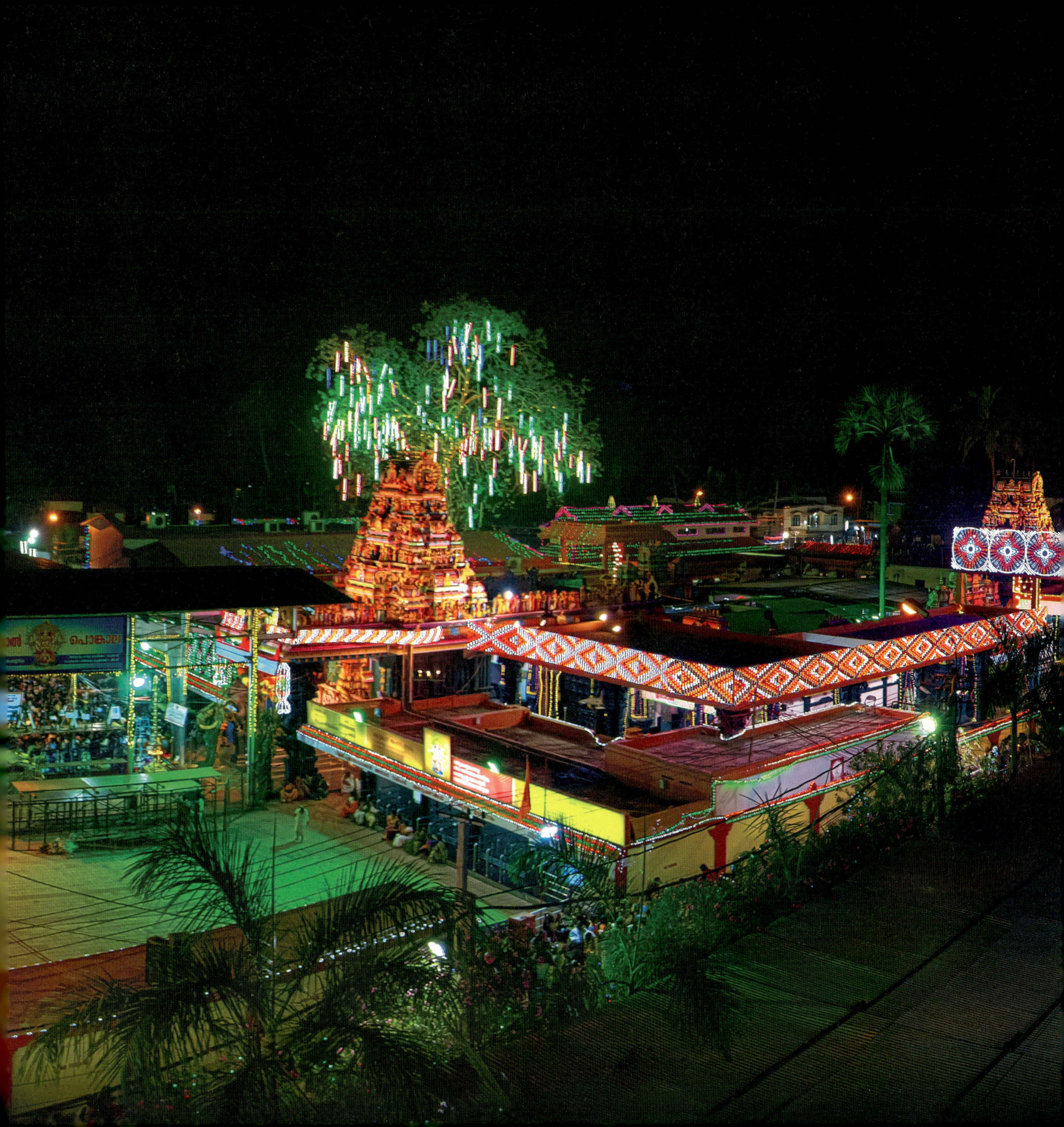
പൊങ്കാല

9

The Ten-day Festival and the Thottam Pāttu

The festival of Āttukāl Amma requires enormous planning because it is marked by the surging humanity from all around towards the temple. Barricades are built from the northern entrance, far away from the sreekovil, in advance, to prevent stampede, and it takes hours to get a glimpse of Āttukāl Amma.

The ABTT and various organizations circulate many booklets carrying the details of the festival arrangements and timings. All leading newspapers bring out Pongala supplements. Many businesses and corporate houses put up their hoardings to welcome the Āttukāl Pongala at every junction.

Vendors of bangles, toys, spices and posters of gods and goddesses line the road to the temple. We can find many temporary tea shops and ice cream parlours too. We can see rows and rows of pot sellers along the streets, all over the city, during the festival week.

Though people have started offering the pongala in stainless steel or aluminium pots, earthen pots are the appropriate vessels for cooking the pongala. The price of the pots goes up astronomically once the Pongala fever is on. A normal-sized pot which costs Rs 50 would go up to Rs 100.

With film songs and announcements blaring out of loudspeakers during the festival days at Āttukāl, it is often difficult to hear the singing of the Thottam Pāttu. The Pāttukār are reluctant to explain what they sing on a particular day or at what point in the story they break off for the day.

In all other versions of Thottam Pāttu, except the one sung at Āttukāl, the story of the slaying of the asura Darikan is recounted. In other versions of Pāttu, Goddess Bhadrakali, whose frenzied rage remains unabated even after She kills Darikan, is depicted as being calmed by Lord Shiva, Her father. Once She calms down, and takes the form of a small girl, Shiva gives Her in adoption to the king and queen of Thekkum Kollam.

Over the last four years, I have listened to the Thottam Pāttu and have managed to understand the narrative content of the song. Here I shall try to explain the song as it is sung over ten days during the annual Pongala festival. In the Pāttu, the Goddess is mentioned as Devi, Amma, Kanyavu, or Kanni, but not even once as Kannaki.

Day One: Beginning of the Thottam Pāttu at Āttukāl[1]

After Kodungallur Bhagavathy is invoked through the singing of the 'Invocation' part of the Thottam song and thus transported from Kodungallur to Āttukāl, and the Kāppu-

The King of Vadakkum Kollam doing penance, standing on tiptoe near a river bank

tying ceremony is over, the singers enter the narrative part of the singing. The first day's song tells the story of the birth of Palakan or Balakan.

King Marayar and Queen Maruthi of Vadakkum Kollam[2] have been childless for a long time. So, the king sets out to do penance, standing on tiptoe near a riverbank. Lord Shiva, who comes to the river to bathe, wakes him up from his trance and inquires the reason for his penance. The king tells him that he and his wife are childless and he is doing penance to invoke Lord Shiva to grant them an heir to the kingdom.

Lord Shiva then tells the king to walk due east. There, he would find a mother plantain tree and a daughter plantain tree; the daughter tree will be bearing a ripe finger bunch of plantains on the top, though normally the plantain bunches at the base should mature first. The king should pluck three plantains from that finger bunch and his wife Maruthi should eat those plantains. On the tenth vinazhika (one vinazhika equals twenty-four seconds) of the tenth nazhika (one nazhika equals twenty-four minutes) of the tenth day of the tenth month from that

ĀTTUKĀL AMMA

Villagers making the huge vilakku or lamp used in vilakkukettu ritual during the festival

the carpenter presents the finely wrought cradle, the king is so pleased with its beauty that he honours the carpenter by giving him a new title 'Thachaguruvazhum Palakan.'

On the seventh day of the child's birth, the king summons the royal astrologer to cast the prince's horoscope. In due course, when the astrologer declares that the horoscope has been completed, the king asks him to announce its highlights.

The royal astrologer declares that the prince would learn to read and write by the time he is five years old, swordsmanship by the age of seven, and horse riding by nine; the boy would construct a market platform by the time he is eleven, preside over it and sell wares by thirteen; and when he is fifteen years old, he would gather his countrymen at the seashore, make them board a ship, set sail to faraway lands and loot gold and riches from those lands, fill the ship with the wealth, sail back to his land, bring the booty to the market platform and reign with felicity. He will marry when he is sixteen. On the date, she would deliver a baby boy who should be given an auspicious name.

The Pāttu here provides lively descriptions of ripened paddy fields and markets where intense trading goes on. The Pāttu refers to Marayar, the king, who visits various places to get the goods needed for his own country. The song narrating the birth of the heir to the throne is carried over to the second day.

Day Two: The Birth and Growing up of Palakan and the Search for a Bride

In the second day's Thottam Pāttu, the narration continues with the story of the birth of Palakan. Queen Maruthi eats the plantains as directed by Lord Shiva and at the appointed hour, gives birth to a son. He is given an auspicious name, 'Palakan.' On the fifth day after the birth of the child, the king summons a carpenter named Vairakhen to make a cradle for the baby. When

Queen Maruti with baby Palakan in the cradle

Kathirukāla, the effigy of a bullock made with fresh paddy, is an offering made to the Goddess during the festival

seventh day after his wedding, when he goes to sell his wares in another land, brigands will pounce on him, rob him of his money, personal jewellery and the wares he was planning to sell, foist on him charges of stealing, murder him at the foot of the gallows and string his body up on the gallows.

The king is incensed by this prediction, and the astrologer, fearing royal wrath, flees to the neighbouring Muthucheri kingdom. As he races down the streets of Muthucheri with the horoscope in his hand, the astrologer is stopped by the king of Muthucheri who is proceeding towards his royal bath. He inquires the reason for the astrologer's flight. The astrologer tells him the story of how his predictions have enraged the king of Vadakkum Kollam who now wants to execute him. The narration does not mention what the astrologer's ultimate fate is.

When Palakan is sixteen years old, the queen instructs the king that when he goes in search of a bride for her son, he should look for one who is suitable in complexion, disposition, wealth and caste, but it does not matter even if she came from a humble background.

The king and his companion leave on a search for a bride for the prince. Unable to find one, the distraught father stops to rest at a wayside inn. He is quite despondent and says, 'I don't want to return to Vadakkum Kollam and see my Maruthi and my son. Let a black panther eat me up while I climb the hills'. He leaves the inn and on his way he sees a dilapidated temple; he enters the temple with his companion and sits under the roof, hoping it will fall on him and end his misery.

There are already two more people in the temple, and they are asleep. When the king falls asleep, his companion wakes up one of them asking who they are and where they are headed. The stranger replies that they are coming from Thekkum Kollam, which is ruled by Narayanar, in search of a suitable groom for the king's seven-year-old daughter. (One variation of the same song says she is six years old at the time of marriage). The companion of the king of Vadakkum Kollam replies that he and his king are also in search of a bride for the prince. The two then wake up their respective masters and apprise them of this information.

The king of Thekkum Kollam, Narayanar, requests the king of Vadakkum Kollam, Marayar, to go to Thekkum Kollam with them, meet the girl, consult the astrologer to fix the auspicious hour for the wedding, and return to his kingdom after partaking of the royal feast. The two kings sail southward from Vadakkum Kollam to Thekkum Kollam in two ships. The young princess, who was in fact gifted in adoption to the king by Her father, Lord Shiva, is standing at Her watchtower in the palace at Thekkum Kollam, looking out to the sea in the west. She spots the ships advancing towards the harbour. When the queen comes to know about it, she assumes that the king has made all the arrangements for her daughter's wedding before returning home.

When the party enters the palace, the queen seats King Marayar on a mat, and seeing he is thirsty, asks her daughter to serve him buttermilk from the golden kindi (a pitcher with a spout), and water from the velli kindi (a silver pitcher). When Devi bearing the pitchers comes close, the king muses: 'This maiden is capable of killing and then resurrecting, enticing, stimulating, attracting evil eye and fecund.' He decides that Her beauty will have to be described properly.

There is a mention here in the narration that Devi reads his thoughts and is angry, and that She then shuts Her left eye and kills the king. But the story goes on to say that She resurrects him by opening Her right eye.

Since the girl has been prophesied to have a happy marriage, King Marayar believes that if his son marries Her, he will escape his fate as foretold in his horoscope. So Marayar summons the astrologer and orders that arrangements should be made for providing a lamp, an idol of Ganapati, niranāzhi,[3] sandal paste, flowers, bunches of coconut flowers, raw rice, and semi-polished rice.

Even though the omens forbid the marriage of Palakan and Devi, the king of Vadakkum Kollam agrees to the auspicious time for the wedding and, Narayanar, the king of Thekkum Kollam, accepts the matching horoscopes. Marayar tells Narayanar that his son would arrive the next day to wed the latter's daughter.

The second day's narration ends here.

Day Three: Mālappuram Pāttu – Devi's Wedding

The Pāttu on this day narrates the wedding of Devi.

Lord Shiva's daughter Kanyavu (the Goddess Bhadrakali) who grew up in the royal household of Thekkum Kollam detests marriage. How could She marry a human youth? Yet, when She is seven years of age, Her foster-father fixes Her wedding with Palakan of Vadakkum Kollam. The Thottam song describes it thus:

> 'On the seventh day from today,
> On the auspicious day, Friday
> At the auspicious moment in Simha Rāsi,
> There is the muhurtam for the sacred wedding
> Of the Divine Virgin of Thekkum Kollam.' [Translated by A.J. Thomas]

Preparing the mandapam for weddings used to be an occasion for a big celebration in those days. The Pāttu describes in detail the offering made to Ganapati – padukka, nirapara, niranāzhi, the golden seat covered with mundu,[4] palli vāl[5] and a variety of wedding garlands. Apart from that,

The wedding of Devi and Palakan

ĀTTUKĀL AMMA

there is also enough evidence about the existence of the dowry system in ancient Kerala. Lord Shiva gives everything he owns to Bhadrakali as dowry. The only difference is that the dowry is demanded and received after the wedding.

Palakan, along with twelve thousand followers, arrives at the kingdom of Thekkum Kollam. They are seated in the Veerāyamani pandal, and Palakan is led to the ceremonial stage. Palakan ascends the stage after addressing all the four directions and seats himself on Devi's right. But when he looks towards Her on his left, he cannot find Her there! Lord Vayu reassures the perplexed Palakan that he would bring back Kanyavu. When Lord Vayu blows, the wind spreads everywhere, but the conch shell does not produce any sound. When Vayu looks inside the conch shell, Kanyavu is found hiding there. He manages to bring Her out through entreaties and seats Her once again to Palakan's left.

When Palakan intends to garland Her and lay claim to Devi's hand, She again vanishes. Devi is not interested in the marriage, because if that happens, She will be given away to a human husband at the end of the ceremony. So, when Palakan picks up the garland to wed Her, She hides under the central lamp. The second time Palakan attempts to garland Her, She hides behind the mirror; the third time, in the decorated pot next to the stage; the fourth time, in the well situated inside the private quarters of the Thekkum Kollam household; the fifth time, under the petal of a lotus in the River Ganga; the sixth time, outside the fortress of Āruthira and the seventh time, under the hood of the serpent situated beyond perumthira, which means, a big wave.

Then Palakan says that he would lose his dignity in front of so many of his own people because of Devi's pranks; Lord Vayu once again assures him that he will bring Her back. When Vayu blows all around, the lotus buds in the pond sway, except one. Guessing that Kanyavu would be hiding in the bud, Lord Vayu opens it and finds Her there. He once again leads Her to the wedding stage and makes Her swear an oath that She wouldn't move away from there.

At that moment, the astrologer declares that it was the muhurtam for the wedding. When Palakan tries to garland Her, it is severed in two and lands in front of Her Father, Lord Shiva, in Kailasam. The Great Lord, when He realizes that this was His daughter's way of informing Him of Her wedding, summons Vishnumāyika to His side and sends through her the thali along with His blessings for Her bright future, and also the garland to be worn by Palakan. As soon as Vishnumāyika arrives in a flying chariot and alights on top of the Veerayāmani pandal, Kanyavu smiles.

The Thottam song describes the scene thus, as Lord Shiva declares:

Panchavādyam during the festival

> 'I have sent my own beloved daughter
> To the earth-world.
> At the tender age of seven
> She is destined to have Her sacred wedding.'
> [Translated by A.J. Thomas.]

Kanyavu picks up the thali that Her Father has sent, and wears it Herself. Thus, there is no actual marriage taking place between Kanyavu and Palakan. As Palakan realizes this, She tells him: 'I have performed a conjuration in front of the eyes of the world's people, my husband!' She tells him that the people saw it as if Palakan had put the garland around Her neck, and that, for the people, they are husband and wife.

Palakan feels aggrieved that Devi wears the thali Herself without waiting for him as per the ritual. Devi then consoles him and goes ahead, leaving Her caprice behind, to complete the other rituals such as 'polivu', the gift-receiving ritual, which consists of drinking milk from the same vessel and the holding of hands. As Lord Vayuvarna proceeds to place Devi's left hand in Palakan's right hand as per custom, Devi, who is enraged at being touched by Palakan, splits the garland into two, throwing one piece into the deep sea and the other into the high mountains and finally Devi adorns Herself with a garland.

Resuming the rituals associated with marriage, She returns to Her parents' house where She serves milk to Her husband. Her father Lord Shiva and She bargain over Her dowry, which includes several types of smallpox seeds. After giving them to Her husband, She tests their efficacy by spraying them on Her foster-father, the king, who is afflicted with smallpox. Following the wailing and weeping of Her foster-mother, Devi resurrects Her foster-father.

The king and queen of Thekkum Kollam construct two citadels where they want Devi and Palakan to be installed separately. Palakan, who is full of love and adoration for Her, however, does not want to be separated from Devi. On hearing this, Devi tells him that they can go to Vadakkum Kollam and spend their days together in leisure, chewing betel leaves. Having decided thus, they plan the details of their trip wherein Devi instructs Palakan and his companions to travel via the hills while Devi and Her attendants will travel via the sea in the golden ship that She has been gifted. Though Palakan wants to travel in the company of his newly-wed wife, Devi consoles him saying that they will be inseparable once they reach their new quarters.

In the course of their travel, Devi and Her attendants come across Palakan's friend who had gone to get the 'komba' and the ring coated with gold. Devi explains to him that Palakan is now Her husband. Taking the ring from him, She proceeds on Her journey.

Thus the bride and the groom travel to Vadakkum Kollam by separate routes. The groom avoids the coast and travels over the hills because he owes some kind of tax to the Goddess of the sea. The bride avoids the hills and goes in a ship because She was originally proposed in marriage to Ayyappan of the hills. Whoever arrives at azheekkal (literally, 'river mouth') first has to wait for the other; this is the arrangement between Devi and Palakan. Devi arrives first and grows anxious because Her husband has not arrived; so She creates rain, thunder and whirlwind. The storm uproots trees that then float down the rivers. Her husband comes riding down the river, to the seashore, on one of those trees. Thus they find each other at last and decide to proceed by sea for the rest of the journey. During their journey together towards Vadakkum Kollam by sea, but by separate ships, to Palakan's home, Devi tests the quality of Her diamond ring by rubbing it against a stone, and in the process dislodges it from its socket. She summons a goldsmith to repair it.

I stood there, near the hymn house, beside the pāttukārs for hours together and listened carefully to what they

ĀTTUKĀL AMMA

were singing to see if the narration matched with what they told me during numerous discussions I had with them over several months. They narrated the stories through the Thottam songs only; they never narrated the content to me during the discussions. It was impossible for me to stay there continuously on all the ten days and nights. I also noticed that women and young girls celebrate the wedding day of Devi; they are all decked up and look cheerful. The crowd also increases on that day. The intricacies of the story and the pain contained in the Goddess having to marry a mere mortal never reach the common devotee.

Day Four: Arrival at Vadakkum Kollam

The Thottam Pāttu narrative on the fourth day describes an incident which takes place during Devi's voyage. Her voyage is interrupted when the wife of Kallakodi Maraykkar, a local chieftain, feels jealous upon seeing the golden ship and incites her husband to seize it. After defeating him in battle, Devi crosses the Maraykkar's coastal territory and finally approaches Vadakkum Kollam where She hears the shots fired by Her husband and his attendants from his ship to announce their arrival; She reciprocates the gesture.

Devi's journey to Vadakkum Kollam after Her marriage

THE TEN-DAY FESTIVAL AND THE THOTTAM PĀTTU

Kuthiyottam boys prostrating before Āttukāl Amma

On the fourth day, they disembark at the palace quarters of Vadakkum Kollam, to find the royal mother Maruthi waiting for them with seven attendants in their traditional hairdo and holding lamps to welcome them. Maruthi brings 'arattha' (a special kind of offering made of turmeric and lime that is deep red in colour, usually waved in circular motion before a newly-wed girl enters her husband's home for the first time) and milk, and worships Devi with a lighted lamp.

After lowering the flame of the lamp, she tells Devi that the king and she will ascend to heaven in seven days' time, and therefore, it is urgent that they go to the temple and make the necessary offerings before that. Thus they bathe and proceed to the temple, where King Marayar and Queen Maruthi make their offerings and retreat. After this, Palakan gives his offerings and is followed by Devi, who then retreats three steps behind Palakan. Following this, the king and the queen hand over all responsibilities to Palakan and Devi and bless them to live just as auspiciously as they had.

At that moment, Lord Shiva's ruby-encrusted chariot descends and the king and the queen ascend it to be transported bodily to heaven with the blessings of Lord Shiva. Palakan breaks down on seeing this; Devi finishes the requisite rituals for the departed and comforts him saying that they have to work hard to maintain the wealth their forefathers have accumulated; '*Irunnundāl kunnum thulayum*' ('If we settle down to eat, even the hills will level out'), she tells him.

Day Five: Devi Tells Her Husband to Sell Her Anklet

On the fifth day, there is a special event that takes place during the festival. The deity of Manacaud temple, Shastha, who is Devi's brother, comes to the temple in a procession (His festival would be on in Manacaud simultaneously), in a ritual called parathendal (begging for paddy on the day of Punartham asterism). Then the Āttukāl Temple's main door is shut against Him, as Devi does not want to see Her brother going about begging. The disappointed brother makes a pradakshinam in the outer balivattom and goes back. However, His other sisters, the Bhadrakalis of Konchiravila and Palkulangara, and other deities of major temples in and around Thiruvananthapuram, receive Him. Āttukāl Amma, while shutting the door against Shastha, promises Him that She will go and meet Him at his temple on the ninth day, and She keeps Her promise by visiting Him during the night of the Pongala.

In the Thottam Pāttu narrative of the fifth day, Devi tells Her husband that they can live with the profits from trade. As they proceed to the market, the Vetās (hunter tribesmen and women) and their attendants standing on the wayside taunt them. Hearing this, Devi asks Her husband to proceed and sell the goods, while She waits for him under a tree, a little further ahead. When Palakan is worried about Her safety, She puts his fears to rest saying that Her sword and spear will protect Her. Having sent him off, Devi closes Her eyes and half opens Her left eye at the taunting women. Immediately, the arrogant womenfolk are afflicted with a host of diseases – chills, fever, malaria, red eye, measles, etc. Terrified, the womenfolk consult an astrologer who tells them that this is the result of their taunting Devi and that they should placate Her on Her way

Devi giving the anklets to Palakan to sell

Jyothi Venkatachalam during her visit to the temple

back by blocking Her way with offerings such as beaten rice, fruits and berries. Accordingly, the women accost Devi with these offerings as She returns with Her husband. They entreat Devi to kill them if their offerings are not acceptable to Her. Devi transforms Herself into Maya and accepts the offerings gladly made by those women. As She closes Her eyes and half opens Her right eye, all their afflictions vanish.

Devi joins Her husband again and they proceed to their palace in Vadakkum Kollam, where Devi instructs Palakan to sell Her anklet along with the other wares that he is about to trade. Palakan proceeds to trade all the wares, including Devi's anklet; he remembers Her words, 'If we settle down to eat, even the hills will be levelled.'

However, other versions of the Thottam Pāttu mention that Palakan, following one of his vices, that of gambling, loses all his wealth through playing dice, and is reduced to such poverty that Devi hands over to him all the wealth She had received from Thekkum Kollam as dowry and Her own personal ornaments. Even these are forfeited and Palakan is reduced to brooding over his loss. To console him, Devi says that She has the two anklets which Her Father, Lord Shiva, has sent Her from Kailasam, and asks him to go to the Pandyan land where one of Her school fellows, a goldsmith, is living in the capital city Madurai, and that he will help Palakan in selling them, and raise enough money to restart his business.

But, Madhu Asan would never think of attributing any vice to Palakan, because he is a god! He would say only that Palakan belonged to a royal family whose main occupation was trade, and so, himself engaged in it. As to why Devi sends him away to conduct trade, Madhu Asan hinted that She wanted him to be away from Her, as She

ĀTTUKĀL AMMA

didn't want to consummate Her marriage and be a wife to a mortal. The poignancy of the tale is inherent in this terrible dichotomy – the tragedy that comes along with such violent wrenching away from emotions and pleasures related to the flesh, while, at the same time, the mind is filled with love and care.

Day Six: The Story of the Stolen Anklet

On his way to the traders' market, Palakan passes by the land of the king of Muthucheri. When the king pays his respects to him, he responds saying that he is not a king, but the son of Marayar of Vadakkum Kollam and that he is on his way

Palakan selling wares in Madurai

THE TEN-DAY FESTIVAL AND THE THOTTAM PĀTTU

Vilakkukettu ritual during the festival nights

to the land of the Pandyan king. The king of Muthucheri tells Palakan that he is his uncle and that it is dangerous for Palakan to meet the Pandyan king. The king takes him home and asks him to rest after instructing his seventh daughter to give him refreshments. However, Palakan escapes during the night. Alerted by the sound of the anklet, the king of Muthucheri comes running to see Palakan escape; 'No one can stop fate on its way,' he says.

En route, Palakan meets the midwife who helped his mother deliver him and asks her for directions to the land of the Pandyan. She points the way with the broom in her hand and Palakan proceeds in the same direction. He meets the Vetās and their attendants and trade with them on the street, finishing his work before he can return home. Later, while trying to sell the anklet, Palakan meets a goldsmith of the Pandyan land. The goldsmith drugs him while offering him betel leaves and takes him home. Reaching his home, when Palakan comes around, the goldsmith pretends Palakan has been intoxicated by chewing betel nuts (this is a common occurrence among betel leaf chewers adding areca nut), and asks him to wait it out. The goldsmith had stolen the queen's anklets to please his wife; he now hurries to the palace to inform the king that he has caught the thief who has stolen the queen's anklet. Palakan is given the name 'The thief who stole from Madurai.'

ĀTTUKĀL AMMA

Palakan being dragged to the King's court

Day Seven: Konnuthottam Describing the Execution of Palakan

In the Thottam Pāttu narration of the day, the Pandyan king tries Palakan for the crime of stealing the queen's anklets, without giving him a chance to explain himself. When the queen tries to intervene, insisting that the anklets found with Palakan were not hers, the goldsmith taunts the king saying that if it was his own wife who went against his word, he would kill her instantly. The enraged king whose manliness was thus questioned, orders that his wife's eyes be gouged out and she be pushed into a well; he thus loses his sense of justice and sentences Palakan to death.

The gallows are prepared, ironically by the same carpenter called Vairakhen who had built his cradle in his infancy! This carpenter is also the executioner. Palakan declares to Vairakhen that he is the husband of Goddess Bhadrakali and yet this fate has come to pass! Even the executioner wielding the axe senses that Palakan is innocent and begs forgiveness of all gods in carrying out his duty. Palakan is hacked to death and then hung up on the scaffold. The executioner engages a young washerman who is washing clothes in the nearby river, to stand guard to Palakan's body on the scaffold, to protect it from predators and vultures. When the washerman asks for wages for this task, the executioner says that the slain man is the husband of Goddess Bhadrakali and he could ask Her for compensation for his efforts, when She comes in search of his body.

Meanwhile, Devi is asleep under the hood of the five-headed serpent. She is startled awake when She has a vision of the execution of Her husband. She leaps out shouting,

> Oh! You damned goldsmith!
> You have played your dirty trick on him!

This is both highly poetic and deeply touching.

Devi, before leaving home to go looking for Her husband, takes leave of the plants and creepers She has nurtured. They are grief-stricken at the Divine Mother's departure. (In the northern variations of Thottam Pāttu, the ancestral home and the family well cave in, just after She leaves). She reaches Kailasam and tells Her Father that She is going in search of Her husband. Lord Shiva tells Her that if She goes in Her natural form, the people will recognise Her and so, to travel in the disguise of the seventy-year-old Variyamma of the silvery hair.

A detailed account of Her grief and search for the husband is narrated in the Pāttu. Goddess Bhadrakali asks everyone She meets on the way, whether they had seen Her husband. The varikka jackfruit tree gives Her the right directions. The Goddess grants it the boon that Her mudi (crown) would be carved out of its live wood.

The sour mango tree doesn't give Her the directions. So, She curses it saying that urchins will pelt stones at it (boys would throw stones at the mango tree when it bears fruit), that its wood will be used for the rituals in the southern portion of the compound (cremation of the family's dead), that its trunk would be hollowed out to make boats, and that the names of the boats would become different as different people board it. For example, when the king boards it, it would become 'Palliththoni' or 'royal boat;' when it is filled with ash, or 'chāmpal,' it will become 'Chāmpaththoni' or 'ash boat.' The implications here are deeply philosophical and mystical.

Small children throw mud at Her as She asks them for directions, so She curses them to eat mud in childhood.

The cow with a white-tufted tail too doesn't give Her directions. The Goddess curses her saying: 'People will kill and skin you, and make a musical instrument using that skin, and the beating on that skin would be necessary for worship in my temple, and even boys will pass you by only after giving a beating on your skin.' (The instrument in question is Chenda, the percussion instrument peculiar to Kerala).

She further bestows boons on a potter, a young woman and so on, on Her way to find Palakan. But none of them recognizes the Goddess. She eventually reaches Madurai. She meets a young Pānan angling in the river. As soon as he spots Her, he throws away the hook and line and comes forward, and prostrates at Her feet. She asks him, 'Why do you prostrate before me?' To which he replies: 'Because you are Mother Bhadrakali.' When She asks whether he has seen Bhadrakali before, he describes Her from feet to crown.

> Merely observing the beauty of Your utterance
> Reciting the name of Narayana
> One can sense that You are Bhadrakali.

Kuthiyottam boys having lunch in the temple

ĀTTUKĀL AMMA

Seeing Your sacred feet, and then Your head
Too, one can gather that You are Bhadrakali.
[Translated by A.J. Thomas]

In the conversation that follows between the young Pānan and the Goddess, She gets to know where the execution has taken place. Seeing the body of Her husband put up on the scaffold, the Goddess wails and laments like an ordinary woman, saying:

O my husband, are you asleep,
Are you asleep on the scaffold?
In the golden Kailasam where I was born
No one has ever died on a scaffold.

O Sri Mahadeva, my good Father
Why did this fate have to come to pass?
My Father, is it so short-lived a husband
That you have given me? [Translated by A.J. Thomas]

The execution of Palakan

Devi chops the tongue of the goldsmith who cheats Palakan

Such lament by the Goddess would drive any one to tears.

Devi who has resolved that She should resurrect Her husband, removes his corpse from the scaffold. Placing his feet on a silver kindi and his head on a golden kindi, She engages two young boys to watch over Her husband's body and goes to Kailasam. She obtains the immortality potion called Kālamegham and sweet water from Her Father and returns to the execution site and bathes Her husband's body. She obtains a cloth from the young Mannān to wrap around his body. Then she sprinkles the immortality potion on the body and asks permission of Her Father, Lord Shiva, and Mother Sri Parvati Devi, to resurrect him.

> O Sri Mahadeva, my good Father!
> May I resurrect my husband?
> O Ganga, Uma, my good Mother Parvati!
> May I resurrect my husband? [Translated by A.J. Thomas]

After this, Kanyavu chants the divine mantra three times into the ear of Her dead husband. At the third chant, life runs into the heart of the dead Palakan. Then he opens his eyes and gazes at the Divine Kanyavu, whom he had wedded. She then proceeds to install Palakan as a deity.

Though She brought Her husband back to life, She is enraged by the violence inflicted on him by the unjust verdict of the king, and is thirsty for vengeance. She splits the scaffold in two, and hurls one piece to the land of the cheating goldsmith, and the other to the land of the Pandyan king.

This part of the song is known as 'Konnuthottam Pāttu', or the 'Thottam Song of the Execution'. Since Her husband's death occurs on the seventh day, as a mark of respect, there are no celebrations in the temple on that day. The temple opens late after the rituals of purification like the otta punyāham are over and chemparuthi thāli[6] and oil are given to the devotees as a symbol of the ritual bath they have to take after a death. The idol of Devi in the gopuram is covered with white cloth and the temple remains closed till late in the morning.

Every year, this part of the Thottam Pāttu churns my mind and heart. This year, I experienced unprecedented peaks of pain and felt the imminence of death. In fact, I felt the presence of death as the only reality in the world. The truth that is Āttukāl Amma, the love that She is, has overwhelmed my heart. My night-long heartache before the Konnuthottam is sung in the Āttukāl Temple, is indicative of the measureless love I have towards my Great Mother. The Goddess of Thottam Pāttu is the eternal Virgin Bhadrakali, one who doesn't want to get married, and once married, doesn't love Her husband. And yet, her lamentation as Her husband lies dead on the scaffold is unbearable. Why does the Goddess, who is omnipotent, and capable of resurrecting Her husband, wail so? I ended up lamenting along with the Goddess the whole night.

Women at the temple precincts on the night before Pongala

Day Eight: Devi's Vengeance

This day's Pāttu is about Devi's vengefulness over Her husband's unjust execution. Devi prepares to kill the goldsmith who betrayed Her husband. He is shivering in fright and hiding inside a chamber in his house. The tottering old woman Variyamma is inquiring about the goldsmith. Thalirmadhura, the goldsmith's wife, tells Variyamma that her husband caught hold of 'the thief who had stolen from Madurai' and that Pandyan had killed him, but that thief's wife is said to have resurrected that thief. As Thalirmadhura asks Variyamma as to why she had come, the old woman tells her that she has brought a lot of gold, for ornaments to be wrought by the goldsmith. Thalirmadhura who secretly plans to get hold of all that gold from the old woman's hands, confers with her hiding husband. As he comes out of hiding to talk to the old woman, she asks him whether he had seen that 'thieving wife' of that thief whom he had caught and got executed. By the time he attempts to escape sensing the danger, Goddess Bhadrakali assumes her cosmic form and roars deafeningly. The entire land of the goldsmith shakes, and the goldsmith and his wife attempt to flee. The Goddess is right behind them. They taste the sharp edge of the Goddess's sacred sword. Mother Bhadrakali who is thirsting for vengeance lays waste the land of the goldsmith and wipes them out but only after bestowing on them the boon of rebirth.

She then proceeds to the land of the Pandyan king. The king who has learned about what has happened to

Devi beheads the Pandiyan King

ĀTTUKĀL AMMA

the goldsmith, takes precautionary measures for his own safety. He posts sentries and bodyguards all around. But Sri Kurumba, who protects all the worlds, overcame all of them. Don't we see the fire dancing in the eyes of Her who was born of the sacred fire of Lord Shiva's third eye? The entire body of Mother Bhadrakali who is wrapped in red silk, is also otherwise reddened by extreme rage. Goddess Bhadrakali roars, as if to crack open all the eight directions. The Pandyan land trembles.

Day Nine: Pongala Day

Devi confronts the Pandyan king. He has set columns of his army against Her. The Goddess is alone on the other side. Only the seven Kalis and the Vetalika are there to keep Her company. The Vetalika has come to consume the blood sacrifice. Mother Bhadrakali kills the soldiers, the king's children and nephews, and all those who oppose Her. Finally, only the king is left. The Pandyan king who looks into Her fire-emitting eyes,

The pandara aduppu before the hymn house is lighted to celebrate Devi's victory and pongala is cooked for Her

Thālappoli ritual

loses his nerve and is defeated in battle. He begs forgiveness of Mother Bhadrakali for his transgression. He begs Her to grant him boons, forgiving his sins committed knowingly and unknowingly and that if She spares his life, he will ensure regular offerings of Thottam Pāttu, Kuthirakettu and Garudan thookkam to Her. But the Mother declares that She will not forgive any of his transgressions, and beheads him with Her divine sword. Vetalika is satiated, lapping up even the last drop of blood that gushed out of his gullet.

At the point in the story when the Devi chops off the head of the Pandyan king, the pongala hearth inside the temple is lit. Punyāham, the purification ritual, is done by sprinkling sacred water all over the temple and the tantri hands over the lamp to the chief priest who lights the pongala hearths in the sacred kitchens in the temple. The junior priest takes the lamp out and lights the fire under the pot, which is called the pandara aduppu (the main pongala hearth), in front of the Thottam singers' hymn house.

The Pongala day at Āttukāl is explained in a separate chapter. Madhu Asan takes over the preparation. He offers the first handful of rice and the temple secretary is allowed to offer the next handful of rice.

Millions of women wait for the announcements from the temple to light their brick hearths. The lighting of the first

ĀTTUKĀL AMMA

hearth is announced over loudspeakers. The announcement spreads all over Thiruvananthapuram city in a matter of seconds, through live telecasts, radio broadcasts, text messages and mobile phone calls, and millions across the city, the other parts of the state and the country where Malayalis offer the pongala, light their hearths almost simultaneously. As millions of hearths are lit together, the Thiruvananthapuram city becomes a yagashala, with smoke obscuring the sun. Many weep, call out 'Amma!' loudly and chant 'Sarvamangala Mangalye' fervently. (In the past, the fire used to be passed from one woman to another in an unbroken chain but the numbers are now so huge that a signal is given on the loudspeaker for women all over the city to light their fires simultaneously.)

The singing of the Thottam songs continues after the Pongala, during Devi's procession to the Manacaud temple and the ritual of Kuthiyottam on the same night.

After killing the Pandyan king, Devi suspends his severed head in the skies and feeds his flesh to the wolves. The king's wife appeals to Devi to kill her too, just as She has killed her husband, the king. Devi, however, does not do this; instead, She severs the queen's breasts and throws one into the deep sea and another into the high hills. Pleased at the penitent attitude of the queen in offering herself to be killed by Devi, She blesses her and asks her to be seated next to Her as Mukkolaykkal Muttāramma and to receive half of all the offerings that are made to Devi. 'Nercha thookkam[7] goes to me, Methāla thookkam[8] goes to you. Pon chooralottam[9] is for me and Velli chooralottam[10] is for you. I will preside over a sreekovil with tiled roof, while yours will have a roof of coconut leaves,' She tells her.

Mother Bhadrakali, roaring as if to break open the eight directions, approaches Kailasam with the severed head of the king. After offering the severed head at the sacred feet of Her Father, Lord Shiva, She lifts it and hangs it beside Darikan's. The Mother is dancing in glee in Kailasam. Her handmaidens welcome Her with Thālappoli. She begs a boon from her

A tired mother and her small girl after performing thālappoli

A baby girl offering thālappoli

THE TEN-DAY FESTIVAL AND THE THOTTAM PĀTTU

Father, Lord Shiva. She tells him that She has decided to reign in the earth-world, and not Kailasam. Therefore, she would acquire some land at Kodungallur in the earth-world and establish Herself there. Shiva hurls his trident and it falls at a spot in Kodungallur; Viswakarma is invoked to create a temple on that spot. Viswakarma disagrees because the five-hooded serpent rests at that very spot; however, he agrees to build a temple nearby.

On Her way to Kodungallur, Mother Bhadrakali grants boons to many people. Mother also grants the young Mannān who watched over Palakan's body and also gave him a change of dress when resurrected, the right to sing Thottam Pāttu, narrating Her story. The Pānan is granted the right to play the musical instrument Murasau, to bring the flags and pennants of Devi, and also to engage in the trade of 'cutting and piecing together' clothes (the tailor's trade).

Goddess Bhadrakali, after consecrating Her husband Palakan, in the Palakan Temple, also installs Her companions, the seven Kalis. Mother Bhadrakali assures that She will come if anyone raises the Pacha Pandal and sings Her Thottam, and invites Her to come over to hear Her story being narrated. But Devi makes the temple Viswakarma creates Her abode; this is the ancient Kodungallur temple. She sets Herself up permanently at Kodungallur, inside the sreekovil, seated on a golden kindi which is placed with its mouth down, on a square altar that is set up on four posts. Goddess Bhadrakali, the daughter of Lord Shiva, sits there thus, facing north, reigning supreme, and granting boons to anyone who seeks refuge in Her.

Kuthiyottam boy from Radhakrishnan Asari's family offering coins as dakshina

There is not a single mention of the names of Kannaki or Kovalan anywhere in the Thottam Pāttu.

Thālappoli

As soon as the Pongala is over, we can see young girls, dressed in the traditional long skirt and blouse, holding platters on which a cut coconut, bunches of the areca tree flowers, a lit lamp and ripe plantains are placed, arriving at the temple. Their numbers can run into thousands. For example, in 2014, there were more than 7,000 girls. Thālappoli is a ritual which is mentioned in ancient texts like *Chilappathikaram*, and even in Thottam Pāttu. The offering of Thālappoli is made to Devi, to obtain good husbands for the girls, and for the general prosperity of the family. There is no specific time for this, but this is also done as an offering and starts soon after the Pongala is over.

Kuthiyottam

The very ancient ritual of Kuthiyottam is conducted at Āttukāl, after the Pongala is over, and after all the women return home. This ritual is performed under the supervision of Radhakrishnan Asari[11] of Valiyavilakam House. He is a graceful sixty-five-year-old. He is one of the permanent presences at the sacred portals of Āttukāl Amma's abode. His recollection about this ritual goes back only up to the time of his mother's grandfather Raman Asari. Like the right of singing Thottam Pāttu, the right to dress up Devi's warriors and to pierce their flanks with silver needles has also come down as a hereditary right to Radhakrishnan Asari.

The boys who perform the Kuthiyottam start arriving around the third day of the festival. They would have followed austerities at least for one week. They bathe together in the temple pond, and come in wet clothes and place seven one-rupee coins each on the sacred wooden seat called pallippalaka in the temple. In the past, the money thus placed used to be twenty-one panams. Once they make this offering, they become Devi's children.

This point onwards, they live and eat inside the temple premises. Severe austerities await them from now on. They have to rise very early in the morning and prostrate before Āttukāl Amma several times a day. These boys, aged between seven and twelve years, have to prostrate before the Goddess 1,008 times, within the span of the next seven days.

In the morning, the boys are given rice gruel (kanji) and green gram curry. At midday, they are given the sadya (traditional vegetarian meal). At night, beaten rice, plantain and tender coconut water are served to them. No food from outside is given to them. No one from outside is even allowed to touch them. Parents must stand afar and see them, if they must, and go back. This would probably be the first time that many of the youngsters are staying away from their families.

Once they finish the evening meal on the eighth day, they are allowed to eat again only after the Devi's nivedyam is over on the evening of the ninth day of the festival.

It is believed that human sacrifice of young boys used to be offered to Devi in ancient times, and the ritual of Kuthiyottam, which involves piercing the sides of the boys with silver needles, is the symbolic re-enactment of the sacrifice.

There are two myths relating to the bloodletting in Kuthiyottam. The first is that when Palakan is killed and Devi is searching for his body, some boys made fun of Her. Enraged, Devi demands a sacrifice of those boys. However, She is satisfied with ritual bloodletting from their bodies. The term Kuthiyottam is derived from the detail of the practice in which the boys' flanks are pierced by silver needles, which are called chooral. 'Chooral' literally means 'cane'. In the old days, cane was used for the piercing instead of silver needles. 'Kuthi' means, 'pierced'. Radhakrishnan Asari, who is in charge of conducting this ritual, told me in a hushed voice, corroborating the common belief: 'This, in fact,

THE TEN-DAY FESTIVAL AND THE THOTTAM PĀTTU

Deepārādhana, the kuthiyottam boys worshipping Āttukāl Amma

is a substitute for human sacrifice … Ammachi[12] wants blood once in a while.'

The second myth is that the boys are the companions (bhootaganas) who followed Devi into battle with Darikan, got wounded, and yet went to meet Lord Shiva to apprise Him of Devi's valiant actions. So, when Devi is taken in procession outside the temple after the Pongala, and as She proceeds to the temple of Manacaud Shastha, Her brother,[13] these boys form the vanguard of the procession.

The piercing of the flanks is done for all the one thousand boys by Radhakrishnan Asari personally. Two silver needles in the shape of Devi's khadgam, interconnected with a silver thread, are used for the piercing. The first needle is pierced through the flesh above the right upper rib. With the second needle fastened to the silver thread piercing the left upper rib area, the ritual piercing is completed.

The piercing is done on the Pongala day, when the day's proceedings are over and the night's nivedyam is done, and the Goddess is about to go out at the head of a procession to the Manacaud Shastha Temple. The piercing begins before the procession starts, making the boys stand facing Devi's threshold in front of the big balikkallu, around one o'clock in the morning.

Submitting boys for Kuthiyottam is a form of offering to Devi made by their parents. This offering would have been

125

ĀTTUKĀL AMMA

made to save them from some terrible disease, or to cure them of extreme mischievousness. The registration for Kuthiyottam begins five months in advance.

Of late, some human rights organizations have come up with a demand to stop this ritual since it subjects the boys to bodily injury, and because it is patently inhuman. Newspaper features condemning this practice, drawing parallels with the banned practice of Garudan thookkam,[14] have been attracting public attention for some time now. What the future holds for this ritual remains to be seen.

Devi's Procession to the Shastha Temple at Manacaud

Since 1994, the state government has provided a guard of honour and an armed escort when the Goddess is taken in procession to visit the Manacaud Shastha Temple on the night of the Pongala. The grandeur of the procession fits the description of Devi as 'Sri Mahārājni' in the *Lalitasahasranama stotram*. The Kuthiyottam boys serve as part of Devi's entourage during this procession.

The first boy is arriving for the Kuthiyottam ritual

For this procession, Devi's thidampu is used. Prior to 1974, it was a silver mask of Devi placed on the shield-like structure called thidampu. After 1974, it was replaced by a golden face mask made by the ABTT, adorned by a golden crown donated by Thankappan Nair of the Sitapuram family, one of the Pāttukār families.

The thidampu is flanked by Devi's gold-coated padavāl, the sword She carries when She goes out into battle. The other sword, the udavāl, on which the Kāppu is tied, is never taken out. The embellishment of the thidampu is another love-filled ritual and it is done under the supervision of M. Bhaskaran Nair of the Keezheperumpally family. He has been doing it for the past fifty-two years, ever since he started serving Devi as the joint secretary of the ABTT, at the tender age of sixteen. His face lights up when he does this. 'This is my Goddess's chella mukham, sweet face,' he says, and looks at it in deep adoration.

After being decorated with flowers and ornaments, the golden mask of the Goddess is taken inside the sreekovil and the chaitanya of Āttukāl Amma is invoked into the thidampu through thooshni āvāhanam.[15] The thidampu is taken out and a priest carries it around the sreekovil once. Then, the thidampu is transferred to the hands of the priest sitting astride the caparisoned elephant genuflecting in front of the valiya balikkallu. The second circumambulation is around the temple, and done with the thidampu on the elephant's back. Then the procession leaves the temple through its southern gate. While returning, it comes through the northern or main gate, and the two processions together, are considered as one pradakshinam. Till the Goddess returns, the sreekovil remains open.

Once out of the temple compound, the procession passes through the streets of Āttukāl and Manacaud, for a distance of about two kilometres. Devotees and their families offer worship to Her, by way of paravaypu,[16] thattam,[17] and fireworks. The procession takes several hours, though the distance covered is very small, as the Goddess receives the worship and adulation of thousands along the route. Reaching the Shastha Temple around eight or nine, the next morning, Devi is taken around the temple once, and after that, around the sreekovil. The thidampu is lowered from the elephant's back, and taken around the sreekovil before placing it right in front of Manacaud Shastha, on a temporary dais. Here, Devi meets Her Brother face-to-face. Thus the Goddess fulfils the promise to Her brother on the parathendal[18] day, that She would come and meet Him. On this occasion, devotees offer silk, gold ornaments and other valuables to Devi.

The Kuthiyottam boys' flanks are pierced by silver needles, which are called chooral

ĀTTUKĀL AMMA

M. Bhaskaran Nair adorning the golden thidampu to be taken out in procession to the Manacaud Shastha temple

Soon after this ritual, Devi's thidampu is taken back on to the elephant and the return journey to Āttukāl begins. This journey normally takes about five hours. Reaching Āttukāl, Devi on the elephant's back makes another round of the outer balivattom, before the thidampu is lowered, taken around the sreekovil once more, taken inside, and the chaitanya is invoked back into the main idol. By this time, seven pradakshinas would have been completed.

Throughout this time, almost twenty-four hours, the Kuthiyottam boys, with their flanks pierced, and on a complete fast, observe their duty as the Goddess's guardsmen. Now, the 'choorals' are removed, the wounds closed with sacred ash, covered with betel leaves, and bandaged with new cloths. The first boy on whom the 'chooral' is pierced, is called 'pandara kuthiyottakkāran' meaning 'Goddess's own kuthiyottam performer'. This boy is invariably from Valiyavilakath, the family of Radhakrishnan Asari.

After the 'choorals' are taken out and the wounds bandaged with betel leaves and a towel tied around their chest, the Kuthiyottam boys return home.

THE TEN-DAY FESTIVAL AND THE THOTTAM PĀTTU

On the Pongala day, there is a change in the pujas offered to Devi inside the sreekovil. When the entire city boils over in love for Her, what else is required! After the pantheeradi[19] puja and deepārādhana at 8.30 in the morning, there is a shudhapunyāham[20] just before the Thottam singers prepare the pongala hearth. Uchha puja (the afternoon puja) is done at around 3 p. m. (the time varies every year) and a combined usha sheeveli (morning procession) and uchha sheeveli is conducted soon after that. After the evening deepārādhana, there are no pujas for Her till she returns from Her visit to the Manacaud Shastha Temple.

Day Ten: Bidding Farewell to Kodungallur Amma

Just as Kodungallur Amma is invoked and installed through music and hymns on the first day, on the tenth day, She is transported through the Thottam Pāttu back to Kodungallur after removing the Kāppu from the sword. The fan-like folded cloth, njorinjāda, is also removed and carefully folded and given back to the ABTT. It is also a tradition that the devotees who witness the Kāppu ceremony on the day of the Karthika asterism, should also witness, ten days later,

The decorated thidampu imbued with the chaitanya of Āttukāl Amma is taken out

ĀTTUKĀL AMMA

THE TEN-DAY FESTIVAL AND THE THOTTAM PĀTTU

on the Uthram asterism day, the ceremony of the untying of the Kāppu, which is accompanied by pinippāttu that describes the various parts of the body, seeking protection from the Goddess for another year. Then, the coconut-breaking ceremony is repeated, to see whether Bhagavathy was pleased with the entire ten-day festival. At night, people gather to bid farewell to Kodungallur Amma; they offer paddy and flowers and pray for their welfare until She returns the next year to bless them again. A gentle breeze wafts through the crowd as She departs. Standing near the sanctum, I felt this unusual breeze on my face, rather strongly.

Now begins the night of the sacrificial offering. Only the oldest members of the family or the temple trust members are allowed to witness this fearsome ritual at midnight. Once a year, Bhadrakali demands blood, a kuruthi (gurusi). Formerly,

Āttukāl Amma's thidampu receiving a grand reception on Her way to Manacaud Shastha Temple

An elephant carrying the thidampu of Āttukāl Amma

ĀTTUKĀL AMMA

The Goddess at the Manacaud Shastha Temple

Āttukāl Amma's thidampu is lowered from the elephant's back, and placed in front of Manacaud Shastha, on a temporary dais

THE TEN-DAY FESTIVAL AND THE THOTTAM PĀTTU

ĀTTUKĀL AMMA

An old picture of the villagers watching stage programmes during the festival. Seated in front is former defence minister V.K. Krishna Menon.

The trust, the intense faith in Āttukāl Amma

it used to be a human or animal sacrifice; now it is a symbolic act of cutting a large cucumber and pouring blood-coloured arattha water prepared by mixing slaked lime and turmeric, and covering it with a bronze uruli. The cucumber is cut with the Goddess's padavāl and the red fluid fills the floor in the darkness of the night, which is an awe-inspiring sight. Women keep away from this scene.

In the past, the temple would remain closed for seven days after the Pongala. Now the temple opens the next day.

After the festival is over, Madhu Asan and a few people from the ABTT stand still before the temple door that is shut at midnight. The whole ambience changes within hours. This is a highly inexplicable feeling. And all those who participated in the festival return home with a feeling no one is able to comprehend. The ten days of fervour and frenzy are over and the Goddess of Āttukāl goes into celestial slumber; people return home gratified by the experience of something they will never forget in their lifetime.

After the conclusion of the festival, there is another one-day festival conducted with great fanfare, exclusively by the temple staff, on a day which is convenient for everyone.

The belief among the people that the Goddess of Kodungallur is brought to Āttukāl by āvāhanam (invocation) via Thottam Pāttu is deep-rooted. They believe that during the ten days of the festival, the pujas are done for Kondungallur Amma at Āttukāl. I have also heard it said that during this period, Āttukāl Amma is replaced by Kodungallur Amma. Actually, through the Thottam Pāttu, the power of Bhadrakali residing at Kodungallur is believed to be invoked to manifest at Āttukāl. Some people express a doubt and ask: 'Where does Āttukāl Amma go at that time?' Discussing time in human terms is quite irrelevant in this context. There is no doubt that during the festival time, the power of the Goddess is intensified.

Āttukāl Amma is Goddess Bhadrakali. Yet, Kodungallur Amma, who is one of the earliest of all the Bhadrakali

The sword of Āttukāl Amma is taken out of the sreekovil to perform guruthi, the symbolic ritual of human or animal sacrifice in olden days

pratishthas of Kerala, is ritually invoked through Thottam Pāttu to be present at the Āttukāl Temple during the Pongala festival. This is supposed to highlight Āttukāl Amma's power (it is similar to āvāhanam from a greater chaitanya). After enhancing Āttukāl Amma's chaitanya during the festival days, the Goddess of Kodungallur goes back.

We may assume that āvāhanam[21] and udhwasanam,[22] which are part of the temple tantra rituals that emerged later, might have been developed from the rituals like Thottam Pāttu. Even in the daily pujas in the sreekovil, there is the ritual of bringing the power of the Goddess from the moola vigraham to the abhisheka vigraham through āvāhanam. The transfer of Kodungallur Amma to the Āttukāl Temple is a similar ceremony. All the pujas inside the temple are offered to Āttukāl Amma only. The pongala offering is also made to none other than Bhadrakali in the form of Āttukāl Amma. Special nivedyams like pānakam are offered only because it is a unique occasion.

So, how do we explain the excitement we feel about welcoming someone special, the ecstasies during the Kāppu kettal and the pain of separation from a beloved that you feel when Kodungallur Amma is given a farewell by the singing of polippāttu?

Such doubts will exist as long as we don't understand the concept of the Goddess, or if we continue to attribute human characteristics to the Goddess. This doubt is one of the many dilemmas we have faced ever since we started trying to figure out and explain the divine that is unfathomable but about whose existence we are certain. We can accept or reject the belief of the common people that Kodungallur Amma comes to Āttukāl during the festival season and also the conclusion of the scholars that, instead, Bhadrakali, the power which pervades the whole cosmos, is invoked at Āttukāl for amplifying Āttukāl Amma's chaitanya.

Soon after the festival at Āttukāl is over, the same Pāttukār sing the same Thottam Pāttu to flag off the festivals in the Konchiravila, Pazhanchira and Mukkolakkal Bhadrakali temples that are not as crowded as Āttukāl. To make up for the bits in the narration I missed at Āttukāl, I have had to go and listen to the Thottam songs sung at those temples too, to get a better grip of the content.

Women, lakhs of them getting ready to light their pongala hearths

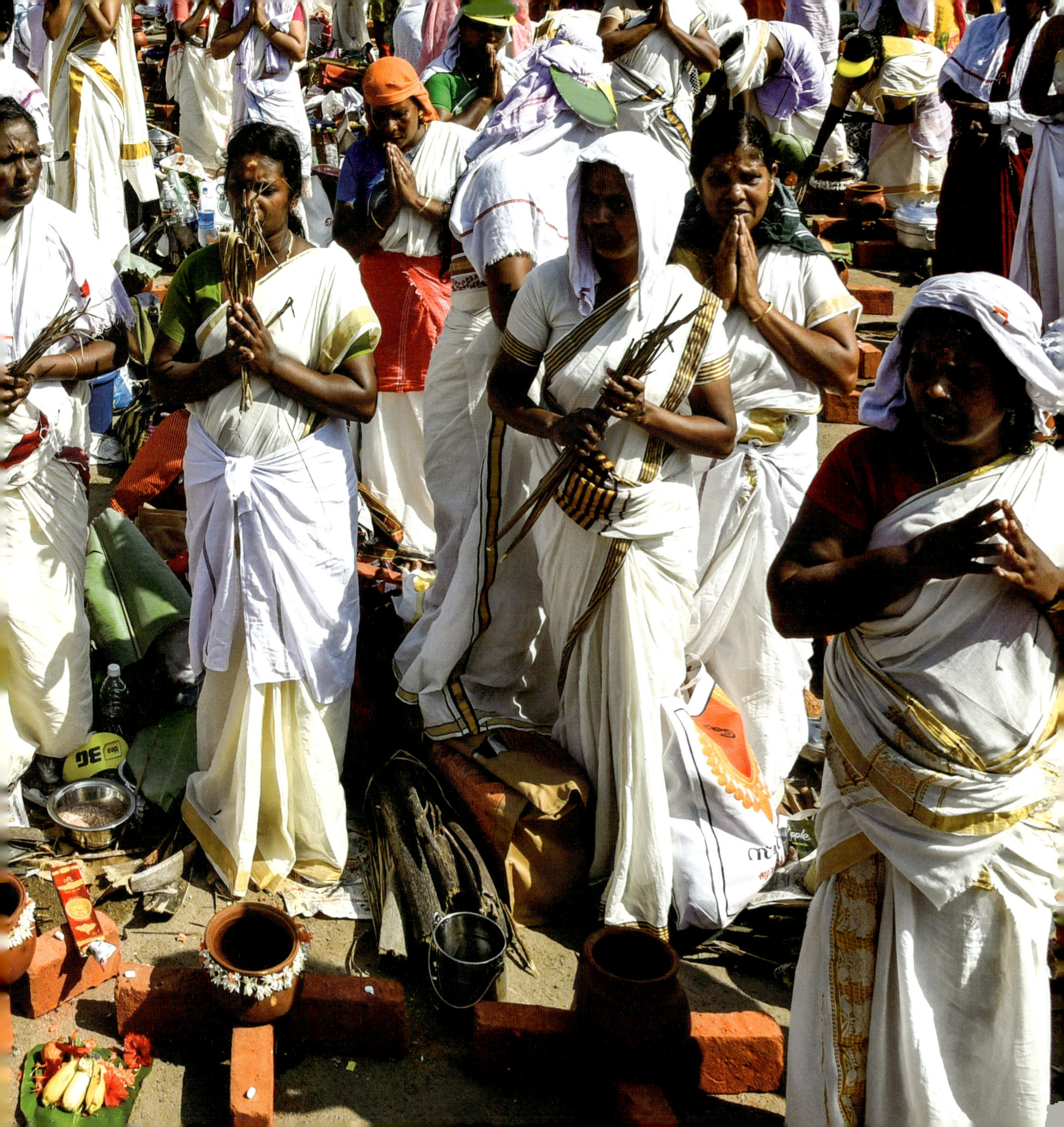
3G

10

Āttukāl Pongala[1]

'Smoke billowed from hundreds of thousands of temporary hearths and hung above the city.'

— The BBC, 2 March 2010[2]

'There is nothing like this anywhere else in the world. It is amazing the way a whole city makes arrangements for women to make this offering. Any woman of any caste, religion, class, or nationality is welcome to participate in Āttukāl Pongala, and almost every woman can afford to do so, because it is a simple, inexpensive offering.[3]

— Dianne Elkins Jenett

The Āttukāl Pongala has made it twice to the *Guinness Book of World Records* as the largest annual gathering of women – in 1997 with a participation of 1.5 million women devotees, and in 2009 with a gathering of 2.5 million. In 2015, the number of participating women rose to four million and it is expected to increase in the coming years.

A festive mood engulfs the city during the festival. All the roads that lead to the temple are full of women, carrying their bags, firewood, rice, jaggery and the clay pot for cooking the pongala. During the festival days, it is mostly local devotees who throng the temple precincts;

The certificate from the Guinness World Records Ltd

An old photograph of women returning home after the Pongala

but on the Pongala day, women in their millions descend on the city from adjoining and even far-off districts.

Those who come from far off places to offer the pongala keep their sparse belongings with themselves, where they prepare the hearth and cook the pongala. Those who come from other districts and from different parts of the country, stay mostly with relatives and friends, and in lodgings available in the city. The women offering the pongala spill over onto pavements, bus stations and the railway platforms too. This is convenient because they can easily return to their homes after the pongala offering. As many as 4,000 police personnel are deployed to ensure the safety of these women. One would wonder how these lakhs of women who arrive in the city at least two days before manage to bathe or fulfil basic needs. But I have also noticed that the government or the temple authorities provide them with basic facilities.

The Āttukāl Pongala festival is, in many ways, a celebration of secular and human values. Several important mosques in the 10 sq. km festival area also provide facilities for thousands of women devotees to make the ritualistic offering of pongala. A. Saifudeen Haji, president of the Vallakkadavu Jamāt and state secretary of the Samastha Kerala Sunni Yuvajana Sangham, said that the Palayam Juma Masjid and mosques at Thampanoor, Chala and Karippottikada, the Central Juma Masjid Manacaud, the Kallettumukku Juma Masjid, the Kamaleshwaram Markaz Masjid and the Juma Masjid at Konchiravila had made similar arrangements for the people who offer the pongala.[4] The importance of the Pongala was specially acknowledged by the Government of Kerala in 1989 when it declared the Pongala a public holiday for the southern districts of Kerala. In the span of two years, the state enhanced its support for the Pongala festival by assigning medical staff, fire services, transport facilities and barricading the area exclusively for the use of women. The district collector is in charge of coordinating the functioning of various departments.

Thousands of women occupy the entire city, move gracefully down the street, chatting and laughing, providing a visual treat for local people and television viewers across the globe. Overnight, Thiruvananthapuram metamorphoses into another world. The city transforms into a temple, and discriminations of caste, religion and colour lose relevance during these days. I personally know many Christian and Muslim women who offer the pongala.

Till 1967–68, men were allowed to accompany women, but that came to a stop with the strict order of a police officer, Parameshwaran Pillai, the then inspector at Fort police station who used to drive away men from this area presumably to ensure women's security. The tradition of giving special passes/badges for volunteers and the queue system for crowd control also were his contribution. The only men who are allowed near the temple on the Pongala day are priests, temple authorities, policemen, firemen, and men with special passes, such as reporters and volunteers who help with crowd control. These passes are difficult to get from the temple authorities and are highly prized.

In confined spaces like the courtyards of houses, only about 2 ft separate the individual hearths; so the latecomers have to thread their way carefully among women with their pots and other belongings, in order to squeeze into any available, vacant space. The possibility of women accidentally setting fire to their own or their neighbours' clothes is high but such incidents are very rare.

Women from all over Kerala arrive in groups

An old photograph of a girl buying a pongala pot

Women buying pots to offer pongala in 2015

In the last couple of years, spaces which were earlier considered inauspicious for offering the pongala have become preferred sites. For instance, it was believed that the pongala can be offered only on the temple side of the River Killi and those areas like Kalady, Nedungadu and places beyond on the other bank of the river were not used. In the legend associated with the origin of the temple, it is believed that Parameshwaran Pillai saw the Goddess in the form of a young girl on the other bank of the river, and he brought Her over to the bank near the temple. The reasoning is that since the Goddess vacated that bank and went over to the other, it is inauspicious to offer the pongala there!

The practice of reserving space for the pongala is a recent phenomenon. The first choice is the vicinity of the temple, and subsequently, all over the city. Just like political parties who reserve advertisement space on the walls in the city anticipating elections, in March 2015, bricks for preparing the hearths began to appear in prime spots, with the name of the devotee written on a paper tied to them, with the admonition, 'Don't touch.' Even some organizations and groups reserve places for the hearths. Political groups and parties also began to squabble for space for the hearths![5]

As the number of devotees began to increase every year, women started to occupy the parts which were on the other side of the River Killi as well. The citizens' forums of these areas vie with one another in providing extra care and facilities to women who arrive in groups, to attract them to their respective areas of jurisdiction, as it is a matter of honour for them to host the Goddess's devotees. There are many police personnel who consider their deployment for security duty during the Pongala festival, a form of votive offering.[6]

The women who wish to offer the pongala, observe a vratam (fast and abstinence), one week before the ritual. Those who expect their menstrual periods during the Pongala festival try to postpone it with medicines; if they

ĀTTUKĀL AMMA

fail, they cannot offer the pongala, and a whole year's anticipation goes in vain!

The dispersion of the crowds into the streets within a radius of over 14 km in Thiruvananthapuram, and the hundreds in their own courtyards in other cities and towns of Kerala, add to the millions already offering the pongala in the temple precincts and public places in the city.

A Typical Pongala Day at Āttukāl

For nearly half a century, Vasudevan Kaniyan from Konchiravila took care of calculating the auspicious time for beginning the Thottam Pāttu, the donning of the Kāppu, kudiyiruthu and lighting of the first pongala hearth. After he passed away, his son was in charge of it and later when he too left this world,

Madhu Asan and his companions keep the hearth and pot ready to offer pongala, before the hymn house

Trustees and other office-bearers wait for the auspicious moment to light the pongala hearth in the cheriya thidappalli

Tantri Chennās Dineshan Namboothirippad bringing the sacred flame to light the pongala

ĀTTUKĀL PONGALA

The chief priest, Neelakandan Namboothiri, brings the sacred flame from cheriya thidappalli to hand over to Keshavan Namboothiri to be taken outside the temple

Keshavan Namboothiri taking the sacred flame to the pongala hearth before the hymn house

Madhu Asan and the priest light the pongala hearth in front of the hymn house

Madhu Asan offering the first handful of rice

M. Bhaskaran Nair, Secretary of ABTT, offering rice

The pongala boils over

ĀTTUKĀL AMMA

The pongala is cooked and Madhu Asan and team wait for the priest to sprinkle holy water

Vijayan Namboothiri, a local astrologer, was given the task of calculating these auspicious hours. The time to light the pongala hearth varies from year to year. It is usually on the Makam asterism or Pooram asterism; but the tradition of the Āttukāl Temple demands that the chooral kuthu ceremony has to begin before the ending of the Pooram asterism, on the same day as the Pongala.

By 9.30 a.m. on the Pongala day, the pots are filled with water and the ingredients are kept ready. The women wait for the signal from the temple to light their hearths. Anticipation mounts as the drums and the repetitive, rhythmic clanging of cymbals accompanying Thottam Pāttu, increase in speed and intensity. When the Pāttukār reach the part where Devi chops off the Pandyan king's head, the tantri hands over the sacred flame from inside the sreekovil to the melshanti who lights the first hearth inside the sacred kitchen within the inner circumambulatory path. Then he lights the hearth at the sacred kitchen in the outer circumambulatory path. Then the melshanti hands over the sacred flame to the keezhshanti to light the pandara aduppu, kept before the hymn chamber of the Thottam Pāttukār. Those who are offering the pongala at their homes far away from the temple follow the live telecast from the temple, and light their hearths accordingly.

The air is filled with the sounds of women's 'kurava,' or ululation, ringing of bells, and the deafening din of firecrackers, mortars and drums as the keezhshantis light the pandara aduppu and the fire is then passed down the line, from woman to woman. I remember standing near the pandara aduppu in 2014. Women who were not near the temple listened to a loudspeaker announcement, lit a fire, and passed the flame down their streets or in their courtyards. As they lit the fire, they were chanting the mantra:

> Sarva Mangala Mangalye Shive Sarvārtha Sadhike
> Sharanye tryambake Gowri Narayani namosthuthe.

('Prostrations to you, Narayani, who is the auspiciousness of all things auspicious, [who is] the protector of all, who grants the devotee all purusharthas, who is capable of giving refuge to all, and who abides as the three-eyed Goddess.') [Translated by the author.]

A woman tying a floral garland before her pongala hearth

Soon the air is filled with the smoke and heat of hundreds of thousands of hearths fired by dry coconut-leaf sheaves. Dried bundles of coconut-palm leaves (choottu) and the outer covering of the coconut flower-pod (kothumbu) are used to fire the pongala hearths. We saw the male volunteers racing on motorbikes with the lighted choottu for the women who were far away from the temple. Most women bring their own choottu and kothumbu along with items like rice, jaggery and other ingredients for the pongala. Before cooking, they wash the rice well making sure that not a grain falls on the ground.

As the hot, thick, white smoke rises, women cover their faces with their upper cloths and wipe away the sweat and tears. They watch the pongala pots and the flames simultaneously to ensure they do not set themselves or other women near them on fire. All the heat and the smoke add to the sweltering feeling. But then the women feel a nice cool breeze caressing their faces. They experience this every year.

After the water begins to boil, each woman takes a handful of washed rice, careful not to spill any, and waves it (uzhiyal) over the pot, puts in three handfuls of rice in succession. Some cry, some chant loudly and then carefully put the rest of the rice into the pot.

As the cooking continues, the women tend the fire, adding just the right amount of kothumbu to bring the rice and water to a complete boil. Creamy white foam slowly rises, expanding, filling the pot until it is barely contained by the lip of the pot. Most women believe it is crucial that the pot boils over, spilling the froth down the side. An old woman who has been doing this ritual for decades acknowledges that while she does not know the exact reason why it is believed that the pot should boil over, she is convinced that the pongala should spill out because only then will the Goddess be pleased. N. Ajithkumar says the word 'pongala' is derived from the Malayalam word ponku-vāla, 'the water boiling over', and it is auspicious if it boils over to the east! As the pot boils over, the elderly women ululate in celebration (kurava) while the others keep praying.

ĀTTUKĀL AMMA

Now, all the women, some of whom would occasionally have been tittering among themselves, become silent and serious, anticipating the 'boiling over' moment of their pongala.

Unbearable heat and mixed emotions crowded my heart too. Something very convincing was happening to me. It was the Goddess, I felt. As I listened to the other women ululating and crying, I felt my own soul empowered and told myself that I mustn't get too involved or I could become lost. This was the predominant feeling not only during the pongala but during the many other rituals I participated at close quarters. I have striven to write down the details of all of them, but the intensity of the bond is often lost in explanation. On such occasions, I always feel like crying.

All this while, a melodious hymn or a song about the Āttukāl Pongala, blares over the loudspeakers. Sometimes it is interrupted by public announcements about the loss of wallets, chains or anklets. On the Pongala day, most women vow not to eat or drink till the offering to the Goddess is completed by late afternoon. By mid-morning, the sun beats down and the temperature soars to over 35 degrees Celsius. According to the tantri, the Goddess is also given only light meals comprising aval (beaten rice) and banana called laghunivedyam and it is not appropriate to eat before She does!

Some women offer more than one pot of rice; there are many who offer one hundred and one pots of pongala, in the sweltering heat, as a thanksgiving for favours received from the Goddess.[7] In 2007, my mother offered the pongala in 108 pots, in the courtyard of my ancestral home in Kadakavoor more than 60 km away from the temple, as an offering for my children who were born after eleven years of marriage. There are many who offer hundred pots of pongala on the roadside.

A fascinating observation to be made with regard to the rice and pulses offered in the form of pongala to the Goddess is that they closely resemble the varieties of rice and pulses mentioned as having special relevance to Devi, as She presides over particular ādhāra chakras of the human body as described in *Lalitasahasranamam*.[8]

According to this stotram (Sanskrit hymn), Sākini Devi presiding over moolādhāra chakra (below the tail bone), and residing in bones, loves rice cooked with green gram; Kākini Devi, presiding over the swadhishthana chakra (below navel) and residing in body fat, likes curd-rice; Lākini Devi, presiding over the manipura chakra (above navel, solar plexus) and residing in flesh, loves jaggery-rice; Rākini Devi, presiding over anahata chakra (heart chakra) and residing in the body's blood, loves

A Malayali lady assists a foreigner to offer pongala

148

rice cooked in ghee; Dākini Devi presiding over the vishuddhi chakra (throat chakra), stays pervaded in the skin and is fond of payasam. Hākini Devi presiding over the ājna chakra (between the eyebrows), and residing in bone-marrow, likes turmeric rice; Lalita Parameswari, in the form of Yākini Devi, presiding over the sahasrāra chakra (the thousand-petalled lotus in the crown of the head), and residing in semen (shuklam), likes all varieties of rice (sarvodānapreetachitta). All the above varieties of rice meals are cooked while offering the pongala at Āttukāl.

The other rice-based delicacies offered to the Devi are therali appam and mandapputtu. Therali appam is a steamed delicacy made by wrapping the dough in cones of therali leaves (bay leaves). The dough is made of rice flour, cane jaggery, green gram powder, dried ginger powder and cardamom, mashed banana and ghee kneaded together. Mandapputtu, which is offered to the Goddess to cure headaches and diseases of the brain, is made with the dough of green gram powder, grated coconut and jaggery. It is also a steamed delicacy. It is fascinating to note that all these varieties of rice and pulse preparations are also offered in the form of pongala to the Goddess.

The women in the temple premises appear to be in a sort of daze, thinking only of the offering. Even as they feel suffocated by the smoke, and tears begin to roll down their cheeks, they are unable to even stand comfortably because the next pot is inches away. Yet, far from being uncomfortable, the women would be smiling and thanking the Goddess for giving them the opportunity to offer the pongala to Her.

As the fire dies, the women cover the pots with banana leaves.

This offering is used in forecasting important events of the succeeding year. Many meanings are read into the offering by the women. Some women believe that if the offering is not made properly, a strong sign that the Goddess is unhappy or angry will appear. Darshana Sreedhar in her essay in the *Economic and Political Weekly* narrates an incident she witnessed, in which a devotee's sari caught fire from the neighbouring hearth and many others accused her of being

Tearful prayers, when the pongala boils over

the subject of the Goddess's wrath![9] But the Pongala is not only for the so-called virtuous or chaste.

Later in the afternoon, the women who had offered the pongala sit together and eat the food supplied to them by various organizations, as they wait for the inauspicious rahukalam to pass. Once this is over, the priests come out of the temple carrying pots filled with sacred water from the temple. They dip the flower of the areca-nut tree in this water and sprinkle it on the pots of the devotees, signalling the end of the ritual.

The women immediately gather their belongings and begin the return journey to their homes with the cooked pongala, to share it with their family and neighbours, as prasadam. After the Pongala ritual is over, men begin to reappear on the streets, distributing water and buttermilk to refresh the departing women. Dianne Jennet mentions in her doctoral

The Pongala offering in front of Padamanabhaswamy Temple
Photo: Anil Bhaskar

ĀTTUKĀL PONGALA

thesis that in the past men used to shower them with flower petals. There is also a rather spectacular and modern ritual – a flower-showering ceremony organized by the temple with the help of the Thiruvananthapuram Flying Club.

The city corporation enlists the services of nearly three thousand sanitary workers, for Pongala-related cleaning work in the twenty wards which come under the festival area. The world's largest gathering of women also offers the swiftest lesson in cleaning. Once upon a time, after the pongala offering was done, the streets used to be littered with the detritus of the mass cooking. For the past few years, however, a cleaning operation with clockwork precision has been put in place. As soon as the ritual draws to a close around 3.30 p.m., about three thousand people fan out across the city and set to work. By around 1 a.m., the streets all across the city are cleared. The main streets are then washed and by daybreak, visitors often wonder if it was the same place they had seen the previous evening.

Making Mandapputtu for the Goddess

Making Therali Appam for the Goddess

151

ĀTTUKĀL AMMA

Another version of the sweet Mandapputtu

An old photo of women offering pongala

The East Fort Paura Samithi offering pongala to Āttukāl Amma, for the successful completion of the Vizhinjam Port. Photo: Anil Bhaskar

Women wait on the roadside, days in advance, to offer pongala for Āttukāl Amma

Now, the irony. The mop-up marvel unfolds in a city where there has been no solid waste removal for the past three years after a popular protest shut down the main garbage dump in 2012. The efforts to find an alternative space for the landfill failed and roadsides have become the new dumping grounds. The cleaning personnel – half of whom are women – say the only motivating factor in the massive clean-up operation is their faith in the Goddess.[10]

Though the Āttukāl Pongala is exclusively a women's festival, in which ladies seek the blessings of the Goddess for the prosperity of their families and loved ones, some notable exceptions, and that too for public causes, have come up in recent times. One such case is that of the Citizens' Committee. For the past five years, the East Fort Poura Samithi has been offering the pongala in East Fort for various causes, such as the development of the capital city, for bringing a High Court bench in Thiruvananthapuram and for the speedy recovery of the extremely popular cine actor Jagathy Sreekumar who met with a near-fatal car accident. During the 2014 Pongala, the Samithi offered the pongala for the successful completion of India's Mangalayān (Mars) Mission![11]

The festival offers a sense of emotional comfort and renewed strength to face the challenges of life throughout the year. Women who offer the pongala in the temple believe that this ritual is extremely fulfilling; their worries and anxieties accumulated over a year is offered to the Goddess along with the pongala, and they return light of heart. Many women believe that Āttukāl Amma comes out of the temple and could very well be one of the women cooking in the crowd!

Like most annual rituals, women who offer the pongala return almost every year, if possible. Although they acknowledge the discomfort of the heat, smoke, and physical exertion, they still want to do it. In fact, the act of offering the pongala has seen a rise in popularity across the world.

ĀTTUKĀL AMMA

Pongala Day the World Over

Outside Kerala, the Pongala is observed in Chennai, Bengaluru, Mumbai, Delhi, and internationally, in Dubai, many cities and neighbourhoods in the US, Europe and the UK. Unknown to the media, pongala offerings are made in the homes all over the world proving that the physical distance from Āttukāl does not deter the devotees.

In the UK, a group of women called the 'Āttukāl Sisters' has been organizing the Pongala in London at the Murugan Temple in Manor Park, East Ham, since 2008. Because of fire regulations in London, the pongala offering is prepared in a single large pot as a symbol of togetherness. The London version of Āttukāl Pongala was started in 1995 by the then civic ambassador councillor Omana Gangadharan.

In Dubai, thousands of women participate in the Pongala festival conducted by Āttukāl Amma Pravasi Seva Samithi; the ritual is usually conducted at Emirates English Speaking School.

Pongala is celebrated in Dubai

Once, in 2007, the timings of the puja and other major events related to the Pongala festival were changed due to the lunar eclipse. These changes were made by the temple office-bearers

A group of women called as 'Āttukāl Sisters' has been organizing the Pongala on the Murugan Temple premises in East Ham since 2008. It was started by then civic ambassador councillor Omana Gangadharan.

according to the directions given by Vishnu Namboothirippad, the astrologer and priest of the Āttukāl Temple.

Over the years, several foreigners have become devotees of Āttukāl Amma. Many Europeans and Americans participate in the Pongala every year. Doris Zizala, an Austrian lady, along with her mother-in-law Karin and sister-in-law Johanna attended the Pongala in 2008. Doris works with an organization that seeks 'to preserve and popularize traditions that are being submerged in the surge of modernity'. 'There was a time when everybody wore jeans and drank Cola. People were sort of ashamed to show their individuality. But things are changing. In many things, including in wearing traditional dresses, people are now prepared to be proud of their traditions,' she said.[12]

Dianne Elkins Jenett lighting the stone lamp at the Āttukāl Temple

Dianne Elkins Jenett*

Dianne Elkins Jenett, a professor at the Sofia University in Palo Alto, in the United States, was instrumental in having the Āttukāl Pongala entered in the *Guinness Book of World Records* for the highest turnout of women in a single location. Jenett, who first visited the temple in 1993, now comes every year to participate in the Āttukāl Pongala. Her doctoral research at the California Institute of Integral Studies in San Francisco was focused on the spiritual experiences of women, and as this was a ritual related to the topic, she visited the temple to witness it personally. Impressed with the devotion of the large number of women from all walks of life, and the community support for them, she wrote her dissertation on the experiences of women who offered this votive offering and the positive values expressed through the Āttukāl Pongala. She has given lectures on the Āttukāl Pongala in various universities and institutes in America. Influenced by this, several regions in America have started observing the Pongala regularly. The main difference is that the Pongala is observed there in moonlight since the muhurtham is observed as per Indian time.

That the Āttukāl Pongala is a festival that transcends all barriers of religion and nationality is proven by people like Jennet who are keen to be a part of this festival of women every year. Having spoken to thousands of devotees, she believes that the festival is symbolic of women's empowerment and it gives them immense power and joy. She has also marvelled at the communal harmony promoted by the festival, noting how even Muslim, Christian and Jain women either helped or participated in the Pongala.

The Āttukāl Pongala, which now extends for more than 14 km in a concentric circle with the Āttukāl Temple at its centre, continues to grow each year, becoming more powerful in reinforcing the relationship between the Goddess and women. Though almost all the temples in south Kerala today observe the pongala as an offering, the Āttukāl Pongala has the singular honour of being synonymous with the ritual across the globe.

The golden brahmakalasham surrounded by herbs grown in the mulayara of the temple and the 1001 parikalashams

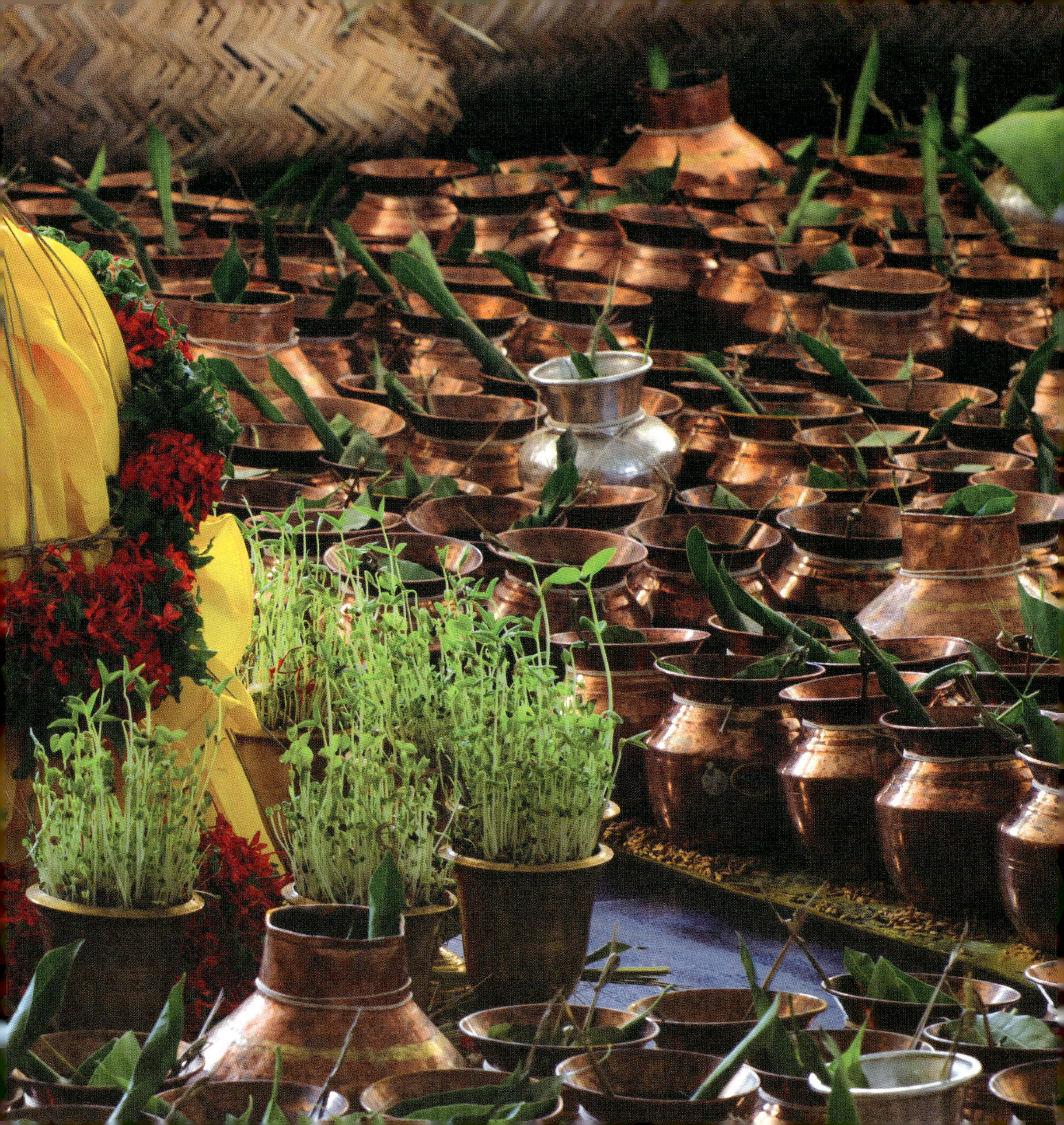

11
Sahasrakalasham: The Rite of Penance and Ritual Cleansing after the Pongala

The rite of penance and ritual cleansing after the Pongala, the sahasrakalasham, meaning 'a thousand pots,' is one of the most elaborate temple tantra rituals conducted at the Āttukāl Temple every year immediately after the Pongala. These rituals, explained and described in the *Tantrasamuchhayam*,[1] are rigorous and meant to restore the sanctity of the temple and to re-imbue the idol with chaitanya.[2] The procedures are long and complex and performed with utmost attention and devotion. Sanctified water and herbs kept in these thousand pots are poured over the abhisheka vigraham of Āttukāl Amma, to the accompaniment of mantras. This also involves a number of homams to restore the sanctity of the idol and the temple. Goddess Bhadrakali is beyond these concepts of pollution and purity but when the patriarchal influence of the Brahmins gained ground in the Kerala temples, even a radically non-Brahminical tantric Goddess like Bhadrakali got co-opted into their system.

The *Tantrasamuchhayam* states that a temple could be polluted in various ways: for example, by death or birth, mostly of animals, insects or birds taking place within the

Chennās Dineshan Namboothirippad performing purificatory rituals at the Namaskara mandapam

temple; or by spattering of blood, urine and sweat in any part of the temple. The entry of unworthy people and creatures like the owl, vulture, crow, dog, donkey, pig, jackal or rat snake is also considered as pollution.[3] Rites of penance should be performed if the idol falls down or breaks, if it is unstable or leans to one side, if it manifests strange signs like sweating, if mushrooms or anthills or beehives are seen on it, and if the daily pujas are not performed, or are missed.[4] In the cases of pollution or of wrongdoings that have not been mentioned here, the appropriate rites of penance in accordance with the nature of the pollution or vikriti[5] have to be performed.

The sahasrakalasham at the Āttukāl Temple is an elaborate ritual performed over six days. The tantri supervises the ritual and the temple staff are involved in the preparation of the materials needed to draw the sacred padmam, the imaginary seat of the deity on the floor, and procure things such as rice flour, turmeric powder, oil, flowers, wicks and the tortoise-shaped stools (āmappalakas) on which the priests sit. If the slightest impediment is encountered, the rituals will have to be done all over again from the beginning. Pots made of copper, silver and gold are used at the Āttukāl Temple instead of earthen pots. The kalasham offerings (paying for these kalashams as an offering) can be booked by devotees well in advance.

Day One

At a serene function on the evening of the first day, soon after the deepārādhana at 6.45 p. m., the office-bearers of the temple entrust the tantri and his assistants with the task of purifying the idols, balipeethams, and the surroundings of the sanctum. The inner balivattom and the nālambalam are meticulously washed and cleaned. Āmappalakas are placed on the namaskara mandapam and the tantri is invited to sit on them. The yajamānan, who is usually one of the office-bearers, places the clothes and other objects that constitute the dakshina given to the tantri and his assistants on the āmappalaka kept for that purpose on the north-east side of the namaskara mandapam.

First of all, puja is offered to Ganapati and the objects to be given to the tantri in dakshina. After this the tantri is offered arghyam,[6] pādyam[7] and āchamaneeyam[8] and given gifts of clothes, pavitra rings,[9] flowers, gold and money. This is called acharyavaranam and it is the mutual contract between the tantri and the office bearers of the temple on the proper conduct of the ceremonies of sahasrakalasham.

The Mulayidal Ritual[10]

As soon as the acharyavaranam is over, the mulayidal ritual which is the most important rite of the sahasrakalasham, starts. A puja is performed to worship the seeds kept in the special chamber called the 'mulayara' which has been

Mulayidal ritual, the sowing of the seeds

prepared on the north-east side of the temple using reed mats. A special padmam of sixteen squares, which signifies the sixteen phases of the moon, is laid either in two rows or in four. Sixteen pālikas[11] are placed on it. Various grains which are appropriate to the deity concerned are sown in these pots accompanied by the chanting of mantras.

The pālikas, made of metal or clay, have six parts: the peetham,[12] the dandam,[13] the galasandhi,[14] the galam,[15] the peethasandhi,[16] and the mukham.[17] After chanting the astramantras[18] of Bhadrakali and washing these pālikas, white cotton thread is wound around them with koorcham[19] and kurumpullu.[20] Then these pālikas are filled with earth from an anthill, sand and powdered cow dung, after which the chaitanya of Mahavishnu is invoked into the pālikas. The seeds can either be sown separately or they can be mixed (called samghātam) and put in all the pālikas, while chanting the prescribed mantras to invoke the deity.

The seeds for each deity are different, says the *Tantrasamuchhayam*. Since Āttukāl is a Bhadrakali temple, nellu,[21] uzhunnu,[22] thina,[23] ellu,[24] thuvara,[25] muthira,[26] cherupayaru,[27] kaduku,[28] chāma[29] and amara[30] are used. In each pālika, the seeds are sown in a specified order after washing them with pure water and milk and Bhadrakali is invoked into these seeds with the astramantra. Washing the seeds with milk symbolizes washing them with nectar.

A punyāha ritual[31] is performed for the pālikas after sowing the seeds. Cantos three to five of the *Tantrasamuchhayam* clearly describe the presiding deities of the grains. These sixteen pālikas have to be placed within the special padmam drawing. It is believed that if the seeds are sufficiently imbued with the divine presence, they will sprout well. Otherwise, the sprouts will be deformed and stunted.

After this, the moon god, Soma, is invoked into the seeds. Then turmeric and ashtagandham[32] are mixed together in water, with the accompaniment of the prescribed mantras, and this liquid is sprinkled on the pālikas containing the seeds. Following this, fresh banana leaves are placed over the pālikas and they are covered with a cloth to protect them. When this mulayidal ritual is complete, a trikāla puja, (the three junctures of the day) is performed to the accompaniment of the chanting of the mantras that invoke the chaitanya of Mahavishnu, Soma and Bhadrakali, the deity of the temple, till the sixth day morning.

If the seeds are spoiled in any manner, they have to be changed, the rituals repeated, and new seeds sown. At the end of the rituals, a puja has to be done to the seeds according to the prescribed rules, and thus the bond of the mantra has to be removed and they have to be arranged around the brahmakalasham, which is kept in a special enclosure made of reed mats, outside the temple, in the prayer hall.

Prāsādashuddhi

The prāsādam[33] and the idol are imagined to be the sthoola shareeram (material body) and sookshma shareeram (astral body) of the deity respectively, be it male or female. Pollution that affects one of these bodies affects the other; therefore, the purification rites have to be carried out for both. Once the mulayidal ritual is complete, the prāsādashuddhi,[34] which is the next step in purification, begins. One would wonder why the prāsādam, which is already clean and untouched by anyone other than the priests, requires such intense cleansing. The tantri told me that impurities accumulate without the knowledge of the priests; even a harsh voice is a pollutant! There is no scrubbing or cleaning involved in this purificatory ritual. This involves the cleaning of the invisible impurities as mentioned earlier.

Prāsādashuddhi begins with the purification rites for the deity's sthoola shareeram, the material body. Ganapati is worshipped to ward off obstacles in conducting the puja, then a garland, made of three strands of darbha grass[35] and three strands of thread wound together,[36] is tied from the north-east of the prāsādam in a pradakshina direction, that

SAHASRAKALASHAM: THE RITE OF PENANCE AND RITUAL CLEANSING AFTER THE PONGALA

is, from the left to the right. The pradakshina circle starts and ends in the north-east, which indicates the head of the deity. After this, the space within and outside the garbhagriha and outside the prāsādam is swept clean with the mushti.[37] It is not the actual cleaning but a ritualistic cleaning.

After this, the mustard seeds[38] and panchagavyam[39] are sprinkled using the mushti in the sanctum and around the temple. The mustard seeds are gathered with both hands and flung three times, first inside and then outside the sanctum. Ashtagandham[40] is then sprinkled. After this, incense and a lighted wick are waved inside and outside the prāsādam.

The astrakalasha puja which follows is meant to guard the place from evil spirits, and to replenish the chaitanya of the idol. For this, a swastika-padmam is drawn on the floor and over it a peetham (seat) is made with rice and darbha. A kalasham (generally a copper or brass pot with cotton twine tied around it) is then kept over this after performing rites known as kumbhasamskara and kalasha puja, and then it is filled with water while reciting the astramantras. After making offerings to this kalasham, the mouth of the pot is covered with a cloth. This is used to anoint the abhisheka vigraham.

Rakshoghna Homam

The rakshoghna homam has great importance in the first day's rituals. It is conducted in the south-east quarter of the temple. This ritual is called rakshoghna homam because it eradicates the presence of evil spirits or rakshasas that may reside in the temple. This is followed by offering katalāti, (Achyranthes aspera) chamata (flame of the forest), ghee and havissu (cooked rice) in the homakundam or the fire pit for sacrifice, reciting respective mantras all the while.

After the rakshoghna homam, rituals like vāsthu homam and vāsthu kalasha puja are done.

Vāsthu Homam and Vāsthu Kalasha Puja

For the vāsthu kalasha puja, two separate swastika-padmams are drawn on the ground and above them a single peetham

Vāsthu Homam

Preparations for Vāsthu offering

made of paddy, rice, sesame and mustard, each separated by plantain leaves, is made. Karuka leaves and kusha grass are kept above the peetham. In addition, two pots, each with cotton thread wound around it, are placed in an upside-down position on the peetham. After the puja, the pots are inverted and filled with different articles: the kalasham on the west with gold and rice and that on the east with gems, gold and pure water. The invocation of these kalashams follows – the mantras of the principal deity are chanted for the western one and those for shanti devata, to the eastern one.

The vāsthu homam which is conducted the same night propitiates the principal deity of the temple and shanti devata. A square area to the north of the sreekovil is daubed with cow dung and fresh sand is spread over it. The homakundam is prepared in this space. The fire for this homam is transferred from the rakshoghna homam with bated breath, to the vāsthu homakundam by the acharya.

Two hundred and fifty oblations of ghee and 108 oblations of karuka sprigs dipped in panchagavyam, as well as semi-boiled rice balls are offered at the vāsthu homam.

Vāsthubali

Vāsthubali is done to propitiate Vāsthupurusha[41] and to seek the blessings of the vāsthu gods. First a vāsthu-mandala padmam (generally of 81 padas or squares) is drawn using three colours: black (from burnt paddy husk), white (rice powder) and yellow (turmeric powder) in a well-defined order. In each pada, karuka akshatam (a mixture of raw rice and paddy) and flowers are placed and puja is done with havissu. The items generally used for the bali (offerings) are havissu (cooked rice) and akshatam.

The vāsthu kalashams are then taken to the sanctum and their contents poured on the idol. Following this, vāsthu punyāham is conducted. This completes the rites associated with prāsādashuddhi and the site becomes free of all impurities. Once the vāsthubali is over, the belief is that the pleased vāsthu gods pervade the entire space within the temple walls.

Day Two

The main rituals on the second day are the purification rites for the idol.

Chathushuddhi

In order to cleanse the idol, the kalasham is filled with materials like darbhamushti (darbha grass tied together), puttumannu (soil from anthill) and nālpāmarappodi (mixture made out of the bark of the four fig trees, viz., Athi, Ithi, Arayalu and Peralu),[42] and a puja and abhishekam are performed. After this, the idol is scrubbed and washed with the materials in the kalasham. Without chanting any mantras, recalling silently the

SAHASRAKALASHAM: THE RITE OF PENANCE AND RITUAL CLEANSING AFTER THE PONGALA

shanti devata mantra so that peace is bestowed, abhishekam is conducted. After this, dhāra is offered.

Mahachathushuddhi

This ritual requires four kalashams. Puttumannu, or earth from an anthill, soil from a theertham or river, and from vilabhoomi (a harvested field) are filled in the first kalasham, three darbhamushtis in the second, nālpāmarappodi in the third and the materials required for a punyāham in the fourth. For the mahachathushuddhi, pujas have to be performed for each of these kalashams to the accompaniment of special mantras, and abhishekam has to be done with the contents of these pots.

Dhāra

For the dhāra, the chaitanya of the goddesses of the seven sacred rivers, the Ganga, Yamuna, Godavari, Saraswati, Narmada, Sindhu and Kaveri, are first invoked. Next, Lord Varuna, the master of all waters, is invoked with mantras. The dhāra, or pouring of holy water, is performed with the kalashams used for this ritual. Various mantras and suktams particular to each deity are chanted while the dhāra is performed and the water is made to fall on the sahasrarapadmam or the invisible inverted lotus on the top of the idol's head. From this spot, the water flows to the sushumna nadi (the astral equivalent of the spinal cord) and then, from there, to all the nadis or veins, conferring mantrashuddhi[43] and nadishuddhi[44] on the deity's idol.

Rice balls offered to Vāsthu gods

ĀTTUKĀL AMMA

Panchaka Kalashābhishekam

It is believed that the body of a deity is created and maintained by tatvams. They are parts or principles or aspects of Nature. Their presence or absence, and combination and permutation play an important role in the creation of the diversity of worlds, their objects and beings, individual bodies, limbs and organs. In short, their aggregation and segregation constitute the building blocks of the whole material manifestations in the world. For the panchaka kalashābhishekam, a puja is performed on five kalashams to the accompaniment of tatvamantras after which abhishekam is done with them.

Puja is performed over the one thousand upturned pots

Day Three

The main rituals on the third day are the prokta homam and prāyashchitta[45] homam. The proktha homam is done in a homakundam shaped like a half-moon. These homams are performed to cleanse and purify the pollution that occurs in Devi's idols and to achieve a powerful enhancement of the chaitanya of the idol.

Day Four

The fourth day is meant for various kinds of shanti homams.[46] If a fire or similar event occurs within the temple, or if cruel creatures enter the precincts, or if there is uncertainty as to which prāyashchitta ritual should be done, a samanya (ordinary) shanti homam is performed and abhishekam is done at the shrine from the kalasham used for it.

Adbhutashanti[47] Homam

This homam is performed when strange or astonishing experiences occur, as when someone feels that the idol of the deity is crying or laughing. This homam is then done as atonement. It is performed to the accompaniment of many mantras that are meant to calm the mind; a bali is offered while chanting the shanti devata mantra and only then is the homam considered to be complete.

Shvashanti Homam

This homam is performed if a dog or other animals come in contact with the sanctum. A homam is performed to the accompaniment of *Sri Suktam*,[48] which invokes Goddess Mahalakshmi and *Bhagya Suktam* which ensures wealth and prosperity. Those who create pollution by bringing in food also harm the subtle state of the temple. This ensures that even if someone enters the temple in a cruel state of mind, this ritual of penance will calm him down.

The Chorashanti Homam

The chorashanti[49] homam is a ritual of penance that should be performed if people, whose state of mind is not sātvic, touch the idol. It should be performed not only if there is

Arranging the water-filled pots

bloodshed, but also if one covets an object within the temple precincts. The idol should be touched only during the puja and while praying. This homam, which is performed with mantras that conceptualize ghee as the mind, the mental state as the yagna spoon and speech as the site, is a ritual of atonement for even the slightest pollution. It restores purity.

Day Five

The homams on the fifth day are very important; the rituals of this day enhance the idol's divinity. Seeds which have sprouted well are moved from the mulayara[50] to the big shed in the prayer hall in the outer circumambulatory path. This is an elaborate ritual and is usually performed jointly by the keezhshantis and the tantri's assistants. The thousand kalashams used for the sahasrakalasham are arranged on the padmam drawing in a particular manner, and decorated. The brahmakalasham made of gold is right at the centre of a large square. There are twenty-four small squares inside this large square, each of which contains forty kalashams. The padmams are drawn with rice powder, and threads are tied around each section. The brahmakalasham has the highest importance. The kalashams which are at the centre of the small kalashams are known as khandabrahmakalashams and the small kalashams around them as parikalashams.

These kalashams are used for performing a puja and abhishekam for Devi with her retinue, and the brahmakalasham is believed to be the brahmandam as well as the Viratpurusha. All the kalashams are filled with pure water, and with banyan leaves, mango leaves and koorcham (bundle of darbha grass). The water is stored in a container called the jaladroni, which is then covered with a cloth. After this, kalashādhivāsa homams are conducted so that all the divinities may appear together. These rituals are conducted in the afternoon on the fifth day.

The adhivāsa homams[51] take place in the shayya, a big shed where the sprouted seeds and the kalashams are stored. Usually, water stored in the kalashams is not used for the next day's puja and the adhivāsa homam is done to ensure the purity of the water. The homakundams used for the adhivāsa homam have beautiful shapes and are prepared as follows: on the eastern side of the shayya, it is a square; on the south-east, it is in the shape of a banyan leaf (yoni, vulva); on the south, it is in the shape of a half-moon; on the south-west, it has a triangular form; in the vayukon (north-west), it is shadkon (six-sided figure) in shape; on the north, in the shape of an eight-petalled lotus and in the north-east, in an ashtakon (octagon) shape. All the assistants are seated on the western side of the homakundams.[52] The main assistant lights the fire from the acharyakundam[53] and places it in a pot; with this flame, he lights the fire in all the homakundams one after another, moving in a clockwise direction. The chamatha,[54] materials and mantras used in each homam are different. The koovala[55] twig is used in the shadkon, the perāl[56] in the vritham,[57] the aythi[58] in the triangle, the arayāl[59] in the half-moons, the karingali[60] in the vulva, the plashu[61] in the samakon,[62] the kumizhu[63] in the ashtakon and the aithi[64] in the lotus shapes. The materials used in the homams are malar (parched paddy), sesame seeds, melted ghee, barley, and sakthu (rice, roasted and powdered).

Tatva Homam

The purpose of this homam is to 'purify' the Goddess of possible defects that may have crept in either due to ignorance or carelessness, or by mistake on the part of the priests, from the first day of the ritual, and got accumulated. (Here we are employing human attributes on the Goddess, though She is beyond human imagination; but all this is done following sankalpa on the part of all involved, and hence common logic should not be sought to be applied here.) To ward off the defects mentioned above, a prāyashchittam (expiation rite), known as tatva homam with kalasha puja, is done.

Tatvam in Sanskrit means 'thatness', 'principle', 'reality' or 'truth' and the temple tantra states that a human being is made up of five senses,[65] five sense organs,[66] five elements,[67] the five parts of the body[68] used for action, and the five involuntary breaths[69] which all add up to twenty-five principles or tatvams. In the temple tantra, they are conceived as the aspects of that particular deity.

It is in order to recreate the tatva mantras connected to the tatvams that respond to the Goddess and the minor deities, that the tatva homam and tatvakalashābhishekam are conducted in the namaskara mandapam in front of the sreekovil.

The procedure followed for the kalasha puja is similar to the earlier one; only the mantras are different. However, rites like lipipankaja puja,[70] moorthi āvāhanam,[71] kāla avāhanam,[72] vidya āvāhanam[73] and tatva āvāhanam[74] are performed, concluding with nivedyam and prasanna puja.[75] After the homam, the sampāta, the mantra-energized ghee, is collected in these kalashams; and nivedyam and prasanna puja follow. During night, the kalashams are kept covered with cloth.

ĀTTUKĀL AMMA

Tatvakalasha Puja

The tatvakalasha puja has great importance. Pujas are done on the brahmakalasham and the parikalashams for purification and prosperity, and then an adhivāsa homam and kalashādhivāsam (the twenty-five principles which are offered as oblation), are performed. Nine homakundams of different shapes are made for the adhivāsa homam. A grand abhishekam is performed to the accompaniment of marappāni, a traditional temple percussion instrument, so that the tatvams strengthen the idol. The day's rituals come to an end after athazha sheeveli, when the acharya, the temple administrators and the devotees gather together and pray that the deities may receive the kalashābhishekams that are going to be conducted the next day and bless them. All the kalashams are then covered with unbleached cloth, with fervour brimming in the minds of the priests.

Day Six

The unbleached cloths are removed from the top of the kalashams in the morning of the sixth day and the tantri then does special puja to the brahmakalasham in the middle of these thousand khandabrahmakalashams. The divinities that had been unified on the previous day are again divided into twenty-four separate khandas. On the morning of the sixth day, for the fulfilment of the divine presence, twenty-four kinds of material, starting with panchagavyam, ghee, honey, jaggery and oil, are used, to perform an abhishekam of the sahasrakalasham. That day, after the pantheeradi puja[76] in the temple, the rituals that will go on for about four hours commence in the presence of devotees. The tantri pours the theertham from each of the kalashams over the abhisheka

A series of homams (adhivāsa homams) are performed around the thousand pots

SAHASRAKALASHAM: THE RITE OF PENANCE AND RITUAL CLEANSING AFTER THE PONGALA

The temple staff is getting ready to take out the sanctified water in the kalashams to perform the abhishekam of Āttukāl Amma

vigraham kept in the mukhamandapam of the sanctum. The kalashams are brought into the sreekovil one by one without a pause. After all the theertham from the one thousand kalashams has been poured out, the tantri and the melshanti together pour the most sacred brahmakalasham and the kumbhakalasham. With this, the elaborate ritual of the sahasrakalasham comes to an end.

By the time the rituals end, the fervour of devotees reaches its peak. Splendid percussion music accompanies this ritual. The rituals come to a close with the drops of theertham being sprinkled over the bali stones during the shreebhoothabali (elaborate version of sheeveli) and the sheeghrashreebali during the last round of circumambulation when the priest and the temple authorities race around (the process has been explained in detail elsewhere in this book), and offer bali to all the minor gods around the temple. The deities in the minor shrines are purified at the same time.

ĀTTUKĀL AMMA

Finally, the theertham used for the abhishekam of the kalashams is poured into the small kalashams which are then distributed to the devotees. The Goddess who has received all these offerings, acquires a divine radiance and beauty, symbolizing Her acceptance of the puja. It is believed that through the sahasrakalasham She is made happy and Her divine presence will reside and grow in the idol.

The beating of marappāni, a sacred wooden drum, seeking permission to take the pots from the shayya, or shed

The procession carrying the brahmakalasham

SAHASRAKALASHAM: THE RITE OF PENANCE AND RITUAL CLEANSING AFTER THE PONGALA

The ritual bathing of Āttukāl Amma's abhisheka vigraham with one thousand pots of sanctified water

171

Niraputhari, offering of freshly harvested paddy to the Goddess

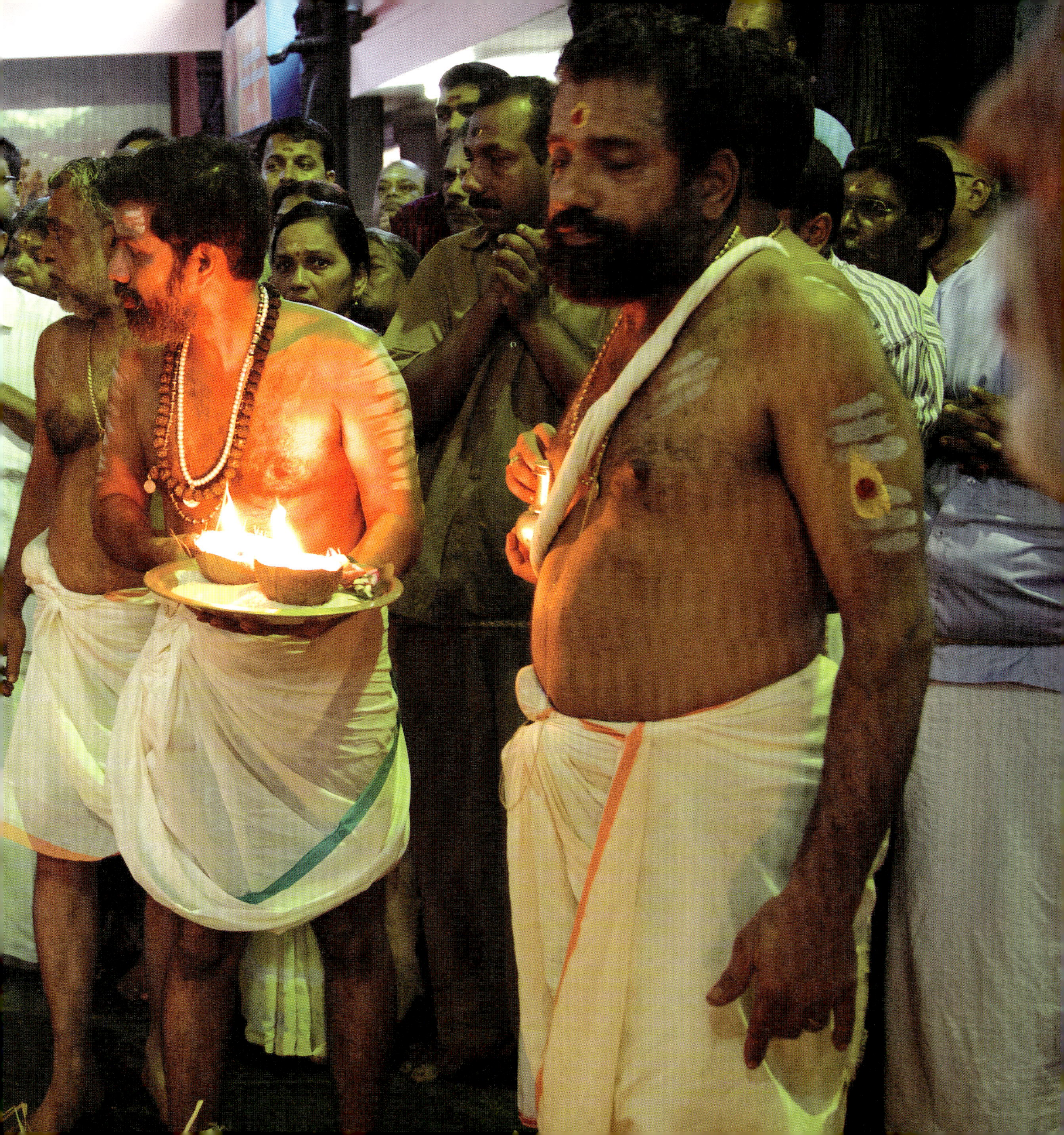

12
Special Offerings to Āttukāl Amma

Every offering made to Āttukāl Amma tells the story of someone's anguish which was overcome with the Goddess's blessing. The offerings made to a deity is known as vazhipādu in Malayalam, which literally means 'the way to remove difficulties' or simply an offering. Sometimes the offering is just a loving gift to the deity – without

Niruba Sathish drawing a huge Kolam of Kodungallur Amma at Āttukāl

demands or expectation. These gifts vary from huge sums of money or diamond necklaces to a handful of flowers or a humble pouch of oil.

According to the Bhadrakali Pāttu, a ritualistic hymn sung in north Kerala, Bhadrakali demands the offerings of roosters, seeds, turmeric, golden thāli, golden eye, Thottam Pāttu, kuruthi, Kuthiyottam, pongala, thookkam, vedivazhipādu, and aivarkali. Aivarkali is a dance drama in praise of Bhadrakali and it is believed that it is Lord Krishna who advised the Pandavas to sing this song and dance to please Bhadrakali who had turned fierce at the killing of Her devotee Karna.[1]

The elders at Āttukāl remember that offering roosters to the Goddess of Āttukāl was usual; prior to that, animal sacrifice was also practised. It is mentioned in *Kali Nadakam* that Darikan comes under the guise of a rooster and Bhadrakali chops his head and drinks his blood.[2] And in Thottam Pāttu there is a mention of Bhadrakali reaching the house of a Thiyya family and asking for the sacrificial offering of their young son. However much we Brahminize Her, the smell of blood still wafts before Āttukāl Amma's sanctum every year during the Kuthiyottam ritual: the stench of blood from the pierced flanks of the boys lingers in the air for a few days.

The rituals and the worship of Goddess Bhadrakali is a separate religion in itself – all the esoteric rituals mentioned in *Kulachudamani Tantra* and many other such tantras involving panchamakarasadhana (an esoteric tantric ritual) mention the use of alcohol, fish, flesh, parched grain and sexual intercourse to please Goddess Kali. Some of them involve the use of blood and corpses and cremation grounds. The wild and unbridled Kali, for whom human sacrifice was commonly offered until the British curbed the practice 130 years ago, has now turned into a goddess who loves payasam and sweet-smelling jasmine flowers at the Āttukāl Temple! She has become the compassionate Mother of millions.

At Āttukāl, people offer Her everything they love, assuming that She too loves them – money, gold, silver, fragrance,

The Āyilyam day at Āttukāl Temple is devoted to the serpent gods
Photo: B. Chandrakumar

The culmination of Akhanda nama japam

sweets, flowers, clothes and lemon. Some make votive offerings (nercha) of silver replicas of body parts or of the whole body (ālroopam) as a gesture of thanksgiving for healing the body of ailments, or as an act of prayer seeking such healing. The vedivazhipādu offering is done with bursting of kathina-mortars. Interestingly, Chemparuthi (hibiscus), Her favourite flower,[3] is not used for pujas at the Āttukāl Temple.

Vestiges of blood and gore, and animal sacrifices, can still be detected in the symbolic offerings made to Her.

The sweet dish Ada, which is offered to Her now is the equivalent of flesh. Goddess Kali likes everything that is ugram (fierce). The blood-loving Goddess is offered a very sweet, thick, dark payasam made with jaggery, which resembles thick blood. The red cloth and deep red vermillion offered to Her again symbolise blood, as Kannan Potti told me.

Garlands made with sweet lemon are offered to Her. There is a saying in Tamil '*Oru kani nālu ātukku samam*' meaning, one

SPECIAL OFFERINGS TO ĀTTUKĀL AMMA

lemon is equal to four goats, and lemon garlands adorn the neck that wears a necklace of decapitated heads. Also the gurusi offering that marks the culmination of the Pongala festival is a symbolic replication of the blood sacrifice as already mentioned.

Besides these, there are a wide variety of sweet dishes that are offered to Her: puffed rice, bananas, beaten rice, sharkarapayasam,[4] aravana,[5] therali appam,[6] unniappam,[7] ela ada,[8] manda puttu,[9] kadum payasam,[10] pāl payasam,[11] vella choru,[12] ilaneer[13] and many more such items. There is also the offering of pongala every day. There are many who offer a hundred pots of pongala to the deity, and the temple does it on their behalf. The pots are distributed as prasadam, after offering to the Goddess.

Usually, the offerings that can be made to the Goddess at the temple are decided during the installation of the idol.

Laksharchana on Karthika asterism is performed every month

ĀTTUKĀL AMMA

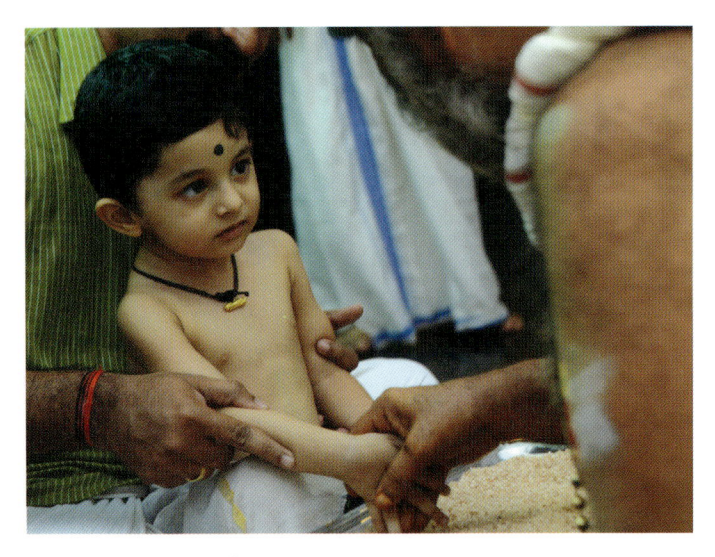

This decision regarding the offerings is known as 'niyamam nischayikkal'.[14] Besides this, many other offerings are allowed since they are established by the devotees or by public demand. These offerings fall into two categories: nityanidānam,[15] and vishesha vazhipādu.[16]

The temple offers the nityanidānam while the vishesha vazhipādus are offerings by the devotees. The nityanidānam at the Āttukāl Temple covers daily rituals like usha puja, sheeveli, various nivedyams, pantheeradi puja, uchha puja, athazha puja and deepārādhana. Most of the offerings and the rituals in practice today were introduced by Vishnutheerthan Potti and the first tantri, Kuzhikkattu Vasudevan Vasudevan Bhattathirippad, some fifty years ago.

Initiation into learning at Āttukāl Temple during Navratri

Thulābhāram using lotus flowers for a small child

Special Offerings

The temple provides a list of offerings from which the devotees can choose what they like. The important offerings are: ālroopam (silver replicas of body/body parts), and saris for the idol of Bhadrakali on the gopuram (the saris are changed seven times a day). The main offering to the Goddess, muzhukkappu (covering the idol with sandal paste) is booked until 2025 CE. Besides these, tying of thali, nāmakaranam (naming ceremony), kunjoonu (the first rice-feeding ceremony for children), thulābhāram (offering things the Goddess likes or used for Her worship, equal to the weight of the devotee), pena puja (blessing the pen), nool japam (a thread energised by mantras to wear around the wrist or neck), thakkol puja (blessing the keys of a new house or a new vehicle), offering in cash, offerings in kind, vidyarambham (initiating into learning), archana (offering flowers), bhagavathy seva (Goddess is invoked into a lamp and offered worship), pushpābhishekam (showering of many baskets of flowers on the Goddess's abhisheka vigraham), kalabhābhishekam (anointing the idol with kalabham) and pidippanam vāral (offering handfuls of coins) are also the favourite offerings made by the devotees.

Those devotees who wish to have these offerings made from long distances, can go to the temple website[17] and remit the requisite amount to the bankers of the ABTT and request that the prasadam be sent to them. The temple authorities conduct the puja/vazhipādu, as the case may be, and send the prasadam by post. Newly produced CDs, DVDs and books are also offered at the temple. Many fondly remember Āttukāl Gopalan Nair, the announcer of events during the Āttukāl Pongala and the contributions of V.S. Sharma and Ezhumattoor Rajarajavarma who edited the temple's magazine, *Ambaprasadam*, for a long time. People also remember Balan Contractor who started the practice of offering vedivazhipādu at the Āttukāl Temple some eighty years ago.

Pidippanam Vāral (offering handful of coins) by the Maharaja of Travancore, His Royal Highness Uthradam Thirunal Marthanda Varma

The sari of the idol on the Rajagopuram is changed seven times a day. Photo: B. Chandrakumar

Offering elephants to Devi, as is the wont in other famous temples in Kerala, does not happen at Āttukāl. The former secretary of the ABTT recalled an incident involving the submitting of a baby elephant named Balakrishnan at Devi's holy threshold, which is called nadayiruthal. The friendly elephant once exhibited unruly behaviour, presumably as the effect of the first appearance of musth. The matter was taken up by an alarmed public, and the district collector seems to have taken a hasty decision, in the interests of many lives which were potentially at risk, and ordered that the elephant be shot. Since then, elephants are not offered as a special offering to Āttuāl Amma.

SPECIAL OFFERINGS TO ĀTTUKĀL AMMA

Niraputhari, freshly harvested paddy, is offered to the Goddess

Aiswarya Puja on full moon days. More than one thousand women participate in it.

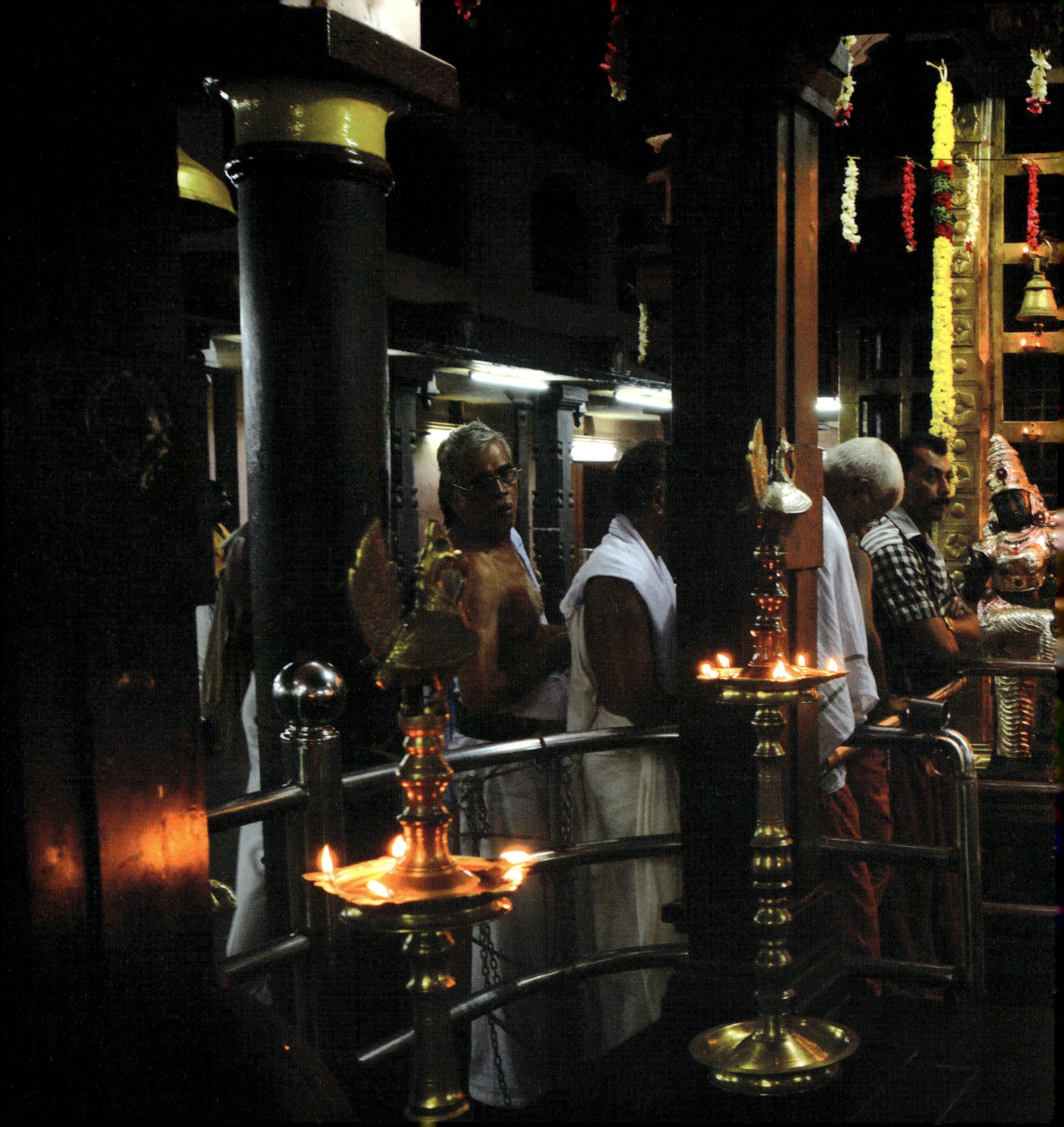

People waiting for the Nirmalaya Darshanam, before the sreekovil at 4.30 a.m.
Photo: B. Chandrakumar

13
Daily Rituals of Worship at Āttukāl*

In a temple, gods and goddesses acquire human attributes – they get angry, need food and nourishment, need to bathe and demand service. Thus the idea of the temple has changed from a place of contemplation of the divinity, to one where prescribed service is ritualistically provided.[1]

The elders at Āttukāl remember a period when the temple did not have the means to light even a wick at dusk or to conduct regular pujas. During the tenure of the first Brahmin priest, Vishnutheerthan Potti, the temple was opened for worship only twice a week, Tuesdays and

Golden and silver pots are filled with water and kalabham to perform abhishekam

Fridays. Later, it began to be opened on the first of every Malayalam month as well. When there was no oil or wicks or incense in the temple, Vishnutheerthan Potti would go to the neighbouring houses and ask for them, so that he could conduct the basic pujas. In those days, only a few women would come with rice, jaggery and coconut for the annual Pongala. Now Āttukāl Amma is offered shodasopachāram[2] and different types of payasam in golden and silver vessels every day! The Āttukāl Temple now owns assets worth millions of rupees and draws global attention during the Pongala.

The daily pujas offered to Āttukāl Amma aim to enhance Her chaitanya and to make sure it is never flawed, says the chief priest Kannan Potti. Pujas are meant to invoke the Goddess and give Her a royal welcome through various oblations and offerings and to please Her. I feel that the multitude of meanings expressed through these rituals, and perhaps the aggregation of all of them, amount to a direct encounter with the divinity propitiated inside the temple.

The Goddess Awakens to a New Dawn!

The agamashastras[3] decree that three hours before sunrise is the ideal time to open a temple. The Āttukāl Temple is opened to the public at 5 a.m. every day except during festival days. The day starts much earlier for those who are involved in arranging the flowers for the pujas, those who prepare the nivedyams[4] and those who get the kalabham[5] and other things ready. Watching the temple waking up to a new dawn in the gentle breeze is an experience one would never forget. Numerous rituals are performed with utmost devotion at the Āttukāl Temple without missing a single detail, from the waking up of the Goddess called palliunarthal in the morning, to the ritual of lulling the Goddess to sleep at night, called palliurakkal.[6]

The Goddess is woken up at 4.30 a.m. when the sky begins to brighten and the ritual of palliunarthal is performed. The conch is blown thrice, and the kazhakakkār[7] play the bhoopala raga, the raga of dawn, using nadaswaram,[8] thakil[9] and thālam.[10] The inner circumambulatory path is swept clean and sprinkled with water, before the commencement of palliunarthal. The lamps are lit before opening the main entrance to the temple. The temples of the upadevatas are also opened at this time.

At 4.50 a.m. the keezhshanti lights the pāni-lamp from the kedavilakku,[11] in front of the sreekovil and leads the melshanti[12] to the temple tank where he takes his ritual bath. After the bath, the melshanti first prays at Lord Shiva's shrine, then goes past the eastern shrine to the southern one and prays to the upadevatas, Ganapati, Mādan Thampuran and the Nagas.[13] He then enters the temple through the western entrance, prostrates in the namaskara mandapam, rings the bell in front of the sreekovil, takes the keys kept on the sopanam,[14] opens the doors and enters the sreekovil.

The pani vilakku and drum

He rings the bell at the entrance, seeking the permission of the Goddess to enter the sreekovil. It is extremely auspicious to be able to see and worship Her at the moment when the door of the sreekovil is opened. There are four lamps that burn throughout the day and night there. The melshanti lights the other lamps in front of the Goddess's idol and prays to Her, amidst the lit lamps, chiming bells and the conch, the bursting of the kathina mortar and the fervent cries of the devotees shouting 'Amma…'. There are many who spend the whole night in the temple courtyard to be able to see Her thus at dawn. This is called nirmalya darshanam.

The garlands and sandalwood paste with which the Goddess was decorated on the previous day would still be in place at this time. It is believed that after the temple closes at night, other gods worship the main deity. Seeing Her, after she has just been worshipped by the other gods is considered very auspicious.

The next ritual is that of removing the previous day's flowers, cleaning the Goddess's idol and preparing it for the day's worship. The abhisheka vigraham and the sheeveli vigraham inside the temple are treated as the Goddess Herself. An ordinary devotee may consider everything that happens inside the temple as puja, but, for the priests, puja involves various temple tantra rituals. There are fixed rules to observe, but the rituals vary from temple to temple, and for different deities; the tantri and the chief priest comply with the tradition of each temple.

Cleaning the idol is followed by the first abhishekam. Before he conducts the first abhishekam in the sreekovil, the melshanti should have performed the temple tantra rituals of dehashuddhi,[15] shankupooranam[16] and ātmārādhana.[17] Through these rituals and the chanting of mantras, the priest who is an ordinary man transforms himself into a being pervaded by divinity, or the deity Herself.

At Āttukāl, the pujas and abhishekams are not offered to the moola vigraham,[18] which is made of wood and covered with the thanka anki.[19] The chaitanya of the moola vigraham is invoked and deposited in the abhisheka vigraham, to perform various pujas and this method of offering puja is called bahubera vidhānam.[20]

This abhishekam is accompanied by percussion instruments like pāni drums, veekkan chenda and thimila as well as the chanting of mantras like the punyāha mantra,[21] the saptashuddhi,[22] thrisudhi mantras[23] and the *Bhadrakali Suktam*. Before the abhishekam inside the sreekovil, āvāhanam from the moola vigraham to the abhisheka vigraham is not done in a detailed manner and it is called thooshni āvāhanam.[24] The abhisheka vigraham is placed on a silver platter inside the sreekovil. The idol is anointed with sesame oil and scrubbed with eenja[25] before the main abhishekam is carried out using water, panchāmritam,[26] milk, tender coconut water, rose water, and sacred water.[27] All these are poured over the abhiskeha vigraham one after the other. The liquids used in the ritual are collected in the silver platter on which the idol is kept. The oil, ādiya enna,[28] which is given to the devotees as prasadam, is believed to have healing powers.

When the abhishekam is over, Devi is ceremonially moved from the silver platter to Her original seat. The pāni-drum falls silent as the conch is blown. Devi is then decorated with flowers and the first nivedyam – aval,[29] malar[30] and fruits[31] – is offered to Her.

Around 5.45 a.m., the keezhshanti performs Ganapati homam[32] in the south-east corner[33] near the thidappalli.[34] No words can describe the feelings evoked by the ringing of the sacred bells, the sound of the conch, the smoke emanating from the burning husk in the homa kundam, the sopana sangeetham with the accompaniment of idakka,[35] and the sweet scent of incense that permeates the surroundings.

The abhisheka deepārādhana[36] takes place at 6 a.m. Usually, anchuthattu vilakku,[37] kumbhavilakku[38] and karpoorathattu[39] are waved thrice at the feet, around the navel and in front of the face, and seven times all over the idol.[40] On all auspicious occasions, parvathavilakku[41] and nagappathi vilakku[42] are

DAILY RITUALS OF WORSHIP AT ĀTTUKĀL

also used. During the deepārādhana, songs are sung in the sopanam style; nadaswaram is played and the conch blown. Deepārādhana is not a puja according to the temple tantra, but this ritual of waving the multi-wick lamps in front of the main idol of the Goddess attracts great crowds.

Soon after this, the pujas for the upadevatas begin. The worship of the upadevatas comprises shortened forms of the offering and pujas done for the main deity. They are offered special pujas and nivedyams during their installation anniversary and on the days that are important for those deities. Ayilyam-puja and noorum-palum[43] are meticulously offered to the Nagas. The Ayilyam asterism in the Malayalam month of Thulam (October–November) is observed in an elaborate manner.[44]

The Intricate Temple Tantra Rituals Begin

There are three methods to offer pujas, according to the temple tantra. They can be offered depending on the convenience of the priest and the time available to perform these. They are padmamāthram, shadpeetham and saparivāram.

Padmamāthram is a descriptive word indicating the form of this particular worship; in this, the deity is invoked

Priest Ramachandran Kunjolam arranging pots for dhāra

ĀTTUKĀL AMMA

on a lotus (in the sankalpa of the pujari) and offered puja. Shadpeetham is the offering of pujas for the Goddess along with six peethams.[45] And saparivāram is the detailed way of offering pujas to the deity along with Her retinue. At the Āttukāl Temple, usha puja is usually padmamāthram and uchha[46] puja is done in the elaborate saparivāram method. The pantheeradi puja and athazha puja[47] are offered according to the shadpeetham method. Each puja includes many rituals conducted by the melshanti. They are dehashuddhi, shankhupooranam, āthmāradhana, peetha puja,[48] āvāhanam, moorthi puja,[49] nivedyam, vaishyam thooval,[50] namaskaram,[51] prasanna puja,[52] deepārādhana, puja muzhumippikkal[53] and layāngam.[54] Shankhupooranam is done only once in the morning and the priest preserves this water for further use. The sanctified water from the conch is poured into the kindi[55] kept at the right-hand side that contains water, and the entire water in the kindi becomes sacred. This water is called shankhupoorana jalam and is used many times during pujas.

Usha Puja

Three bells are rung at 6.30 a.m. for the usha puja, which is one of the four main pujas at Āttukāl. The melshanti does the temple tantra rituals of dehashudhi and ātmārādhana, and proceeds to peetha puja.[56] The Goddess is invoked in the

Keshavan Potti doing the worship of Naga Idols

DAILY RITUALS OF WORSHIP AT ĀTTUKĀL

The drawing of the sacred Padmam

A floral crown for Āttukāl Amma

abhisheka vigraham, with the sankalpa that She is placed on a lotus (or, Her peetham is a lotus) that has eight to one thousand petals. Jalam,[57] gandham,[58] pushpam,[59] dhoopam[60] and deepam[61] are offered to the peetham. This is peetha puja.

Then comes āvāhanam, in which the chaitanya of the Goddess is invoked into the abhisheka vigraham from the moola vigraham, using the prescribed mantras and mudras.[62] Then the chaitanya is invoked from the priest's moolādhāram[63] imagining that a part of his life force – jeeva – is separated and that it rises from his moolādhāra chakra, and passing through various chakras above that, it comes to the point of exit. This exit is through exhalation. The priest breathes in air, and the pure prānavayu[64] is exhaled through the right nostril (pingala) and is instilled into the flowers, akshatham,[65] sandal paste, and the water from the shankhu kept in his half-closed fist and held close to the bimba hridayam, the heart of the deity (idol). The belief is that the priest's prāna is merged with the deity's. Immediately after the idol is infused with the priest's prāna, it is immediately fastened on to the idol using suitable mudras and mantras, such as the āvāhana mudras and shadanganyāsam,[66] chandassu nyasikkal,[67] and ayudham.[68] The priest prays, recites the dhyanashlokam[69] and moolamantra,[70] and offers flowers to the Goddess.

Then the Goddess is offered shodasopachāram that consists of the sixteen upachārams (articles of worship), including everything that would satisfy Her. These are like the items we offer to an honoured guest. For Bhadrakali they are pādyam,[71] arghyam,[72] achamanam,[73] madhuparkkam,[74] punarāchamanam[75] and snānam,[76] punasnānam,[77] vastram,[78] angavastram,[79] yanjnopaveetham,[80] bhooshanam,[81] gandham,[82] pushpam,[83] dhoopam,[84] deepam,[85] nivedyam[86] and vandanam.[87]

Offering to the deity till the tenth upachāram, i.e., 'bhooshanam,' is done using the shankupoorana jalam[88] and again, the deity is offered pādyam, arghyam and āchamanam with the same. Then the deity is adorned with sandal paste on the forehead[89] using a tulsi leaf. Then the moorthi puja starts. The deity is offered shadupachārams – jalam, gandham, pushpam, dhoopam, deepam, and again jalam, accompanied by mantras. Then the nivedyam of payasam and white rice is offered.

The devotees are asked to move to one side, as vella nivedayam[90] and payasam are brought in. It is believed that there is an unseen link between the thidappalli (temple kitchen) and the sreekovil and to protect the sanctity of the link, the devotees are not allowed on that side while keezhshantis bring the nivedyam in from the thidappalli. The conch is blown as the food is brought to Devi, but none should look at it, or pay attention to it. (In the past, the keezhshantis used to run with the nivedyam from the thidappalli to the sreekovil without even drawing their breath). The melshanti then purifies the nivedyam, and transforms it into amritham, through rituals like amrithamudra and does prānahuti (reaching it through the incantation, 'swaha') to the Goddess, and mānasa puja, assuming that the taste of the nivedyam reaches the Goddess's tongue.

Then the priest comes out from the sreekovil, chants the dwarapalaka mantra,[91] offers water to the dwarapalakas or doorkeepers and goes to the bali stone representing Agni at the southeast corner and chants the dikpalaka mantras for Agni,[92] and offers bali on the bali stone on the southwest.[93] He then goes to the namaskara mandapam, prostrates,[94] recites the aparadha shanti mantra[95] and moolamantra eight times, seeking forgiveness for any mistakes he might have committed, washes his feet and face,[96] rings the bell, offers water[97] to the dwarasthans,[98] opens the shrine, enters the sreekovil, closes the door behind him, and offers the nivedyam to the Goddess by giving water and flowers to the Nirmalyadhāri inside the sreekovil, who is present as the unseen power situated at the angle between the north-east and the north (uduthi padam). Then the Goddess is offered gandooshadi āchamaneeyantha arghyam.[99]

From top to bottom: 1. The burnt husk is mixed with ghee and given as prasadam after the Ganapati homam, 2. Lamps in halved coconut on rice after performing neerajanam, 3. Payasam and unni appam used for Ganapati homam

DAILY RITUALS OF WORSHIP AT ĀTTUKĀL

The next part of the usha puja is the prasanna puja,[100] which means the puja to please the Goddess. She is offered the shadupachāram,[101] thrice, along with the chanting of the moolamantra. Then she is offered vettila, adakka, pazham, unni appam and pāl. (betel leves, areca nut, plantain and milk) At Āttukāl, this is offered in sankalpa through mantras during the morning prasanna puja. (These are again offered, for real, to the Goddess at the prasanna puja during the athāzha puja).

Devi is now propitiated and worshipped using the peetha puja mantra, moorthi puja mantra, and yadhāshaktimoolam.[102] Now, Her favourite suktams[103] are sung; this is the time for offering Her various types of archana.[104] Again, the chanting of the moola mantra is done eight times and an offering of flowers is made.

Then comes poorna pushpanjali, meaning everything that has been done so far, is offered to the Goddess. The shankupoorana jalam, gandham, akshatham and flowers are offered at Her feet. This is also accompanied by the prayer seeking forgiveness for any errors that might have crept in during the pujas, using the aparadha shanti mantra. Next, the Goddess is offered prasannārghyam.[105]

Then, theertham is made. The priest invokes Goddess Ganga into the conch. He takes water from the conch and grips the Goddess's feet, with the belief that by doing so, he is taking the nectar from Her feet in the form of theertham. With this theertham in hand, he meditates on his guru. Then, chanting mantras, he sprinkles the theertham on the Goddess in the north-east, the asuras in the north-west, the pitrukkal[106] right in front, and himself.

After this, the melshanti performs usha deepārādhana for which the karpoorathattu alone is used. After that, the theertham is sprinkled on the dwarasthas (doorkeepers), and all the people who are standing outside with their palms joined in devotion; along with this, the lighted camphor is taken outside for the devotees to worship and inhale.

Kadum payasam and ila ada for the Goddess

An old woman praying to Āttukāl Amma

ĀTTUKĀL AMMA

Hari Thirumeni offering Bali to Saptamatrukkal

Next, the melshanti goes inside, offers one more poorna pushpanjali[107] and avasaneeya arghyam.[108] Then the chaitanya that has been invoked to the abhisheka vigraham through āvāhanam at the beginning of the puja is returned to the moola vigraham. He seeks forgiveness again, chanting aparadha shanti mantra, and offers pushpanjali to the moola vigraham. Then he secures the chaitanya in the moola vigraham by attributing vyāpakam.[109]

He then worships the six angas[110] with mantras addressed to the moola vigraham. He chants the chandassu[111] and does tālatrayādi dashadigbandhanam (clapping the hands thrice, securing the ten directions around the chaitanya).

Once again, he chants the aparadha shanti mantra, touches the feet of the idol and chants the moolamantra eight times, and takes the flowers to distribute among the devotees as prasadam. Then he takes a flower, inhales and throws it away. He takes another flower and keeps it on his head, and makes the sankalpa that one-sixteenth of the chaitanya he has already infused to the chaitanya of the deity from his being, is returned to him. Then he does prānayama with the moolamantra. Again, he repeats the vyāpakam[112] with the moolamantra, shadanganyāsam, chandassu, tālatrāyadi dashadigbandhanam and chanting of the moola mantra eight times. He also chants the

DAILY RITUALS OF WORSHIP AT ĀTTUKĀL

chandassu for the divinity he infused within himself. This is called layāngam.

After this, the bell is rung twice for the usha sheeveli. On ordinary days, giving the dikpalakas and the dwārastas light food at the time of the puja is called sheeveli. In all the important temples in Kerala, the sheeveli is conducted three times a day. The special drums, called the purappadu pāni, accompany this procession.

The bali stones seen around the sreekovil are an essential part of the temple architecture. During the sheeveli, we see the pleasing sight of Āttukāl Amma who is happy with the nivedyam and prasanna puja offered to Her, Who comes out to check the well-being of Her retinue and to find out if they have been given food. These offerings represent the panchabhootas – jalam for Water, gandham for Earth, pushpam for Sky, dhoopam for Air or Vāyu and deepam for Fire or Agni. The melshanti carries water in sheevelippāna and sandal paste in chandana odam; the keezhshanti carries in a silver plate, havissu (rice boiled-over seven times) and flowers from kaivatta.[113]

The devotees who are not directly connected to the temple, are not permitted to stay inside the temple during the sheeveli.

For the sheeveli, in most temples, the divine presence of the deity is invoked from the moola vigraham into the sheeveli idol. But at Āttukāl, it is just a sankalpa and the actual āvāhanam is not performed.[114] A replica of the Goddess's idol, which is called a thidampu, is taken out ceremonially by one of the junior priests. He carries it around the temple, to the accompaniment of the pāni drum escorted by someone holding aloft a kuthu vilakku.[115] The belief is that Devi has eight dwarapalakas or doorkeepers; two each at the door of the sreekovil facing the front door, and the three imaginary doors to the right of the deity – Sundari and Sumukhi in the east, Viroopa and Vimala in the south, Anthaki and Vandaki in the west, Purandari and Pushpamardani in the north.[116]

Preparing garlands for Āttukāl Amma

Noorum pālum, a mixture of turmeric powder, milk, tender coconut water and rice powder, is offered to the serpent gods

The sheeveli is done within the akathe (inner) balivattom first, with three circumambulations, and then within the purathe (outer) balivattom, again with three circumambulations. During the first circumambulation of the sheeveli within the akathe balivattom, bali is offered for all the unseen deities mentioned above to the accompaniment of moolamantraksharas (mantras corresponding to each goddess).

During the second circumambulation, bali is offered for Vetala (Devi's vehicle) in the namaskara mandapam and for the preta shakti behind the sreekovil (prishthabhagam). Again, the bali is offered for Devi's vehicle, the Vetala, in the namaskara mandapam and for Ganapati and Dakshinamurthi, the unseen powers at the south. Then bali is offered for the dikpalakas – on the north for Soma and Vaishravana, in the north-east for Ishana, on the east for Indra, on the south-east for Agni, on the south for Yama, on the south-west for Niryathi, on the west for Varuna and on the north-west for Vayu.

The third circumambulation in the inner balivattom comes next. Bali offerings are scattered to Brahma and Ananta and then the melshanti returns to Veerabhadran and Ganapati (exists in sankalpa), and then to Saptamatrikas and, to the west of the Saptamatrikas, to Shastha, Durga, Subramanyan who is next to Durga, and to Nirmalyadhari.

The thidampu is taken out from the sreekovil when the offering of bali is done for the Saptamatrikas. After this, the thidampu is taken to the outer balivattom through the northern entrance, and the priest carries the thidampu on his head.[117] As the Devi goes out, bali is offered for Jaya and

Vijaya, the invisible sabhā dwarasthar[118] on the right and left of the corridor, and then for Devi's retinue outside. Prayers and flowers are offered.

Next, bali is offered for dhwaja devatas around the chuttambalam – the Bheeshanabhairavan who is below the valiya balikallu facing the shrine, Samhārabhairavan in the north-east, for Asithangabhairavan in the east, for Rurubhairavan in the south-east, Chandabhairavan in the south, Krodheeshabhairavan in the south-west, Unmatthabhairavan in the west and Kapālibhairavan in the north-west.

The procession, after making the first circumambulation within the outer balivattom, reaches the valiya balikkallu.[119] Next, bali is offered on the peethas of the valiya balikkallu. It has the same retinue who have been honoured separately inside the inner balivattom. There is no flagstaff here; yet the bali offerings are made before the sankalpa of the Vetala, Devi's vehicle, on top of an imaginary flagstaff.

When the second circumambulation within the purathe (outer) balivattom begins, the melshanti enters the nālambalam after offering bali to the kshetrapala.[120] Then he washes his feet, does āchamanam,[121] prostrates in the namaskara mandapam reciting the aparadha shanti mantra and chants the moolamantra eight times.

The keezhshanti carries the sheeveli vigraham and the devotees accompany the sheeveli procession, and finish the second circumambulation to the accompaniment of instrumental music; then they perform a third circumambulation. Then the priest who carries the sheeveli vigraham goes inside, goes around the sreekovil, rings the bell, opens the sreekovil and enters. He places the sheeveli idol on the right side of the moola vigraham. When the sheeveli vigraham is brought inside the sreekovil, the chaitanya is returned to the moola vigraham, in sankalpa.

In all the major temples, there would be five pujas – usha puja, ethirthu puja,[122] pantheeradi puja,[123] uchha puja and athazha puja. At Āttukāl, there are only four main pujas, and the morning oblation is not considered a puja. This is again another error that might have crept in during the changes that happened in the temple administration or thorough neglect. Usually, pujas should be in odd numbers.

After this, the melshanti goes to the place where the golden pot filled with kalabham is kept and gives dakshina for keezhshantis (muhurtha dakshina) and does archana to their hands with the padma mantra. Then the brahmakalasham for the ashtadravya and the golden pot filled with kalabham are given to them. A muthukuda[124] shields the procession which is preceded by the beating of pāni drums. The pradakshinam starts with a person carrying the pāni vilakku, a keezhshanti carrying neerajanam[125] in a silver plate, and the melshanti carrying a conch, chanting the *Swasti Suktam*,[126] or *Mangala Suktam*. The keezhshantis carrying the pots containing the kalabham and water walk behind the melshanti, and usually someone from the temple administration would join them. People who made the offering of kalashams would also join the procession. All of them would proceed to the accompaniment of the blowing of the conch and nadaswaram.

Then the priest enters the temple, anoints the abhisheka vigraham, ceremonially placed in the mukhamandapam, with kalabham. Nivedyams are offered then. Uzhiyal (waving in a circular motion) with neerajanam is done before and after all abhishekams. The abhisheka vigraham is cleaned and taken inside the sreekovil. Pāni drums and the blowing of the conch accompany this. Then the remaining rituals of the shodashopachāram continue till layāngam (as mentioned in the usha puja).

Pantheeradi Puja

Pantheeradi, means twelve steps, and it determines the time of the puja based on the human shadow measuring twelve steps in the morning, which will correspond to five nāzhikās (two hours) after sunrise (roughly between 8 and 8.30 a.m.). As the bell is rung for the puja, the melshanti performs the temple tantra rituals of dehashuddhi, āthmārādhana, peetha puja, āvāhanam and then offers shodashopachāram.[127] At the time of offering snanam (bath) to the Goddess during the pantheeradi puja, She is given an elaborate bath – not as sankalpa as in usha puja. Devi is ceremonially installed in a platter/peetham, in the outer part of the sreekovil, the mukhamandapam. The conch is blown. Abhishekams are done on the idol with kunkumam, panchagavyam, navakābhishekam and parikalashangal, or ordinary pots which are filled with water. After each abhishekam, nivedyam, usually payasam, is offered to the Goddess. All this is done with the accompaniment of the pāni and other instruments, the uruttu chenda[128] and ilathālam.[129]

The passage from valiya thidappalli to the sreekovil is swept and sprinkled with water, and the entire amount of payasam made with ghee and jaggery is brought from the kitchen to be offered to the Goddess in a big vessel. The conch is blown to herald this. After nivedyam is removed, the place is swept and sprinkled with water. The ashtadravya abhishekam[130] (in nine pots – eight parikalasham and one brahmakalasham) with eight dravyas is conducted only after this.

First, Bhadrakali's ashtadravyas in the parikalashams are offered – the ashtadravyas are pure water, milk, curd, ghee, honey, sugar cane juice, tender coconut water and kalabham. The nālambalam is swept and sprinkled with water again. The melshanti lights the pāni lamp from the lamp at the main shrine, rings the bell and gives the drummers permission to play the pāni drum. The drummers pray to the Goddess and circumambulate the temple once, beating their drums.

From 8.30 to 11.30 a.m., the Goddess can be worshipped by the devotees without any restraint.

Uchha Puja

Uchha puja (puja at noon) is the third main puja. It is a lengthy one since elaborate purifying rituals have to be done and also because it is a puja performed to the Goddess along with Her full retinue.[131] There is a difference in the way dehashuddhi is performed in the saparivāram method of conducting a puja. In the uchha puja too, the steps for conducting the puja are similar to those during the usha puja – but in the uchha puja, dehashuddhi is done in an elaborate manner.

After doing the dehavyāpakam[132] during dehashuddhi, lipinyāsam[133] is performed. After that, panchatatvanyāsam is performed. It involves attributing the five tatvas of Bhadrakali on the five parts of the body[134] – sirassu,[135] mughavaktram,[136] hridayam,[137] nābhi[138] and padadvayam.[139] Then comes moolāksharanyāsam.[140] This is followed by hrillekhādhi panchamoorthi nyāsam. The panchamoorthis (associated with Bhadrakali), are Hrillekha, Gagana, Raktha, Karalika and Mahoschukshma. These five moorthis are installed on the five angams or body parts of the priest.

Various other nyāsams, as in usha puja, are performed after this and vyāpakam is done between all the nyāsams. The next step is ātmārādhana, or the worship of the self. The priest mixes the sandal paste with the water from the shankhupoorana jalam, and smears it on five spots of his body (temple, neck, both the shoulders and heart), and keeps flowers on his head five times. Then chandassu japikkal, dhyanam, mānasa puja, yathāshaktimoolam and again chandassu japikkal are performed. Through this chain of rituals, all that has been offered to the deity is again offered to the priest, who is imbued with the chaitanya of the Goddess. Of course, all these are offered in sankalpa.

Peetha puja also is elaborate in nature during the uchha puja, as shadupachāram is offered to the parivāra devatas using around forty-two mantras, for the same number of devatas in their position in the peetham. Then āvāhanam is done. Here too, the rituals done during dehashuddhi nyāsam for the priest's body are repeated for the deity's body. The chanting of the dhyanashloka and giving shadupachāram are similar to the shadpeetham method of offering the usha puja, but there is an increase in the number of mantras.

Moorthi puja differs from the usha puja with respect to the usage of mantras. Shadupachāram is offered thrice with pranava mantra; then upachāram is done just once as in usha puja and moola mantra is chanted thrice. The pranava puditha moolāksharam[141] is offered to the deity. And then, upachāram is done to Hrillekkhādi panchamoorthis. Next, upachāram is done on hramādishadāngam (on the deity's hridayam and other five parts) and āyudham (weapon of the deity). The offering for the parivara devatas is done together with this from the east, on eight positions in the peetham. These positions are Vashinyadi moorthi āvaranam (Vashinya, Kameshi, Modini, Vimala, Aruna, Mahayakshi, Sarveshwari, Kaulini); angāvaranam using the mantras of shadanganyāsam in the appropriate places in the peetham; Brāhmanyādi moorthyāvaranam (Brahmani, Maheshwari, Kaumari, Vaishnavi, Vārāhi, Indrāni, Chamundi, Mahalakshmi); Asithāngādi moorthyavaranam (Asithangabhairavan, Rurubhairavan, Chandabahiravan, Krodheeshabhairvan, Unmathabhairavan, Kapālibhairvan, Bheeshanabhairavan and Samhārabhairavan); Indrādi dasadikpalakar (Indra, Agni, Yama, Niryathi, Varuna, Vayu, Soma, Ishana, Ananta, Brahma); Vajrādi (the weapons of the dasadikpalakas – vajra, shakti, dhandu, khadgam, pāsham, ankusham, gada, trishulam, chakram, padmam); and Nirmalyadhari (Sheshika). Appropriate mantras to the devatas in these positions are offered to the peetham (these are repeated six times with jalam, gandham, pushpam, dhoopam, deepam and jalam and are called jalādi jalāntham).

Then the offerings such as nivedyam, vaishyam thooval, namaskaram, nivedyam muzhumippikkal and prasanna puja (using the same peetha puja mantras and moorthi puja mantras, suktams, yathāshaktimoolam, which are used for

Priest Narayanan Namboothirippad with Devi's sheeveli idol

ĀTTUKĀL AMMA

Kannan Potti doing deepārādhana during athāzha sheeveli

pushpanjali also) are done till layāngam in the same way as in usha puja.

The devotees feel that Āttukāl Amma attains Her fullest radiance at this time. The uchha deepārādhana is conducted at noon and bali offerings are made to the retinue in the same manner as for the usha sheeveli in the morning. The shrine is closed at 12.30 p.m.

All the major pujas include invoking the Goddess's chaitanya into the abhisheka vigraham and pleasing Her and dissolving the chaitanya returning to the moola vigraham through the temple tantra rituals. The melshanti then comes out and gently closes the three doors, locks them and hands over the keys to the temple official. Then he prostrates before the sreekovil. The devotees are urged out after this.

The temple suddenly falls silent and the divine presence permeates the entire precincts. The shrine is reopened only at 5 p.m., but the kazhakakkār begin their tasks at 3 p.m. These tasks include cleaning and preparing the objects and materials needed for the puja in the sreekovil, preparing everything necessary for the nivedyam. They also carry the pāni lamp and remove the offerings from the balikkallus.

All the four doors of the temple are opened at 4.40 p.m. and the devotees are allowed inside. Around 4.45 p.m., the shrines of the upadevatas also are opened. At 5 p.m., the melshanti, after taking the ritual bath in the temple pond, opens the shrine, lights the lamps, changes the garlands and offers trimadhuram to the Goddess. This is the time for japa, the recital of various sacred shlokas and keertanas.

The conch is blown three times to indicate sunset. This is followed by the sandhya deepārādhana at 6.45 p.m. The crowd in the temple is the biggest during the evening deepārādhana. A multi-tiered lamp with sixty-four wicks is

DAILY RITUALS OF WORSHIP AT ĀTTUKĀL

lighted and waved up and down and around the Goddess. The Goddess's idol, the mysterious smile and the thanka anki shine so brilliantly, and it is the most heartening moment in the temple. Instrumental music and songs in the sopanam style accompany this ritual.

Deepārādhana is followed by the Bhagavathy seva. This is an important and popular puja offering as is evident from the fact that it has been booked by devotees for the next thirty years. Bhagavathy seva is a temple tantra ritual in which the Goddess is invoked to the padmam and the lamp, which is used as a seat for Her. It is interesting to note that all the temple tantra rituals conducted inside the sreekovil are performed here too. This is a parihāra kriya.[142]

Another offering to Devi, the pushpābhishekam, is also conducted every day. For this ritual, which is a veritable vision of beauty, many baskets of flowers of various kinds are showered over the Goddess's idol.

7. 30 p.m. – Athāzha Puja

This is the fourth and the last main puja, which is conducted at night. This puja is conducted in any of the three methods[143] depending on the convenience of the priests. At the time of

Kannan Potti doing Bhagavathy seva

the prasanna puja, as mentioned earlier, vettila, adakka, etc., are offered. This is followed by the athāzha deepārādhana at 8 p.m. and the athazha sheeveli follows.

During the sheeveli, offerings are made to kshetrapala (the guardians of the temple). Before commencing the second circumambulation, a special deepārādhana is done for the Devi's idol in front of the valiya balikkallu. After this, the melshanti enters the nālambalam through the northern entrance and prostrates in the namaskara mandapam and chants aparadha shanti mantras.

The second and third circumambulations are then done; the sheeveli idol enters the temple after making a circumambulation around the sreekovil. The priest carrying the sheeveli idol, rings the bell at the door and enters the sreekovil. The sheeveli vigraham is kept on the right side of the moola vigraham and the chaitanya is sent back to the moola vigraham via the thooshni method.

The Goddess Goes to Sleep

The Goddess slowly slides into sleep listening to the Neelāmbari raga on nadaswaram. Regular devotees call out, 'Amma!' Many of them are reluctant to leave, and beseech Her not to abandon them. The melshanti comes out and gently closes the shrine, locks the doors, rings the bell, and hands over the keys to the temple official. Then he prostrates before the sreekovil. The kazhakakkār removes the alankāram; the nālambalam is swept clean and water sprinkled.

The most striking part of all the rituals in the temple is the soulful instrumental music or the pāni. Starting from the waking up ceremony to the ritual of making the Goddess sleep, playing the Neelāmbari raga on nadaswaram, the temple's ambience is full of life with music. The temple drummers Sadasivan and Ramesh, in fact, make it a stirring experience.

At all the three times of the day, the pujas to the upadevatas are conducted at the same time as the pujas are performed inside. Deepārādhanas are conducted for Lord Shiva just after those performed for Devi in the morning, noon and at dusk, followed by the sheeveli offerings.

The Origin of *Tantrasamuchhayam* and the Temple Tantra Rituals

The *Tantrasamuchhayam* is the main source of instructions regarding the temple tantra rituals and practices. The *Tantra Shastra* is the sadhanashastra (spiritual text) that sheds maximum light on the inner spaces of human beings and the universe, and transforms the powers that lie within each of us to elevate ourselves to the state we desire, the state of identifying with God.

It is said that the temple tantra tradition in Kerala starts with Parashurama. The *Tantra Shastra* that he is supposed to have composed is also known as *Parashuramakalpa Sutra* and is the basis for the *Tantrasamuchhayam* and other texts that followed later. There are several manuscripts that explain the *Tantra Shastra* and many of them, like *Tantrasamuchhayam* (1427 CE), *Sheshasamuchhayam, Sharadatilakam, Prapanchasaram, Bhuvaneshwarikalpam, Prapanchasāratantra, Kuzhikkattupacha, Saparivarapujakal* and *Tantradarpana* are based on the *Parashuramakalpa Sutra*. Among these, the text that is most used in the temples of Kerala is *Tantrasamuchhayam* compiled by Chennās Narayanan Namboothirippad. There is another sacred text called *Pudayur Bhasha enna Kriyadeepika* written in Malayalam by Vasudevan Namboothirippad of Pudayur Illam near the Thalipparambu Temple, which is older than *Tantrasamuchhayam* as Kanippayyoor Shankaran Namboothirippad says in the Preface to the second edition of the former text.

Keshavan Potti is doing the puja before the pushpa abhishekam at night

The members of the family of Narayanan Namboothirippad of the Chennās Illam used to conduct all the puja rituals in the temples that were under the administration of the Samootiri of Kozhikode. Narayanan Namboothirippad was one of the renowned poets belonging to the Samootiri's court. Once, after an argument between the Samootiri and Narayanan Namboothirippad, the Samootiri decided that the Namboothirippad had to be punished for something he said. Those days it was considered a sin to punish Namboothiris and the only punishment the Samootiri could devise was to ask Narayanan Namboothirippad to write a book on all the puja rituals conducted in Kerala till date. The Samootiri's malicious hope was that the writer would commit a mistake in this task and thus be subjected to a divine curse. However, the *Tantrasamuchhayam*, the flawless text that Chennās Narayanan Namboothirippad compiled, collecting data that spanned over six centuries, still remains the main text for the tantra rituals practised in the temples of Kerala. The story concerning the Samootiri intending to punish him notwithstanding, it is said that Chennās Narayanan Namboothirippad wrote the *Tantrasamuchhayam* with the explicit aim of bringing order and clarity to the confused state into which the temple tantra rituals had lapsed.[144]

An ordinary person can never comprehend temple tantra, however much he tries. 'It is an ocean,' as Chennās Dineshan Namboothirippad, the scion of the illustrious lineage and one of the most prominent of the tantris in the history of Āttukāl, whose tenure came to an end just recently, told me during our discussions. But by closely observing the rituals and while attempting to learn a small portion of it, I was convinced beyond any doubt, that there is a mysterious meaning and indescribable power embedded in temple tantra.

However, sometimes simple yet deep love is enough to bring Her amidst ourselves. She emerges from within ourselves and not from outside.

Old documents related to the land and the rules of the temple administration

No. G.C.572/21/L.A.

FROM

THE Division Peishkar, Trivandrum.

To

THE Registrar,
 Huzur Secretariat.

Subject:— Acquisition of lands for the Attukal Bhagavathy temple.

Reference:— G.O.ROC.No,670/46/Rev.dated 13th May 1947 and ROC.No.2071/47/Rev.dated 26-7-23.

SIR,

The draft declaration and valuation statements received from the Tahsildar, Trivandrum connected with the above acquisition are sent herewith. It is seen that the declaration has been prepared for the actual area found at the spot. I request that the declaration may be arranged to be published in the Gazette.

As regards the petition put in by Paswari Amma Saraswathi Amma against the acquisition, it is seen that the acquisition was sanctioned by Government on a representation from Mr.Raman Pillai Krishnan Nair and others after considering the pros and cons of the question(Vide G.O. ROC.No.670/46/Ref.dated 13th May 1947). Hence the petiti

P.T.O.

14
The Growth of the Āttukāl Temple and Its Administration

Sitting: Front row from left to right.
T.D.P. Nair of Govardhanam, P. Bhaskaran Nair of Vadakke Veedu, R. Narayana PIllai of Lakshmi Mandiram, R.N. Damodaran Nair of Ushus, P. Raghavan Pillai of Kurunkudi, R. Sankara Pillai of Seethapuram, M. Bhaskaran Nair of Keezheperumpally,

Middle row, Left to right
K. Sukumaran Nair of Chekkalavilakam, C.R. Thankappan Nair of Thekke Vilakam, R. Gopinathan Nair of Sasi Nilayam, K. Velukkutty Nair of Velan Vila, P. Madhavan Nair of Thekkeveedu, K. Parameswaran Nair of Manimandiram

3rd row, Left to right
K. Kumaran Nair of Kannettilveedu, N. Sreedharan Nair of Banglowil House, K. Krishnan Nair of Mynaduveedu, G. Bhaskaran Nair of Vasanthikam, R. Sadasivan Nair of Thekkevilakam.

Kuzhikkattu Parameswaran Vasudevan Bhattathirippad, the new Tantri of Attukal Bhagavathy Temple

K.P. Ramachandran Nair
Chairman of ABTT

V.L. Vinod
President

K. Girija Kumari Amma
Vice President

N. K. Sreekumar
Joint Secretary

The office-bearers during the time of writing this book

During the writing of this book, it was a blessing to find that at least a few old people still cherish the memories of the old Āttukāl village with perennial ponds full of crystal-clear water, rivulets that never stopped flowing, vast coconut groves and country roads filled with the sweet fragrance of flowers. They remember a small mudippura, surrounded by paddy fields, a few small thatched huts, four or five padippuras[1] with tiled roofs; people swimming and bathing in the River Killi, children playing country games like kuttiyum kolum,[2] kilithattu[3] and vattukali[4] – that was the picture of the old Āttukāl. Āttukāl was part of a larger area called Manacaud. Even now, Āttukāl has the characteristics of a village. Cherukaraveedu, Kuruppacham Vilakam, Keezheperumpally, Muthuvalliveedu, Valiya Kizhakkathu, Kurunkudiveedu, Kanchipuramveedu and Sitapuramveedu were some of the Nair families of Āttukāl, about fifty years ago.

My account of the temple's growth and its administrative system is based on the recollections of a few people who have been both witnesses and contributors to the expansion of the temple. Prominent among them are K.P. Ramachandran Nair, T.D.P. Nair, R. Gopinathan Nair, M. Bhaskaran Nair, K. Krishnan Nair and G. Ramachandran Nair.

M. Bhaskaran Nair, the secretary of the Āttukāl Bhagavathy Temple Trust when I was writing this book, remembers that in his childhood, during the monsoons, the water from the River Killi would reach the temple. In those days, the temple was only a tiny thatched hut. Sandalwood paste and kanmazhi[5] were applied on the wooden idol. 'A beauty adorned with ornaments – that is the Goddess, for me,' Bhaskaran Nair smiled.

K.P. Ramachandran Nair, the president of the ABTT remembers that, in those days, there were performances of Thiruvathirakkali, Chakyarkoothu, Ottanthullal and Pādhakam during the festival and before the deepārādhana at night; people making a lamp offering called 'theru vilakku' would circumambulate the sreekovil to the accompaniment of a variety of instrumental music. The practice was to throw the offered lamps backwards over one's shoulder after circumambulation. Nowadays, the lamps that were once made using vazhapola (plantain-stem swathes), the thāzhampoo flower, frangipani flower and kuruthola (tender fronds of the coconut tree) are being made from plastic and thermocol. 'During the festival, a group of young children would start fund raising. In the 1950s, we used to get coins of denominations of nālana (four annas) and ettana (eight annas) as donations. We would collect those coins in our palms or in a tin box and hand them over to the adults, who were in charge of conducting the festival. The Thottam Pāttu was sponsored by several families and there were people who backed out from conducting the Pāttu as they couldn't raise enough funds.' An elderly member of the ABTT had this to say.

ĀTTUKĀL AMMA

Administration of the Temple in Earlier Times

During the 1940s, ten to fifteen families that lived around the temple would meet once every three years to form an administrative committee, to discuss and take decisions regarding the conduct of the daily pujas and the annual Pongala festival. They raised funds for the festival, and each year, after the festival, their meeting would approve the accounts of the income and expenses related to it maintained in an ordinary notebook.

As the temple grew in terms of wealth, fame and the ever-increasing number of devotees, the management of the temple gradually grew into a complex affair, triggering controversies related to administration and representation. The ABTT has become an interesting case study in what happens when money-related power and prestige overtake the simple, faith-based set-up of a humble, rural shrine. A deity that was worshipped by all castes following the rituals of the lower castes, a temple on whom no one can make any exclusive claim, is now under the control of the Nair community.

Vishnutheerthan Potti giving prasadam to Abhedananda Swamikal

THE GROWTH OF THE ĀTTUKĀL TEMPLE AND ITS ADMINISTRATION

Until 1963, the temple was without compound walls and it was surrounded by the lands of people of various castes. Later, some land owned by Valiya Kizhakkathil family, located to the south of the temple, was purchased by the administrators of the temple, to add to the public space around the temple. A compound wall was soon built, enclosing all the temple property. But there was resistance from the people of the area regarding this purchase and the compound wall being built around the temple, as it blocked free access to the adjacent plots and the temple. It escalated into a very serious issue, with the political leaders of that area aligning themselves with the two opposing sides.

As a result of these protests by the locals against the exclusive control of the temple administration by a particular set of people, a trust was formed in 1970 to bring about an equitable approach by the inclusion of all interests. The trust deed was prepared by Mannar P. Gopalan Nair. Ironically, the trust deed, while addressing the protests of the local people, ensured that the control of the temple remained exclusively in the hands of the Nairs. A senior citizen of Āttukāl, who doesn't wish to be named, revealed that the members of the committee were forced to form such a body to prevent the possibility of losing control over the temple! This subterfuge did not go unnoticed. There was unrest again. This time, the locals protested by printing and circulating handbills calling the trust deed 'a silver-coated fake legal document'.

The Āttukāl Bhagavathy Temple Trust (ABTT) was registered with the number 2249/1970 on 26 June 1970, after the required fee was remitted at the Chala sub-registrar office. In 1979, this twenty-eight-member trust was given the stamp of approval by the Thiruvananthapuram district court and as per OS number 01/1979 scheme decree; the needed amendments were made in the bylaws for the temple administration.

As the population of Āttukāl increased, disputes over the administrative posts of the temple arose. Prominent persons among the new settlers in the area, K. Velukkutty Nair, R. Narayanan Nair, A.N. Gopala Pillai, K.P. Ramachandran Nair, R.N. Damodaran Nair and N. Gangadharan Nair filed cases demanding the expansion of the trust, to have themselves included. The twenty-eight-member trust didn't welcome this. Possibly because of the influence of the prominent people in this group, Bhuvanachandran Nair, the assistant commissioner of police (law and order), directed the police to surround the temple. They entered the trust office and made all the locals sign in the minutes' book of the trust. Thus the breach of the exclusivity of the trust (which was till then in the hands of a coterie) was effected. The devout R. Narayana Pillai, the secretary of the ABTT then, and others who were intimidated by all the happenings, wanted the twenty-nine-year-old M. Bhaskaran Nair to take over the administration of the trust in 1976. In fact, no one else was willing to accept that position because the situation at Āttukāl then was extremely volatile.

As soon as he took charge, he had a notice pasted on the Trust notice board declaring that the trust was rejecting the interference of the police as it was against the law. The assistant commissioner immediately summoned Bhaskaran Nair to the police station. He went along with his close friend M.M. Alexander who was the commissioner of police (traffic), to meet the angry assistant commissioner Bhuvanachandran Nair. Everything turned out positive as he welcomed them well.

But the court cases went on endlessly. Finally, under pressure from well-wishers, the trustees of the temple agreed to a compromise decree. The Āttukāl Bhagavathy Temple Trust Scheme with the addition of eighty-nine new members came into existence and was recognized by the Thiruvananthapuram district court on 12 June 1997. The list of new members was added as the first schedule and the names of the twenty-eight old members were included in the second schedule.

Only five out of the second-schedule members are alive now. (T.D.P. Nair, R. Gopinathan Nair, M. Bhaskaran Nair, K.

Krishnan Nair, G. Ramachandran Nair) and the membership of the trust has come down to eighty-nine, from the original 117. As per the bylaws approved by the district court, once every three years, an executive committee with twenty-eight members and a chairman is elected from among the eighty-nine trustees. From among the executive committee, the president, vice-president, secretary, joint secretary and treasurer are elected. They carry out the administration of the temple for three years. The trust members are all life members, while the elected offices are for three years; they have the right to resign and the trust board has the power to disqualify any member.

Anyone who reads the trust scheme now will wonder why the Nair community is mentioned in it many times over. The most glaring partiality perpetuated by subterfuge is borne out by Clause C of the third item in the objectives of the trust, which states that activities for the advancement of the Nairs of the Āttukāl Pitāka should be initiated. Isn't the inclusion of such a clause in a trust scheme recognized by the court, a mockery of history itself when the temple thrives on the money of the people belonging to all castes?

In a bid to gain exposure, the temple authorities have, of late, begun calling the Āttukāl Temple as the 'Sabarimala of Women'. Sabarimala is a temple that is dedicated to Lord Ayyappan which is open to people of all castes and creeds, but women between the age of ten and fifty are not allowed entry. At Āttukāl, except for offering the pongala, men participate fervently in many forms of worship during the festival and at other times, all through the year. Therefore, the epithet 'Sabarimala of Women' is clearly inaccurate. But the temple trust procured the trademark for it, seeking to establish exclusive rights over it.

Paradoxically, there are at least two other 'Sabarimala for Women' existing now! Recently, on my way to Ponmudi, a hill resort east of Thiruvananthapuram, I noticed a hoarding that said 'Welcome to Chakkulathu Kavu, the Sabarimala of Women.' The Mandaikadu Bhagavathy Amman Temple in Kanyakumari district, is also known as 'Sabarimala for Women.' From ancient times, women used to visit this temple with the Irumudi (a bundle divided into two sections, containing puja items similar to those carried by the male devotees going to Sabarimala).

The Trust and Its Role in the Development of the Temple

The revenue from all the institutions controlled by the trust, the income from the properties of the trust, the income from the temple, the donations made by individuals, institutions and organizations, grants, and other assets are all considered part of the trust fund. The accounts of the trust and its institutions are audited annually to ensure financial transparency and discipline.

The farmlands and dwellings around the temple were acquired to expand the space available for the Pongala. The roads leading to the temple were widened. A hospital was built in the vicinity.

The trust has also constructed a shrine dedicated to Chattampi Swamikal, a great saint of modern Kerala, and daily offerings, pujas, prayers and bhajanas are held there. After the renovation of the temple, a memorial hall for Sri Chattampi Swamikal, a decorative passageway, compound wall and a threshold too were constructed.

There is also a publication wing under the trust to collect, develop and bring out religious literature. A spiritual magazine titled *Amba Prasadam*, published by the trust, has been in circulation from October 1999 and is well received by the devotees and the public.

The procession to the Shastha Temple has also gone through a few changes. Earlier, it was characterized by the lighting of the lamp and the offering of the 'thattam', a big plate full of fruits and flowers to be offered to the Goddess. Now, devotees throng both sides of the roads with pandals decorated with electric lights and niraparas (caskets filled with grain, used during auspicious occasions), placing the thattam offering inside them. The pushpābhishekam (worship with flowers) is done along the way. It is miraculous that over a short span of fifty years, the Āttukāl Bhagavathy Temple rose to become one of the most important temples in Kerala and one of the most famous temples in the world itself, through the popularity of the Pongala festival.

My Goddess

It took me four years to complete the book, and holding the printout of the completed manuscript close to my bosom, I stood at the western entrance of the temple once again, basking in the warmth of feeling closer to Her. I again watched the uchha sheeveli of the Goddess going past me; the temple drummers and the priests in the procession, smiled at me.

My Goddess, my Amma, I whispered. From within my heart, I heard Her reassuring beat. Her. Mine. Ours.

The former secretary of ABTT M. Bhaskaran Nair and treasurer Kannettil Krishnan Nair with the golden thidampu of Āttukāl Amma

Notes

Preface

1 The deity's noon procession around the temple to check on Her retinue.

2 The special idol that is taken outside the sreekovil, in the sheeveli procession.

3 Sweet pudding, sandalwood paste or kumkumam given to the devotees; it literally means divine grace.

4 Percussion instruments are divided into two: devavādyam and asuravādyam. Chenda is called an asuravādyam, which means it cannot go in harmony.

5 Imagination; conception or idea or notion formed in the heart or mind.

6 Pongala means 'to boil over' and refers to the ritualistic offering by women, for Goddess Bhadrakali, and it is made of rice, jaggery, coconut gratings and plantains.

7 The systematic method of offering worship to various deities.

8 A grateful offering to a teacher.

1. The Temple through Legends

1 The River Killi originates in the scenic hills of Ottakombu and flows across the north-west boundaries of Nedumangad. Like the Ganga from the Himalayas and the Pamba from Sabarimala, the Killi has been flowing for centuries. Its name evokes memories of an ancient Dravidian Goddess as well as the family name of a Chola dynasty. Nedumudi Killi, for instance, was the name of a king from the Chilappathikaram period. There are a number of Devi temples located along its banks, such as the Udiyannur Devi Temple, Maruthankuzhi Bhadrakali Temple, Valiyashala Temple and the Mahadeva Temple at Sasthamangalam. Details available at http://www.thehindu.com/sci-tech/energy-and-environment/and-quiet-flows-the-karamana-the-rise-and-flow-of-killi/article4031048.ece, by Achuthsankar S. Nair.

2 Sreekanteshwaram G. Padmanabha Pillai (1864–1946), lexicographer and scholarbest known for his Malayalam dictionary Shabdatalralvali, says that 'Āttukāl' means the 'kāl' (feet) of the 'āru' (river), or the tributary of a river. This word is often interpreted by artists and local newspapers without much clarity during the festival.

3 Gate house.

4 A raised platform for the sacred basil plant, where a lamp is lit at dusk every day.

5 Umayamma Rani reigned from 1677 to 1684 ce as regent on behalf of her nephew Raja Ravi Varma.

6 Ettuveettil Pillamar (Nobles of the Eight Houses): The eight-member oligarchy alliance of madampi (aristocrat) families who rebelled against the royal family. Accusing them of acting against the well-being of his subjects, King Anizham Thirunal Marthanda Varma defeated and killed them in the eighteenth century; their homes were razed to the ground and ponds dug at their sites. Their women had to undergo 'thurayilettu', or being handed over to the fishermen of Valiathura, in the 1730s.

7 Land measuring 6.25 cents was awarded for establishing the temple through a royal decree that gives the allottees' name as, 'Pandārakāryam Cheyvārkal'. ('Those who look after divine worship connected with the royal family'); the original record is believed to be lost. A copy of the pattayam (land deed) is available at the village office of Manacaud (Thandapperu 784, Survey number 1057).

2. The Dispassionate Gaze of History

1 The ritualistic ballad sung by three men from the lower castes, in the Bhadrakali temples of southern Kerala during the festival season.

2 Sale Deed No. 3925, dated 25 September 1973.

3 Caldwell, Sarah, *Whose Goddess? Kali as Cultural Champion in Kerala*, Opera Minora, Harvard Oriental Series, 1999, p. 86.

4 Personal interview with N. Ajithkumar.

5 Ibid.

NOTES

6 Washerman caste.

7 Sanctum sanctorum.

8 Kesava Pillai, K. C. (dramatist, poet and a disciple of Brahmananda Shivayogi), in a letter to Shivayogi, dated 7 Dhanu 1088 (Malayalam Era [ME]), says: 'As I had been tied down with official duties, it was only yesterday that I completed reading *Mokshapradeepam*. ... After reading, the first thought that came to my mind is that it is essential to have a copy of this book in each and every household; especially, in the house of Nair nobility. At Āttukāl, here in Thiruvananthapuram, there is a temple dedicated to Goddess Bhadrakali. In this temple, in the Kumbham month every year, there is a ritual; it begins with songs and after ten days ends with animal sacrifice to propitiate the deity. For this, more or less hundred goats and five hundred cocks are killed. Neither the speeches of people like me nor the verses in my book *Subhashitha Ratnakaram* were potent enough to oppose these. It was at that time that your *Mokshapradeepam* came to the possession of one of the citizens. Is there a need to explain further? It had been unanimously decided that the cruel practice must not be conducted from this Kumbham month. Moreover, in order to prove its inhumanness, it has been decided that a poster, together with excerpts from *Mokshapradeepam*, is to be printed and circulated.'

Anandashram, Palakkad, *Brahmananda Shivayogi* (1988), pp. 363–68, has the following passage: 'Shivayogi was very particular that the struggle against the social evils should never acquire a violent dimension. He believed in enlightening people and changing minds through debates and logically placed arguments. In the book *Mokshapradeepam*, he pictures a scene where the fateful sacrificial-animal pathetically pleads to its executioner – man who is supposedly more intelligent – to show some mercy.

'Having been attracted to this particular principle of Brahmananda Shivayogi, his disciples have worked to stop this evil practice and had accomplished it to some respect. An instance of this is the ceasing of animal-sacrifice in Āttukāl Temple of Thiruvananthapuram through their efforts.'

9 Aiyappan, A., *Social Revolution in a Kerala Village*, Madras, 1937, p. 115.

10 *Proceedings of the Sri Mulam Popular Assembly*, Travancore, 11th to 15th Sessions, 1916, p. 120.

11 Sri Chithira Thirunal Bala Rama Varma, Maharaja of Travancore, Temple Entry Proclamation of 1936.

12 Interview with local villagers and confirmed by M. Bhaskaran Nair.

13 Docket sheet for DIS files, Government of Travancore, Revenue Department, No. D. Dis 1267/48/rev dated 26 April 48.

14 The simple temple tantra practice of divining the deity's will in specific situations. It is done by gathering white and red flowers from the idol's feet and keeping them in two separate packets. The devotee is asked to pick one packet from it and it is auspicious to get the packet with white flowers.

15 Kunjikrishnapillai, S. in his book, *Shankara Kavikal* (1941). The author is the grandson of Shankaranatha Jyotsyar.

16 Jenett, Dianne Elkins, 'Red Rice for Bhagavathy – An Ethnographic/Organic Enquiry of the Pongala Ritual at Āttukāl Temple, Kerala, South India', Doctoral Thesis submitted to the California Institute of Integral Studies, San Francisco, CA, 1999.

17 Shankaranathan had a son with Lakshmikutty Amma who was known as Āttukāl Shankara Pillai. Having taken after his father in scholarly pursuits, Āttukāl Shanakara Pillai completed the translation of *Devi Bhagavatham* into Malayalam. He served as the munsiff of Travancore. His son, Shankaran Nair, became known as a leader of the People's Movement in Travancore against the oppressive regime of Diwan Sir C.P. Ramaswami Iyer. He is also known to have served jail terms for being part of the uprisings.

18 Kunjan Pillai, Shooranadu, in an article in the Annual issue of *Manorajyam Weekly*, 1989.

19 An uprising in the Malabar area, by organizations of tenants against powerful landlords, during the 1920s.

20 Circular cookware made of bell metal.

21 Literally, handing over the horoscope; as part of confirming a marriage proposal.

22 Interview with M. Bhaskaran Nair, secretary of the Āttukāl Bhagavathy Temple Trust (ABTT). Chattampi Swamikal (1853–1924), along with his contemporary and friend, Sree Nārāyana Guru (1856–1928), strived to reform the heavily ritualistic and caste-ridden Hindu society of the late nineteenth century Kerala.

23 Tulu speaking region spread over parts of present-day Karnataka and Kerala states.

24 Personal Interview with Vishnutheethan Potti's son.

25 Ibid.

26 An umbrella made of talipot palm leaf.

27 Ritual bathing of the deity.

28 A mixture of ghee, honey, plantain, sugar lumps

3. ĀTTUKĀL AMMA

1 http://www.thehindubusinessline.com/blogs/blog-rknair/attukal-pongala/article5695570.ece

ĀTTUKĀL AMMA

2 A lamp with oil and wick within the cut half of a lemon turned inside out.

3 In Hindu mythology, Vetalika is the vehicle of Bhadrakali. It is a bloodthirsty female spirit who haunts cemeteries and takes possession of corpses.

4 One of the oldest Nair families around the temple; this family has a representative in the Temple Trust.

5 Trident.

6 Sword.

7 Shield.

8 Chalice.

9 Ferocious.

10 The idol used in the sheeveli procession.

11 The idol used for ablutions.

12 Original and ancient idol.

13 The ritual of clearing the previous day's flowers from the idol.

14 Front chamber of the sanctum.

15 Ablution

16 Personal interview with M. Bhaskaran Nair.

17 Ibid.

18 Attributes or nature.

19 Personal interview with M. Bhaskaran Nair and Kanippayoor Krishnan Namboothirippad.

20 Personal interview with Jyothish Kumar, former secretary, ABTT.

21 Personal interview with M. Bhaskaran Nair.

22 A miniature, temporary structure erected during the renovation of the sanctum, to house the idol.

23 Ashtabandham is a Sanskrit word which means a mix (bandham) of eight (ashta) ingredients. The process of applying ashtabandham to the idol is done every twelve years and it acts as sealant. It is a paste made of eight natural ingredients for fixing an idol. Preparing the mixture is a forty-one-day long procedure and the eight ingredients that go into it are finely powdered conch, gall-nut, sealing wax, gooseberry, resin of 'pinus dammar', two varieties of gravel from the Bharathapuzha (a holy river in north Kerala, India) and from the confluence of three rivers (Triveni), and cotton.

24 S. Jayashanker, *Temples of Kerala*, Census of India, Special Studies, Kerala, 1997, p. 175.

25 The gold-plated outer casing of the wooden idol.

26 An astrological ritual to ascertain the deity's will about matters related to the temple and faith. Ashtamangalyam consists of a group of eight auspicious materials and it varies according to the context.

27 The bhava after annihilating the demon Ruru.

28 Interview with Kanippayoor Krishnan Namboothirippad.

29 Eight sacred serpents.

30 Personal interview with M. Bhaskaran Nair and Kanippayyoor Krishnan Namboothirippad.

4. THE ORIGIN AND DEVELOPMENT OF THE BHADRAKALI CULT IN KERALA

1 Caldwell, Sarah. 'Margins at the Center: Tracing Kali through Time, Space and Culture', in *Encountering Kali: In the Margins, at the Center, in the West*, edited by Rachel Fell Mcdermott and Jeffrey J. Kripal, Delhi: Motilal Banarsidass Publishers, 2005, p.255.

2 Personal interview with Dr N. Ajithkumar.

3 The primal energy or life, located at the base of the spine.

4 The Shakta tradition specifically worships Goddess Shakti in Her various forms such as Parvati, Durga, Kali, etc.

5 'Margins at the Center: Tracing Kali through Time, Space and Culture', in *Encountering Kali:In the Margins, at the Center, in the West*, edited By Rachel Fell Mcdermott and Jeffrey J. Kripal. Delhi: Motilal Banarsidass Publishers, 2005, p. 255.

6 Vishnu Namboothiri, M.V., *Folklore Nighantu*, Thiruvananthapuram: State Institute of Languages, 2000.

7 Personal interview with Dr N. Ajithkumar.

8 Radhakrishnan, Shweta, 'Sanitising the Profane,' *Sub/Versions — The Journal of Emerging Research in Media and Culture Studies*, Vol.1, Issue.1, (2013), Mumbai: School of Media and Culture Studies, Tata Institute of Social Sciences, pp.202–34.

http://subversions.tiss.edu/wp-content/uploads/2013/12/Shweta_Radhakrishan_Subversion_pdf.pdf

5. THE ĀTTUKĀL TEMPLE

1 Binumol Tom, 'The Physicality and Spirituality of the Hindu Temples of Kerala', https://www.google.co.in/?gws_rd=ssl#safe=off&q=binu+mol+tom+the+spiritualiy+of+kerala+temples. If the deity is male, the platform should be female and vice versa. This can be identified by the sculptors alone. They identify it by the sound the stone produces when hit with a hammer or how they feel it.

2 S. Jayashanker, *Temples of Kerala*, Census of India, Special Studies, Kerala. 1997, p. 41.

3 Sreedhar, Darshana, 'Myth and Modernity in a Ritualistic Space', in Shiju

NOTES

Sam Varughese and Satheesh Chandra Bose (eds), *Essays on Kerala Modernity: Interdisciplinary Perspectives*, Hyderabad: Orient Blackswan, 2015, p. 152.

6. The Commencement of the Ten-day Festival

1 The state festival of Kerala.
2 The New Year's Day or the first of the month of Medam in Kolla Varsham (the Malayalam calendar), usually in the second week of April.
3 In which young boys, whose flanks are ritualistically pierced with silver needles, parade as Devi's guard.
4 Personal interview with M. Bhaskaran Nair.
5 Ibid.

7. Āttukāl Amma and Kannaki of *Chilappathikaram*: Different Entities?

1 'Āttukāl Pongala, Myth and Modernity in a Ritualistic Space', *Kerala Modernity: Ideas, Spaces and Practices in Transition*, Hyderabad: Orient Blackswan, 2015, p.151.
2 Kurup, Deepu P., 'Bhadrakalippāttu: History, Society and Culture', Doctoral Thesis in Malayalam, submitted to the University of Kerala, 2015, awaiting publication from the State Institute of Languages, Thiruvananthapuram, Kerala.
3 Sreedhara Menon, A., *Kerala Charitram*, (Malayalam), Kottayam: D. C. Books, (Revised edition), 2007, p.75.
4 Ibid., p.81.
5 Adarsh, C., *Kodungallurinte Vyāvahārika Bhoomishāstram* (Malayalam), Shukapuram: Vallathol Vidyapitham, Distributors, National Bookstall, Kottayam, 2013, pp. 48, 96 and 111.
6 http://temple.dinamalar.comennew_en.phpid=479, accessed on 18 November 2015.
7 https://en.wikipedia.org/wiki/Pattini, accessed on 18 November 2015.
8 https://en.wikipedia.org/wiki/Kannagi, accessed on 18 November 2015.
9 http://www.thehindu.comtodays-papertp-opinionin-praise-of-citizen-Kannakiarticle3119956.ece, accessed on 18 November 2015.
10 https://www.google.co.in/?gws_rd=ssl#safe=off&q=eric+miller+kannaki, accessed on 20 November 2015.
11 A survey was conducted by the East India Company and published in St George Gazette of 15 November 1883.
12 http://www.thehindu.comnewsnationaltamil-nadutemple-for-Kannaki-a-picture-of-neglectarticle4651234.ece
13 Adarsh, C., *Kodungallurinte Vyāvahārika Bhoomishāstram* (Malayalam), Shukapuram: Vallathol Vidyapitham, Distributors, National Bookstall, Kottayam, 2013, pp. 32, 87.
14 *Travancore State Manual*, Vol. II, p. 19.
15 Ilayathu, Kunjukuttan, *Kodungallur Kshethrethihasam*, Devi Books, Kodungallur, 2003.
16 Sreedhara Menon, A., *Kerala Charitram*, (Malayalam), Kottayam: D.C. Books, (Revised edition), 2007, p. 84.
17 Chandran, V.R., *Sree Kodungallooramma – Charitravum Āchārānushtānangalum*, (Malayalam), Kodungallur: Ayyappa Seva Sangham, 1990.
18 Rajendran, P.G., *Kodungallur Bhagavathy: Aithihyavum Charitravum*, (Malayalam)
19 Gopalakrishnan, P.K., *The Cultural History of Kerala*, Thiruvananthapuram: State Institute of Languages, Kerala, 2010.
20 Gentes, M. J. *Scandalizing the Goddess of Kudungallur*, Austin, Texas: University of Austin at Texas, available at https:// nirc.nanzan-u.ac.jpnfile1735, accessed on 26 November 2015
21 Ibid.
22 Induchudan, V.T., *The Secret Chamber: A Historical, Anthropological and Philosophical Study of the Kodungallur Temple*, Thrissur: Cochin Devaswom Board, 1969, pp. ii and iv.
23 Jenett, Dianne Elkins, 'Red Rice for Bhagavati, Cooking for Kannaki: An Ethnographic Organic Inquiry of the Pongala Ritual at Āttukāl Temple, Kerala, South India', Doctoral Thesis, California Institute of Integral Studies, 1999.
24 N. Ajithkumar, 15 December 2015.
25 Kurup, Deepu P., 'Bhadrakalippāttu, History, Society and Culture', Doctoral Thesis in Malayalam, 2015, awaiting publication from the State Institute of Languages, Thiruvananthapuram, Kerala, p.30.
26 Ibid., pp.31–32.

8. Thottam Pāttukār

1 Old lady.
2 She.
3 Very old lady.
4 A mixture of plantain, ghee, sugar, honey.
5 Thick payasam made of rice roasted in ghee and cooked in jaggery.
6 Kurup, Deepu P., 'Bhadrakalippāttu, History, Society and Culture', Doctoral Thesis in Malayalam, 2015, awaiting publication from the State Institute of Langauges, Thiruvananthapuram, Kerala, p. 64.

9. The Ten-day Festival and the Thottam Pāttu

1 On the first day of the Pāttu, expenses for the pujas and the Pāttukār are sponsored

by Nediyavilakom family. On the second day it is by the Thekkeveedu family, on the third day by the Velanvila house. From the third day, the expenses for conducting the festival increase dramatically because from this day until the ritual of Kuthiyottam is performed on the ninth day, food and accommodation have to be provided for about one thousand boys. The fourth day's song is sponsored by Panayil Veedu Family, the fifth day's by Sitapuram House, and the sixth day's by two families, Kurumkudi House and Kshatriyakkudi House. On the seventh day it is by the Charuvilaveedu. Vadakkeveedu and Kannettilveedu sponsor the eighth day's Pāttu. Chandralayam House and Kancheepuram House sponsor the ninth day's song. The tenth day's Pāttu is sponsored by the ABTT.

2 Near the present-day Panthalāyini, Vadakara, Malabar.

3 A small bushel, ritually filled with grains.

4 The traditional garment of Kerala.

5 Sacred sword.

6 A herbal shampoo made from hibiscus leaves.

7 Thookkam is an offering and a ritual art form performed in the Kali temples of south Kerala.

8 Unclear.

9 Kuthiyottam with golden hooks.

10 Kuthiyottam with silver hooks.

11 'Asari' can be a carpenter or mason. It is the name of a caste.

12 Endearing term for mother.

13 Lord Ayyappan is the son of Lord Shiva and so he is the brother of Goddess Bhadrakali, who is also Shiva's daughter.

14 Garudan thookkam (Eagle hanging) is a ritual art form performed in the Kali temples of south Kerala. People dress up as Garuda and perform the ritual dance. After the dance, they are made to hang from a shaft with a hook, by the skin on their back

15 Thooshni avahanam is a sankalpam that Devi's chaitanya is invoked in the thidampu, without using mantras.

16 Para is the biggest measuring unit; nirapara is a para filled with rice grains and is used in all auspicious occasions.

17 A big tray full of flowers, fruits and delicacies.

18 The deity comes out begging.

19 The puja offered to the deity when the human shadow measures twelve feet.

20 A purificatory rite.

21 Invoking the chaitanya of a deity.

22 Sending back the chaitanya to its source.

10. ĀTTUKĀL PONGALA

1 The Āttukāl Pongala is celebrated on the penultimate day of the ten-day festival and it falls on the Makam/Pooram asterisms of the Malayalam month of Makaram–Kumbham (February–March). The pongala is an offering of rice, boiled until thick white foam spills over the top of the pot, which represents an excess, or 'more than enough', and it is offered to fulfil a woman's vow to the Goddess. The ingredients are simple, and almost any woman can afford to do it. Rice, after being boiled out in the open in a new red earthen pot over a hearth of bricks, is sweetened with jaggery, a dark brown, unrefined sugar from the palm tree. This form of offering by women to the fierce Goddess Kottavai appears in the Sangam literature of the fifth century. (*The Chilappathikaram of Ilanko Atikal: An Epic of South India*, trans. R. Parthasarathy, from Asian Classics Series, New York: Columbia University Press, 1993).

2 http://news.bbc.co.uk/2/hi/south_asia/8544038.stm

3 Jenett, Dianne Elkins, 1999, 'Red Rice for Bhagavati/Cooking for Kannaki: An Ethnographic/Organic Inquiry of the Pongala Ritual at Āttukāl Temple, Kerala, South India', Doctoral Thesis, California Institute of Integral Studies. Dianne is a core faculty member and co-director of the Women's Spirituality Program at New College of California.

4 *The Hindu*: http://www.thehindu.com/todays-paper/tp-national/tp-kerala/mosques-open-their-doors-to-pongala-devotees/article2965840.ece, accessed on 28-11-2015.

5 *http://www.thehindu.com/todays-paper/tp-national/tp-kerala/appropriating-space-to-offer-pongala/article6980910.ece, accessed on 28 November 2015.*

6 Sreedhar, Darshana. 'Āttukāl Pongala: Youth-club, Neighbourhood Groups and Masculine Performance of Religiosity', *Economic and Political Weekly*, Vol. XLIX, No. 17, 2014. p. 53.

7 Jenett, Dianne Elkins, 1999, 'Red Rice for Bhagavati/Cooking for Kannaki: An Ethnographic/Organic Inquiry of the Pongala Ritual at Āttukāl Temple, Kerala, South India', Doctoral Thesis.

8 *Lalitasahasranamam,* Verses 98 to 110.

9 Sreedhar, Darshana, 'Āttukāl Pongala: Youth Clubs, Neighbourhood Groups and Masculine Performance of Religiosity', *Economic & Political Weekly,* Vol. XLIX, No. 17, 26 April 2014.

10 http://www.telegraphindia.com/1150307/jsp/nation/story_7328.jsp#.VY_lhkZMLok. Accessed on 30 November 2015.

11 http://www.newindianexpress.com/cities/thiruvananthapuram/Pongala-for-Mangalyān/2014/02/17/article2060388.ece. Accessed on 30 November 2015.

12 http://www.thehindu.com/todays-paper/tp-national/tp-kerala/austrians-on-pongala-trip-to-city/article1207604.ece. Accessed on 30 November 2015.

11. Sahasrakalasham: The Rite of Penance and Ritual Cleansing after the Pongala

1 *Tantrasamuchhayam,* written by Chennās Narayanan Namboothirippad in the fifteenth century CE, specifies the implementation of vāsthu in temple construction. This book is the main source of authoritative instructions for the temple tantra rituals and practices. The *Tantrasamuchhayam* decrees that if the signs of destruction or danger are perceived in the idol that enshrines the deity who is meant to bless devotees, the rites of penance must be performed as atonement. The *Tantra Shastra* is the sadhana shastra (spiritual text) that sheds maximum light on the inner spaces of human beings and on the universe, and transforms the powers that lie within each of us to elevate ourselves to the state we desire, the state of identifying with God.

2 Divine vitality.

3 *Tantrasamuchhayam,* Canto 10 Verse 2.

4 Ibid., Canto 10 Verse 3.

5 Rites that have been clearly prescribed for certain faults.

6 Water to wash hands.

7 Water to wash feet.

8 Water to wash mouth.

9 A gold ring with a mythical tradition.

10 Sowing seeds for germination.

11 Small flower pots in metal.

12 The base.

13 The stem.

14 The neck joint.

15 The neck.

16 The base joint.

17 The cup.

18 'Sleem pashu hum phal' is the astramantra of Goddess Bhadrakali

19 Darbha grass tied together.

20 Two darbha grass blades, cut into three parts (six pieces), two with the pointed ends and two base parts.

21 Paddy.

22 Urad dal.

23 Millet.

24 Sesame seeds.

25 Lentil.

26 Horse gram.

27 Green gram.

28 Mustard.

29 Little millet.

30 Beans.

31 Sprinkling the water that has been sanctified by mantras.

32 A mixture of eight fragrant herbs.

33 The sreekovil and its surroundings.

34 Purification of the sreekovil and surroundings.

35 *Desmotachya bipinnata*

36 Kapotha-mala.

37 A tiny broom specially made for this task, made of palasha (*Butea monosperma*).

38 The presiding deity of this seed is Shiva.

39 A mixture prepared by adding five products of the cow: cow dung, cow urine, milk, curd and ghee. Panchagavyam is one of the most important ingredients in the purification rites.

40 For Bhadrakali, they are pachakarpooram (raw camphor), sandalwood, sindooram (vermilion), gorochanam (a stone or 'bezoar' found in cattle), kandivenna (the first feces excreted by a newborn elephant-calf), jadamanji (Alerina root), kachoorikizhangu (aromatic ginger) and akil (a wood like sandal).

41 The Vāsthupurusha and the Vāsthu mandala provide the foundation for classical vāsthu. The *Matsya Purana* describes how a weird personality emerged from a drop of Lord Shiva's sweat as he fought a war with the asuras. This peculiar person was cruel and when Shiva granted him the boon to eat anything from the three worlds, he devoured everything he found on his way. The devas were terrified and approached Lord Shiva. The Lord grew angry and kept the creature pressed under his foot till the war was over. When this person finally surrendered to Lord Shiva, He named him Vāsthupurusha (Vāsthu god). He ordered him to go to Earth and reside there in every place/house. In return, Shiva promised that he would bless all the occupants with health, wealth and prosperity, that every occupant would worship Vāsthu and allow him to lie down comfortably in his house. Four devas then collectively caught hold of

ĀTTUKĀL AMMA

Vāsthupurusha and hurled him to Earth, his face downwards, his head in the north-east and his feet in the south-west. Forty-five devas held down his body, thirteen from within and thirty-two from outside. In this way, the Vāsthupurusha and the forty-five devas form a Vāsthupurusha mandala, which is the most important spiritual aspect of vāsthu evaluation.

42 *Ficus racemosa*, *Ficus gibbosa*, *Ficus religiosa* and *Ficus bengalensis*.

43 Purification by mantras.

44 Purification of the veins.

45 Oblations in fire seeking penance.

46 Oblations in fire seeking peace.

47 Oblations in fire seeking a balancing effect.

48 A Vedic chant propitiating Goddess Lakshmi.

49 Oblation in fire to cleanse the impurities on account of the touch of thieves.

50 Temporary hut to germinate the seeds.

51 A homam to preserve the sanctity of the kalashams, to be used the next day.

52 Oblation pit.

53 The main oblation pit.

54 Firewood.

55 Bael tree.

56 Indian banyan.

57 Circular oblation pit.

58 East Indian screw tree.

59 Peepal tree.

60 Black catechu.

61 *Butea monosperma*.

62 Squaire shaped oblation pit.

63 *Gmelina arborea*.

64 *Helicterus isora* Linn.

65 Of smell, taste, touch, seeing and hearing.

66 Nose, tongue, skin, eyes, and ears.

67 Akasham, vayu, agni, jalam and bhoomi (Sky, wind, fire, water and earth).

68 Mouth, hands, feet, anus, and the organ of procreation.

69 Prāna, apāna, samāna, udāna, vyāna.

70 It is the symbolic representation of the creation of Hrudayapadmam in the Brahmanda.

71 Invoking the chaitanya of the Goddess.

72 Different aspects of paradeha are invoked.

73 This is the invocation of sookshma deha (subtle body) of the deity.

74 This universe is believed to be made up of twenty-five tatvas. By invoking them, the creation of the subtle body of the deity is complete.

75 Offering songs, sweets, etc., to please the deity.

76 The puja performed inside the sanctum when the human shadow measures twelve feet.

12. Special Offerings to Āttukāl Amma

1 Personal interview with N. Ajithkumar.

2 N. Ajithkumar, *Kali Nadakam,* Thiruvananthapuram: State Institute of Languages, Kerala, 2015, p. 133.

3 According to a legend in the *Devi Bhagavatam*, Jasun was an ardent devotee of Devi. When the gods asked Devi to assume the form of Kali to destroy evil, Jasun donated the red colour of her flowers to Goddess Kali's eyes so that She could show Her anger. Kali was pleased with Her devotee's sacrifice. She told Jasun to ask Her for any favour and it would be granted. 'I wish to serve you forever,' said Jasun humbly. 'You shall be my flower,' Devi granted her wish. 'From today you will be known by many names: Jathon, Deviphool, Japākusum. Whoever gives me an offering of your flowers shall be blessed by me.' Since then the hibiscus flower is offered by devotees to Kali. (From *Brahma's Hair: On the Mythology of Indian Plants* by Maneka Gandhi, Yasmin Singh [PDF, internet]).

4 Rice cooked with jaggery.

5 Rice fried in ghee and cooked in jaggery, a thick payasam.

6 Mixture of rice flour and jaggery steamed in cones made in bay leaves.

7 Fried sweet dumplings made of rice, bananas and jaggery.

8 A delicacy, consisting of dough made of rice flour, with sweet fillings, steamed in banana leaf.

9 A steamed sweet dish prepared from rice flour, jaggery and green gram.

10 Very thick, dark, sweet payasam.

11 Rice kheer.

12 White rice.

13 Tender coconut water.

14 Deciding the code of conduct in the temple.

15 Daily rituals.

16 Special offerings.

17 The temple's website www.attukal.org.

NOTES

13. DAILY RITUALS OF WORSHIP AT ĀTTUKĀL

* This chapter was done under the scholarly supervision of Kannan Potti, melshanti of the Attukal temple, 2014-15.

1 Krusche, Krupali and Vinayak Bharne, *Rediscovering the Hindu Temple: The Sacred Architecture and Urbanism of India*, Cambridge, UK: Cambridge Scholars Publishing, 2014, p. 1.

2 Sixteen types of offerings.

3 They contain rules for worship, temple construction, spirituality and rituals.

4 Food for the deity.

5 The sandalwood paste mixed with other perfumes to anoint the idol of the deity.

6 The ritual of waking up the Goddess with the accompaniment of music.

7 The temple staff, the musicians here.

8 A pipe instrument.

9 A percussion instrument.

10 Hand cymbals.

11 The lamp that burns continuously, night and day, in the temple.

12 Chief priest.

13 Serpent gods.

14 Steps to the sanctum.

15 The ritualistic cleaning of the outer and inner self of the priest to enable him to offer pujas to the deity.

16 The water imbued with mantras that is stored in a conch. This is used for the puja during the rest of the day.

17 The ritual in which the priest, with the prescribed mantras, becomes a body that is pervaded by divinity, to offer pujas to the deity.

18 Main idol.

19 The golden outer casing.

20 The presence of more than one idols in the sanctum where chaitanya is transferred to a smaller idol to perform pujas, as a precautionary method mainly not to damage the ancient idols. The abhisheka vigraham of Āttukāl was made in 1966.

21 Vedic mantra that cleanses.

22 Seven mantras from the Rig Veda to purify the idol.

23 Three mantras from the Rig Veda to purify the idol.

24 In the sankalpa that the deity comes to the abhisheka vigraham; this is done without mantras or mudras and is different from āvāhanam.

25 The fibre of *Acacia caesia* plant.

26 It is a mixture of five sweet ingredients, usually honey, sugar, plantains, raisins and ghee.

27 From the conch, the shankupoorana jalam.

28 Literally, the first oil. Here it refers to gingelly oil.

29 Beaten rice.

30 Puffed rice.

31 Varieties of plantain like kadali, nentran or poovan.

32 A homam to propitiate Lord Ganesha.

33 Agnikon.

34 Sacred kitchen in the agnikon.

35 An hourglass-shaped drum.

36 The worship by waving lighted lamps soon after the abhishekam.

37 Five-tiered lamps.

38 Round, pot-shaped lamp.

39 A brass lamp with a long handle to burn camphor.

40 Personal interview with Kannan Potti.

41 A lamp with many tiers that is pyramidal in shape.

42 A serpent-hood-shaped lamp.

43 Mixture of turmeric powder, milk, tender coconut water and rice powder along with coconut flowers offered to Nagas, on a specially drawn padmam. It's meant to cool the snake gods.

44 The birth star of the Naga deity, Ananta.

45 Ādhārashakti, vidyabdha, rathandweepa, sumangala, manimandapa and kalpakavriksha.

46 Midday.

47 Puja at night.

48 Worshipping the base on which the idol is placed.

49 Worshipping the deity.

50 Offering bali to Lord Agni so that it reaches all the deities through Him.

51 Prostration.

52 Puja to make the deity pleasant.

53 Completion of the puja.

54 Offering puja to the priest's self. It is similar to what he offers to the deity. This is an act of unifying the Goddess's self and the priest's self. It involves taking a small fraction of the chaitanya into the priest's body.

55 Pot with a spout.

ĀTTUKĀL AMMA

56 The preparation of the place for the invocation of the Goddess.

57 Water.

58 Sweet smell.

59 Flower.

60 Incense.

61 Light.

62 Hand gestures.

63 The first chakra where kundalini resides.

64 Life breath or life itself.

65 A mixture of washed rice and paddy.

66 Attributing six body parts in the idol. Five of them are – heart, head, the tip of medulla oblongata, calf muscles, eyes and one imaginary part, asthram (in this case, arrow) to prevent impurities from entering again.

67 Touching the head, above lips, and heart.

68 Weapons for the Goddess.

69 This means the physical description of the deity being worshiped. In this case it is: *Kaleemeghasamaprabham* ..., etc., as described in an earlier chapter.

70 Om aim kleem souh: hreem Bhadrakalyai namah.

71 Offering water to Her feet.

72 Giving water for washing the hands.

73 Giving water to wash Her mouth.

74 Offering a mixture of curd and honey.

75 Giving water to wash the mouth again.

76 Instead of an actual bath, prokshanam is done, which is sprinkling of water from the conch which is equal to a bath.

77 Bathing again.

78 Giving Her new clothes.

79 Giving the upper cloth.

80 Sankalpa of adorning with the sacred thread or poonool.

81 Giving Her ornaments.

82 The perfume of sandal paste.

83 Flower.

84 Incense.

85 Lighted lamp.

86 Food.

87 Greetings.

88 Water from the conch.

89 Upachāram11 and 12.

90 Cooked rice.

91 Mantra's to propitiate the doorkeeper deities.

92 Mantra's to propitiate God Agni.

93 Vaisyam thooval for Agni with the belief that it reaches all the gods through Agni.

94 Sixteenth upachārams.

95 Mantra seeking forgiveness.

96 Āchamanam.

97 Arghyam.

98 The doorkeepers.

99 Giving water to clean the teeth, tongue, mouth, face, hands and feet.

100 During this time, the sreekovil remains closed till the deepārādhanā at 6.40 a.m., approximately for five minutes.

101 Six methods of honouring the Goddess.

102 The number of times the moolamantra should be chanted is not mentioned here; that is why it is called yathāshakthimoolam, meaning, as many times as one can.

103 Hymns from the Vedas.

104 Offering of flowers.

105 Water from the conch.

106 Departed souls of ancestors.

107 Offerings of flowers, sacred water, sandal paste, rice and grains of paddy in handfuls with special mantras.

108 Informing the deity that the puja is concluding.

109 Touching the moola vigraham from the head to feet along with the chanting of the moolamantra.

110 Shadanganyāsam.

111 Reciting the name of the sage who created the mantra, the rhyme of the mantra and the deity invoked.

112 Spreading the chaitanya of the mantra into the deity's self.

113 The vessel in which all these are placed.

114 Only thooshni āvāhanam is done. The Goddess's thidampu was made in 1968.

115 A lamp with a long handle and a horse's face at the lower tip; it is also called pāni vilakku and the horse figure on it represents vāyu, the vehicle of Agni.

116 All are in sankalpa; they are all unseen deities.

117 In the old days, there would have been a separate roof for the valiaya balikkallu

NOTES

which is lower in height and to avoid the collision with it the sheeveli idol would be carried in the hand and when the priest comes out of the inner balivattom to the outer balivattom, he would keep it on his head. Here in Āttukāl, there is no separate enclosure for the valiya balikkallu, but the priest follows the custom that has become a rule through long usage; though there is no chance of colliding with a roof here.

118 Doorkeepers.

119 A miniature representation of the sanctum and all the bali stones, right in front of the sanctum, in the outer circumambulatory path.

120 The guardian spirit of the temple.

121 A symbolic bath where he ritually wets his lips, eyes, nose, and ears twice.

122 To welcome the sunrays.

123 When the human shadow lengthens to twelve steps.

124 Ceremonial umbrella.

125 Rice and broken coconut lumps and karuka grass (Cynodon Dactylon)

126 The mantras chanted while beginning a journey.

127 Sixteen types of honouring.

128 A kind of percussion instrument.

129 Hand cymbals.

130 At Āttukāl, kalabham is used in place of water and water is taken in a separate pot called brahmakalasham.

131 Saparivāram method.

132 Spreading the moolamantra on the priest's body which is also called moolavyāpakam.

133 This is done by infusing the old Malayalam alphabets in the spiritual body of the priest. Each alphabet is a beejamantra, which are organized together as mantras later.

134 Angams.

135 Head.

136 Above upper lip.

137 Heart.

138 Navel.

139 Feet.

140 Spreading each sound of the moolamantra of Bhadrakali to nābhi, hridayam, sirassu, ears, eyes, lips, nose and spreading it from the heart to the hands and then from the heart to the feet.

141 Adding pranava mantra before and after each letter of the moolamantra – Om omom namah, Om aimom namah…bham-dram-kam-lyaim-nam-mam.

142 Penitential rtual.

143 Padmamāthram, saparivāram or shadpeetham.

144 Seth, Pepita, *Heaven on Earth: The Universe of Guruvayur Temple*, New Delhi: Niyogi Books, 2009, p. 64.

14. THE GROWTH OF THE ĀTTUKĀL TEMPLE AND ITS ADMINISTRATION

1 Entrance gate to the better-off houses.

2 A crude form of cricket.

3 Hopscotch.

4 A game using marbles.

5 Eyeliner.

Tamil girls offering Thālappoli to Āttukāl Amma

Acknowledgements

Achha, I believe that you extend your hands from a place afar to touch this book, hold me close, and look at me once. I prostrate before your memory.

Amma, for raising us in a home where God is a living presence.

My maternal aunt, K. Swarnalatha, my Thankamma, for all the love.

Adityan and Bhadra, my children, for calling me Amma. For blessing my life. Both of you were six years old when Amma began writing this book and now you are ten years and you always asked me, 'Whom do you love the most, Āttukāl Amma or us?'

M. Bhaskaran Nair, the secretary of Attukal Bhagavathy Temple Trust (ABTT), whose affection and advice during the course of writing this book, helped shape this book, especially at the final stages.

Jyothish Kumar, former secretary of ABTT, for giving me the permission to do the book. The temple staff, for their abiding interest in the progress of the book.

My valiyachhan, late K.G. Sudevan, for introducing me to the world of gods and Sanskrit texts at a very tender age. Guru Nitya Chaitanya Yati, for guiding me to explore esoteric wisdom when I was barely twenty. Acharya K.K. Nair, my guru, for making me familiar with temple tantra and for making me believe it is something I have to do. Dr B.C. Balakrishnan, for the blessings, for the guidance.

Dr A.J. Thomas for showing me the path. For the light. For the limitless love and the most valuable guidance, all these years.

Dianne Janett, for the affection, for sharing her doctoral thesis on Āttukāl Pongala, unconditionally, which made my work a lot easier.

Dr Shashi Tharoor for the valuable observations, Soorya Krishnamoorthy for the trust in my work.

P.I. Sheik Pareeth, IAS, director, Department of Tourism for realizing the worth of this book and giving the recognition it deserved almost instantly.

P. Prabhath for being my best friend. You told me you know the text by heart now. Thank you for the unwavering support, advice and patience.

Kavitha Valsala and Abhilash Nair of Paithrika Homes for holding the book close.

Anees Salim, for the friendship, for coming up with the title of the book.

V.K. Karthika, chief editor and publisher, HarperCollins *Publishers* India, Antony Thomas, Bonita Shimray, Arijit Ganguly, Supriya Mahajan and other staff at HarperCollins, for the uncompromising adherence to perfection. I worked very hard because I didn't want to fail you. Keerti Ramachandra, for editing, for the support and for the invaluable suggestions that make the book flawless.

ĀTTUKĀL AMMA

Bikash Niyogi and Niyogi Books, for the work experience.

Mini Krishnan, R. Vijayaraghavan, K. Satchidanandan, Rani Mohandas, for the affection and support.

Meena Kandasamy for being mine.

G. Binulal, Balan Madhavan, Hari Thirumala, Manoj Vasudevan and Sajan K.S., brilliant photographers, for being with me along the tough journey. Artist Madanan, for finding time to be a part of the book, for the sketches that make the book unique. Thank you B. Chandrakumar, Anil Bhaskar, Aswin, Ragesh Nair, Krishnakumar, Dhanya Studio Vijayan, Vineeth Nair Muttappalam, Sajan Chirayinkeezhu, Gavas Kanjiramnilkunnathil and Sethu Menon and the many unknown photographers whose pictures I have treasured and used in the book.

Dr N. Ajithkumar for the scholarly advice. For clearing my endless doubts. I am fortunate that I met you.

Raj Purushotthaman, P.P. Sathyan, Dr Deepa Manoj, Aswathy Karanavar, Soni Somarajan, Amit Kumar, K.P. Kailas, Babita Pillai of State Bank of Travancore, Dr Parameswaran, Dr Samadarshi, Gopika Govind, Liza George, Thottam singer Madhu Asan and his troupe, former tantri of Āttukāl, Chennās Dineshan Namboothiripad, the present tantri Kuzhikkattu P. V. Bhattathirippad, Kanippayyoor Krishnan Namboothiripad, the previous melshantis of the Āttukāl, Temple Gosala, Balamurali, Hari Thirumeni, Neelakandan Namboothirippad, vāsthu expert Sunil Prasad; the temple's staff, especially Sreekaryam officer S. Udayakumar and store manager P. Sivaprasad, P.K. Krishnan Nair, Kannettil House, Keshavan Namboothiri, Eswaran Namboothiri, Ramachandran Kunjolam; the temple drummers, Sadasivan and Ramesh, security staff, the sweepers, flower sellers, footwear keepers, auto drivers, everyone in and around the temple. I owe you a lot.

Kannan Potti, melshanti of Āttukāl, when I was concluding the book, for sharing such valuable information and correcting the temple tantra part of the book. I am indebted to you for the long discussions. For the patience. For the peace and grace you brought into my work, my home and life.

Dr Eric Miller, for sharing his scholarly research findings on Kannaki.

Editors of *Vanitha, Kerala Kaumudi, Mathrubhumi, The Hindu, The Indian Express, The Sunday Guardian* and *Malayala Manorama*, who publish my articles; it has been a huge encouragement. V.S. Rajesh, Premlal and Remya of *Kerala Kaumudi,* G.R. Indugopan of *Malayala Manorama*, P.V. Chandran, managing editor, *Mathrubhumi,* Thomas Jacob, editorial director of *Malayala Manorama,* Paul Mathew of *Gulf Today,* Subhashchandran of *Mathrubhumi*, for the support.

You always have a very special place in my heart: T.K. Vinodan, Padmashree Dr G. Vijayaraghavan and Nalini Vijayaraghavan, Geeta Krishnankutty, Dr Sarada Devi, Dr Samadarshi, Dr Thankom Varma, late Abraham Eraly, Kanishka Gupta, S. Gopalakrishnan, Chandini Santhosh, Niruba Sathish, late Prof. O.N.V. Kurup, Pradeep Suthan, Sumana Roy, T.N. Seshan, Jaya Seshan, Dr Lakshmi Priya, Geetha Saji, Shalini Krishnan, Vishnu. R. Krishnan, Sreekanth Velikatt, Suneetha Balakrishnan, Dhanya, Prema George, Aparna Thomas, Rajashree Warrier, Amit Kumar, Krishna and Ammu, P.L. Lathika, Mamang Dai, Prema Manmadhan, Bijukumar Alakode, Shylan, Malayinkeezh Gopalakrishnan, Dr Achuthsankar S. Nair, Sanjeev Sivan, Meera Bhushan Iyer, Sreejith V.T. Nandakumar, Nandan Kizhakkeveettil, Fatima, and Sucharita Dutta Assane.

Sajeev, Venugopalan Nair, Ajith – thank you for driving me safely to the temple and back home hundreds of times, in the past four years.

Rakesh Viswaroopan, for connecting me with the family of Judge Attukal Govinda Pillai. I am indebted to you.

Padma Shri K.S. Chitra and husband G. Vijayashankar, K.S. Beena and husband C. Venugopal and the family of late Attukal Govinda Pillai for their support.

My brother Sujumon, his wife Indulekha, and children Vinayak Sujathan and Sidharth Sujathan and my sister

ACKNOWLEDGEMENTS

Rani and her husband Captain Aswanikumar and children Govindan and Meenakshi, my sister's in-laws, Advocate K. Gopinathan and Leela Gopinathan, my apologies for being away, immersed in the book for the past four years. I missed many important moments in your life but I am sure the great Goddess I wrote about will protect you in times of need. You were never more than a thought away. My cousins, my uncles and aunts and everyone at my village Kadakavoor.

My domestic help Vijayamma Chechi for everything she did to make me comfortable and work peacefully.

Smt. S. Kausallya, my mother-in-law, Maya Chechi, Prasannan Chettan, Sanjeev Annan, Ratna Chechi, Anu, Meenu, Anosh, Dilu, grandchildren Venika and Dev and the members of my husband's family. Thank you. Your role in my life has been remarkable.

My friends on Facebook. A big thank you!

Authors of the hundreds of books I read, referred to, studied and collected.

I took four years to complete the book, starting from 2012. The happiness I celebrated in my Preface underwent a perceptible change during the last few months of finalizing this book, owing to certain factors, which I do not intend to elaborate here. It will remain a painful memory.

Rajeev, thank you, for instilling a sense of pride in me, without which I wouldn't have been able to complete anything in this life. Thank you for making me bold, righteous and hard-working. I needed all that to survive, to write. I am indebted, for the appreciation, love and the comforts you gave me all these years.

G. BINULAL
PHOTOGRAPHER

MADANAN
ARTIST

SAJAN K.S.
PHOTOGRAPHER

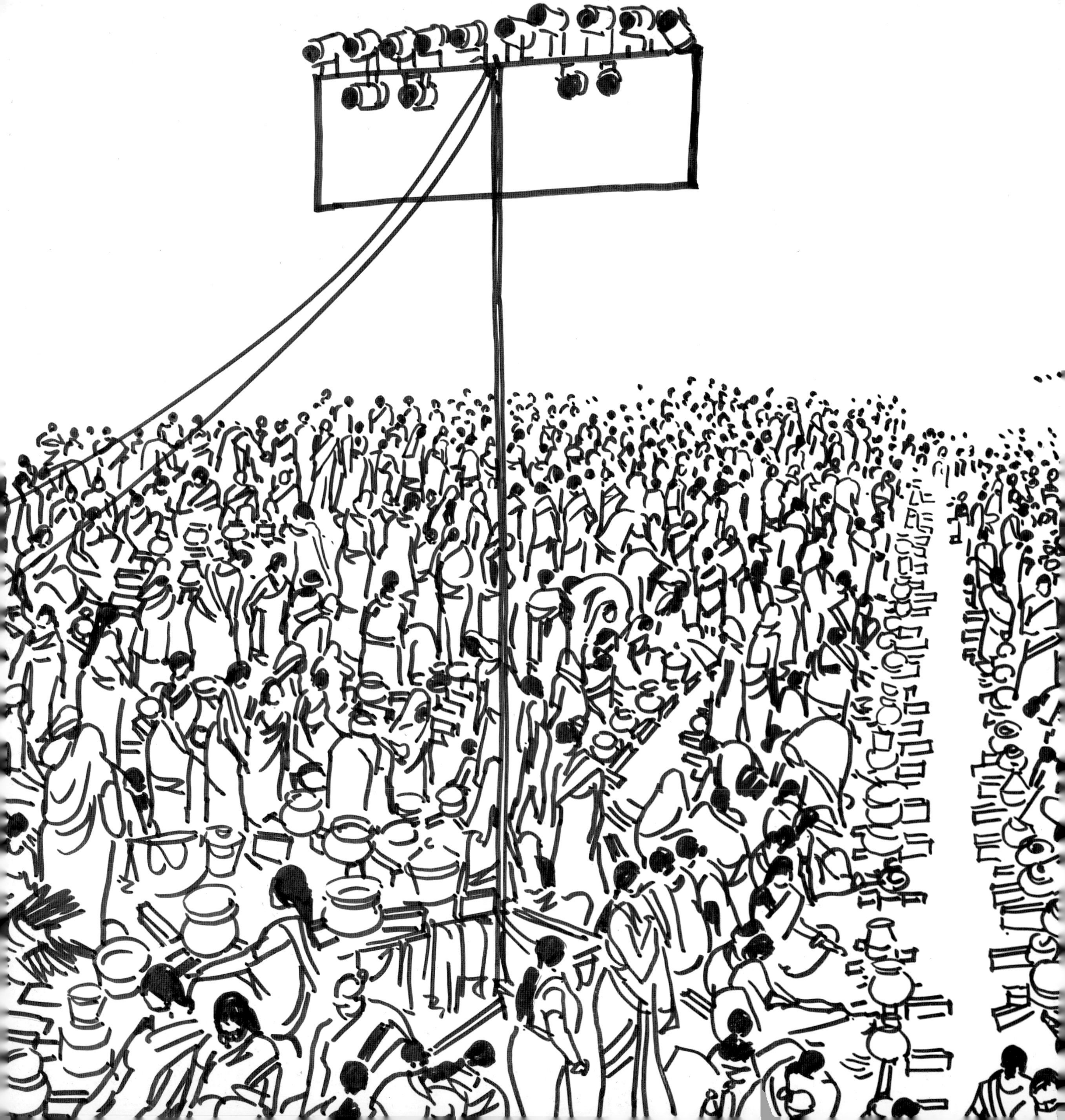